War and Democratic Constraint

War and Democratic Constraint

How the Public Influences Foreign Policy

Matthew A. Baum

Philip B. K. Potter

PRINCETON UNIVERSITY PRESS

Princeton and Oxford

Copyright © 2015 by Princeton University Press
Published by Princeton University Press, 41 William Street,
Princeton, New Jersey 08540
In the United Kingdom: Princeton University Press, 6 Oxford
Street, Woodstock, Oxfordshire OX20 1TW

press.princeton.edu

Jacket image: CodePink protester Medea Benjamin holds up
an anti-war placard as US secretary of state John Kerry arrives
to testify before the Senate Foreign Relations Committee on
Capitol Hill in Washington, DC, December 9, 2014.
Photograph © Jim Watson / AFP / Getty Images.

Library of Congress Cataloging-in-Publication Data

Baum, Matthew, 1965–
War and democratic constraint : how the public influences
foreign policy / Matthew A. Baum, Philip B. K. Potter.
pages cm
Includes bibliographical references and index.
ISBN 978-0-691-16498-4 (hardback) — ISBN 978-0-691-16523-3 (paper)
1. International relations—Public opinion.   2. International relations—Decision
making—Citizen participation.   3. Political participation.
I. Potter, Philip B. K.   II. Title.
JZ1305.B384 2015
327.1—dc23
2014028841

British Library Cataloging-in-Publication Data is available

This book has been composed in Minon Pro

Printed on acid-free paper. ∞

Printed in the United States of America

1 3 5 7 9 10 8 6 4 2

To my father, Richard Denis Baum

And to my kids, Téa and Alec

My circle of life—M.A.B.

For Rachel, my best friend through thick and thin

And Hazel, who puts everything else in context—P.B.K.P.

CONTENTS

FIGURES AND TABLES

FIGURES

TABLES

ACKNOWLEDGMENTS

Having reached the end of this journey, we begin by taking a step back to acknowledge the people who helped us to our final destination, such as it is. In this instance, the road has been long, winding, and uncertain, with many unexpected forks along the way. Progress has not always been smooth. The first recognizable kernel of the final product appeared a full decade ago, in a 2004 conference paper. The two illustrious discussants—Larry Bartels and Ken Schultz—commented something along the lines of "really cool results; great that they support all the hypotheses; but we don't believe any of it."

While disappointing, the message was both apt and delivered with grace and constructive intent. As painful as the medicine was to swallow, if it hadn't been administered this book would not exist in its current form. For their honesty and thoughtfulness, the authors are grateful to Messrs. Bartels and Schultz. Their double-barreled rebuke led directly back to the drawing board (no passing "Go," no collecting two hundred dollars, nor even a third-tier journal article) and ultimately to a series of productive collaborations between the authors over the past six years that have culminated in this volume.

A great many other individuals contributed to this project along the way. To begin with, for his methodological insights, creativity, and tireless work ethic on the news content analysis data employed in chapter 5, we thank Yuri Zhukov, who began as a research assistant and quickly became a valued collaborator. For additional research assistance, we are grateful to Kuyoun Chung, Jamie Georgia, Shuhei Kurizaki, Claire Lehnen, Peter Li, Rohan Mehta, Alan Potter, Daniel Quan, Kristin Van Ausdal, and Michael Yates. For their thoughtful comments and feedback on drafts of the manuscript, individual chapters, theoretical or empirical approaches, or just random thoughts, we thank Jamie Druckman, Julia Gray, Tim Groeling, Michael Horowitz, Patrick James, Stephen Kosack, Jonathan Ladd, Tarek Masoud, Quinton Mayne, Lorelei Moosbrugger, Ryan Sheely, and Marc Trachtenberg. We also wish to thank the participants at workshops and seminars at UCLA, Stanford, Duke, Texas A&M, the University of Texas, Austin, the University of Michigan, the University of Virginia, and Harvard.

Various stages of this research were financially supported by grants from the UCLA Academic Senate, the Harvard Kennedy School, the International Policy Center at the University of Michigan, and the Weatherhead Center for International Affairs at Harvard University. All that said, for better or worse we are entirely responsible for the results of this endeavor. As Frank Sinatra famously sang (pardon the paraphrasing), we did it our way. And as Rodney

Dangerfield slightly less famously said in response to Sinatra, "What other way is there to do it?"

Finally, we turn to the most important people. From Matt: I wish to thank my daughter Téa for her wit, kindness, and creativity, and for her uncanny ability to always make me laugh, and my son Alec for his limitless energy and joie de vivre. Though they don't realize it, this is where I find meaning every day. Finally, I also wish to dedicate this book to my father, Richard Baum, for teaching me how to laugh, write, persevere, throw a curveball, and *always look on the bright side of life* . . . . From Phil: I thank my wife Rachel for her unfailing encouragement and love. She supported this project wholeheartedly right when her own academic career was heating up, and without her help this book would not have been possible. By extension, our daughter Hazel has had to put up with too much parental typing, but has been a constant source of joy and a reminder of what is really important in life. My hope is that she will not remember her contributions to this project, but I thank her nonetheless.

War and Democratic Constraint

1

Introduction: Looking for Democratic Constraint

In February 2003, British citizens opposed to the war in Iraq held the largest public demonstration ever seen in the United Kingdom. The protest brought London to a standstill—no mean feat in a country with a long and storied tradition of public protest. In the three months preceding the war, only a third of the British public on average supported a military attack on Iraq, compared to nearly half (47 percent) opposing it. Public support bottomed out in the month prior to the war (February 2003), falling to 29 percent, with opposition rising to 52 percent. Indeed, as late as March 16, four days before the US-led invasion, 54 percent of the British public considered war against Iraq unjustified, while only 30 percent considered it justified.

Despite strong public opposition, Tony Blair—a Labour prime minister whose left-of-center politics made him no obvious ideological ally to Republican US President George W. Bush—proceeded to commit forty-five thousand troops to the conflict. Blair maintained that presence—a force second in number only to that of the United States—in the face of opposition that intensified in the years that followed. In short, despite substantial opposition from his own electorate, Blair prioritized the strategic relationship with the United States, which was pushing very hard for contributions to its "coalition of the willing."

The British public was not alone in disapproving of the Iraq War. Prior to the war's outbreak, an overall average of two-thirds of respondents across sixty-two countries surveyed—in some cases over 90 percent—opposed a military attack on Iraq.[1] Protests of comparable magnitude to those in London sprang up in many Western countries in the first half of 2003, but the domestic responses to them varied widely. Canada—a country with equally deep cultural, military, and financial ties to the United States—withheld support for the conflict, as did France, a long-standing ally. Both cited domestic opposition as a primary reason. Italy and Spain initially committed forces, but withdrew them in the face of the same sort of mounting opposition that Blair withstood.

---

[1] Baum (2013).

How should we understand this variability? When it comes to foreign policy, why are some leaders seemingly constrained by public opinion, even in the earliest stages of policy formulation, while others are more insulated from it? These are the questions that motivate this book.

The problem is substantial. Republican forms of government, by design, put distance between leaders and voters. Citizens voluntarily delegate some of their sovereign power, for limited periods of time and in limited domains, to elected representatives. In theory, this allows leaders to make considered decisions by insulating them from popular passions. In the longer term, however, representatives must either faithfully represent the deeper preferences of the citizenry or be replaced through elections. In an era of mass democracies in which millions hold the franchise, we are inevitably speaking of such republican arrangements in which the few represent the many. Yet the variability that we have just described in the way American allies responded to calls for contributions to the coalition of the willing suggests that not all democracies are alike when it comes to insulation and responsiveness.

We argue that this distinction arises from the way diverse institutions modulate the flow of information from leaders to citizens. There are important differences among democracies on this dimension. Some foster the flow of information much more effectively than others, and these distinctions are important. With information comes democratic constraint. Without it, democracies are in some important regards functionally equivalent to autocracies.

Most existing work on democratic conflict behavior assumes that information flows easily and responsiveness is automatic. These assumptions might approximate the realities of direct democracy in ancient city-states such as Athens, but they bear little resemblance to democratic processes in modern mass democracies. As is so often the case, the result is a mismatch between theory and practice that undercuts the validity and usefulness of academic research on this subject. In practice, citizens cannot perfectly constrain their leaders. The best evidence suggests that, more often than not, they fail to even come close. This is because, once in power, leaders have powerful incentives to prevent citizens from holding them to account. In some cases they also possess institutional tools enabling them to do so.

Nowhere is the gap between elected representatives and the public larger than in the "high politics" of international affairs, particularly in matters of war and peace. Most citizens have little or no firsthand knowledge of events taking place abroad. In this sense, the Iraq example is more the exception than the rule in that citizens worldwide were at least aware and mobilized enough to have preferences and make them known. More commonly, leaders make foreign policy decisions without any meaningful public scrutiny. Citizens generally lack the time and incentive to inform themselves about distant events with uncertain implications for their daily lives. This leaves them dependent upon political and media elites to tell them what they need to know about foreign policy.[2] Consequently, political and media institutions that systematically foster both robust opposition elites and the flow of information from them to citizens enhance democratic responsiveness, whereas their absence tends to insulate leaders from their citizens.

WHY DEMOCRATIC INSTITUTIONS MATTER

While an extensive body of empirical research explores how and why states become embroiled in international conflict, very little of it differentiates among democracies. For example, the voluminous literatures on the democratic peace and domestic audience costs—which we grapple with in this book—generally identify states as either democracies or autocracies, thereby smoothing over any institutional differences within democracies as a group. This can be a useful simplification for answering some questions, but it also means that puzzles like the aforementioned variability in nations' responses to the Iraq conflict generally escape scrutiny. Within democracies, this body of work tends to implicitly assume that the foreign policy process is perfectly transparent to attentive voters, that these citizens easily "hire and fire" their leaders, and that this translates into relatively high leader responsiveness and consistent constraints on foreign policy behavior. Indeed, the mechanisms underpinning the audience cost and democratic peace propositions actually *require* that these assumptions meaningfully approximate reality. The initial departure point of this book is to challenge their universality.

Given the extent of executive insulation in the United States when it comes to foreign affairs, it is perhaps unsurprising that the long-dominant, made-in-the-USA paradigm in international relations, neorealism,[3] holds that it is possible to understand and explain states' interactions with one another, including decisions to go to war, while simultaneously "black boxing"—that is, ignoring entirely—everything that goes on within the state. A common neorealist analogy thus likens the international system to a billiards table, with states—the only meaningful actors on the table—as balls moving around independently while occasionally bumping into one another (that is, interacting). Neorealism thereby treats states—regardless of regime type—as "functionally undifferentiated units." The implication is that scholars interested in studying international interactions, including international conflict, can safely model autocracies and democracies in the same way while ignoring the institutional differences between them, or among democracies.

---

[2] Baum and Groeling (2010); Brody (1992); Berinsky (2009). In the US case, the incongruity between relatively potent and autonomous leadership in foreign affairs and more constrained leadership in domestic politics underlies Wildavsky's (1966: 23) well-known "two presidencies" thesis, that "[t]he United States has one president, but it has two presidencies: one presidency is for domestic affairs and the other is concerned with defense and foreign policy."

[3] Waltz (1979).

Challengers to this perspective have sought to pry open the black box to better understand how variations in the linkages between citizens and leaders might influence states' foreign policy activities. This led to the rediscovery of Kant's democratic peace thesis, according to which democracies are—due to their pacific norms or institutional checks and balances—either less likely to fight wars or less likely to fight wars against one another, or both.[4] More recently it has spawned a large scholarly literature focused on determining whether and when democratic citizens will be inclined to punish their leaders either for foreign policy failures or for failing to live up to their foreign policy promises. According to the theory, such potential punishment—commonly referred to as domestic audience costs—makes democratic leaders more credible to adversaries than their autocratic counterparts.[5] The reason is that democratic leaders will tend to issue threats only when they mean business, because once they make a public threat citizens will punish them at the ballot box for backing down.

While these literatures are substantial in size and influence, nearly all work purporting to consider the role of domestic political institutions in international interactions has simply replaced the realist black box—that is, the simplifying assumption that in explaining the interactions between states it is possible to assume away all the nuances of politics within states—with two slightly smaller ones: democracy and autocracy. Yet, as others have established for autocracies,[6] democracies are far from an undifferentiated class. We argue that there is actually a great deal of consequential variation within these categories and that by taking such variations into account, we can substantially improve our understanding of the conditions that lead to variation in citizens' abilities to hold their leaders to account in foreign affairs.

THE ROLE OF POLITICAL INFORMATION WITHIN DEMOCRACIES

We contend that the reliability of the flow of information from elites to the masses most directly determines the degree to which citizens can constrain their leaders. Two basic conditions must be present for citizens of mass democracies to hold their leaders accountable. First, there must be independent and politically potent opposition partisans that can alert the public when a leader missteps. This is the part of the system required to counteract leaders' incentives to obscure and misrepresent. Second, media and communication institutions must be both in place and accessible sufficiently to transmit messages from these opposition elites to the public.

---

[4] Kant ([1795] 1983); Doyle (1986); Maoz and Russett (1993); Russett and Oneal (2001).
[5] Fearon (1994); Schultz (2001b); Potter and Baum (2010); Smith (1998).
[6] E.g., Weeks (2008); Geddes (2003).

Scholars of international relations have long recognized the importance of information and variations in its quality in mediating interactions between states. Influential theories of international conflict, in particular, turn on questions of the transparency, reliability, and availability of information to the actors involved in disputes.[7] After all, states cannot prevail in crisis bargaining or negotiations unless they are able to successfully communicate their intentions and resolve. Yet scholars have devoted scant attention to the process by which states disseminate information internally. In effect, most international relations research assumes (implicitly or explicitly) that among democracies, information passes efficiently from leaders' mouths or actions to the intended recipients.[8] If so, the only remaining uncertainty—which underpins much of the formal literature on international conflict—concerns what information a leader transmits or withholds and whether or not the intended recipient considers it reliable. As noted, this assumption is problematic in an era dominated by mass democracies.

Throughout the post–World War II era, democratic citizens have primarily learned about their governments' activities via the mass media. The past decade has witnessed the emergence of new political information sources, like social media, that may in some cases serve as alternatives and in other cases as complements to traditional mass media. However, a great deal of data, some of which we introduce in later chapters, clearly indicate that at present, mass media—especially television, but also newspapers and radio—remain the predominant sources of political information for the vast majority of people around the world.

This raises the questions of whether and how the mass media influence states' behavior in international conflicts. The few scholars of international relations who have investigated this question have mostly emphasized the possibility that a press free from government influence might facilitate peaceful conflict resolution by raising the domestic political costs to leaders of engaging in war abroad.[9] The trouble is that nearly all democracies feature a free press, so press freedom alone cannot help resolve the puzzling variability in democratic constraint that we introduced at the start of this chapter.

Communication scholars and journalists have shown greater interest in this question.[10] Nonetheless, while avoiding the unstated assumptions of the international conflict literature, they have in at least one important respect drawn a similar conclusion, at least for the United States (the case upon which research in this area is largely based). That is, they typically agree with international relations scholars that the media frequently do not exert very much independent

---

[7] E.g., Putnam (1988); Fearon (1995); Powell (1993); Slantchev (2003); Lake and Rothchild (1996).

[8] For an exception, see Baum and Groeling (2010).

[9] E.g., Van Belle (2000); Slantchev (2006); Choi and James (2006); Potter and Baum (2010).

[10] Among communication scholars see Mermin (1999), Jakobsen (2000), and Wolfsfeld (2004). For a journalistic perspective see Sharkey (1993).

influence in foreign affairs. Instead, the prevailing view is that in most instances the (American) media index their coverage of foreign policy to the tenor of elite rhetoric on whatever issue elites are publicly debating.[11] This means that when elites are united across party lines in support of a president's foreign policy, media coverage will reflect this harmony and the public will tend to support the policy. In contrast, when elites engage in partisan conflict, media coverage will reflect this partisan discord and the public will consequently divide along partisan lines. In such cases, the president's fellow partisans will tend to support the policy while opposition partisans oppose it.

Others such as Entman, however, hold that in at least some circumstances the media can play an important proactive role, even in the archetypal US case.[12] Yet in many such situations, contrary to the international relations literature, communication scholarship emphasizes the propensity of media to *exacerbate* military conflicts by, for example, pressuring democratic leaders to use military force for humanitarian purposes. According to this so-called CNN Effect hypothesis (an admittedly outdated term), public opinion, driven by dramatic images of human suffering, can pressure governments to take military or humanitarian action abroad that they would otherwise be inclined to avoid.[13] That said, with the exception of some anecdotal accounts of the US-led intervention in Somalia in 1992,[14] most of the related research finds no consistent evidence of such a pattern, leading to the current prevailing wisdom that the supposed CNN Effect is either incorrectly specified or perhaps the imaginings of self-congratulatory journalists overestimating their own importance.[15]

Despite the substantial body of work, there remains a disconnect between the understanding of communication and international relations scholars concerning whether, when, and how the media are likely to matter in situations of actual or potential international conflict. We argue that by properly situating the media within the larger context of the information transmission process between governments and citizens, it becomes possible to reconcile these seemingly contradictory arguments concerning how media might influence international interactions in potential conflict situations. We contend that media influence can cut multiple ways. In some circumstances it can reduce the likelihood of conflict between states; in others it is more likely to raise the odds of a military clash, while in still others the media are unlikely to exert any significant influence on policy makers.

[11] Bennett (1990); Berinsky (2009); Baum and Groeling (2010).
[12] Entman (2004).
[13] Livingston and Eachus (1995); Mermin (1999); Strobel (1997); Jakobsen (1996).
[14] E.g., Sharkey (1993); Maren (1994).
[15] Communication scholars have also broadened the search for evidence of an independent media effect on foreign policy to include structuring the environment surrounding peace negotiations (Wolfsfeld 2004) or as a means by which leaders can go over the heads of foreign leaders to speak directly to the publics of foreign nations (Goldsmith and Horiuchi 2009).

THE RECIPE FOR DEMOCRATIC CONSTRAINT

We identify two aspects of democratic systems that affect both the generation and the flow of information about foreign policy by influencing the extent of independent political opposition and their ability to reach the public with their messages. These aspects are political opposition and media access. Our argument, which we introduce here but develop more fully in chapter 2, is that these forces work in conjunction with one another and that their effects are thus conditional—both are required for meaningful and consistent democratic constraint.

Institutions and the Flow of Information: Political Opposition as Whistleblowers

The primary source of quality foreign policy information challenging the executive's policy frame is a strong and independent political opposition. Political systems that feature robust and diverse opposition have effective whistleblowers who can relay news of a leader's foreign policy miscues to the media.

Independent and robust political opposition can come from many sources. For example, it might emerge in the context of a close election between parties that are near power parity. Alternatively, high-profile individual political dissidents or provocateurs—like Lech Walesa in Poland, Andrei Sakharov in the former Soviet Union, Fang Lizhi in China, Martin Luther King, Jr. in the United States, or Mahatma Gandhi in India—can sometimes apply more pressure on a regime than any organized group. In other circumstances, nonprofit organizations, like Human Rights Watch or Amnesty International, can serve this role by carefully monitoring government actions and sounding the alarm when a government commits a transgression. However, when speaking systemically across countries and over time, opposition arises most reliably when there are multiple independent, robust, and diverse political parties.[16] Throughout this book we therefore rely on the number of parties in a political system as our primary empirical indicator of the extent of elite political opposition.

A robust and diverse opposition changes the nature of media institutions and content, as well as the electorate. Research has shown that multiparty electoral systems engender more diverse and policy-oriented media coverage of

---

[16] It is worth noting that this assertion may not hold at the extremes. For instance, Anderson (2000) argues that extreme fragmentation in party systems can prevent citizens from attributing responsibility for policy failures to individual politicians or parties, thereby weakening their ability to hold leaders accountable for poor performance at the ballot box. Moreover, not all opposition parties have equal incentives to blow the whistle on the incumbent government, particularly if they anticipate being included in a future coalition with the incumbent (Kunicova and Rose-Ackerman 2005). However, despite these and other potential exceptions (some of which we discuss in chapter 2), on average more and more potent opposition parties tends to mean more potential sources of opposition messages.

politics,[17] and consequently better informed and more politically sophisticated citizens, relative to two-party systems.[18] Therefore, citizens in multiparty systems are less likely to uncritically accept a leader's foreign policy pronouncements. All else equal, this should reduce leaders' willingness to accept the risky gamble of a war, make risky threats, or otherwise ignore the expressed or latent foreign policy preferences of the electorate.[19]

Throughout this book, we use the term "whistleblower" to invoke the monitoring role that we argue elite opposition can play in the foreign policy process. While this is useful shorthand for the theoretical mechanism we propose, it is admittedly a partial departure from the typical usage of the term in the principal-agent and bureaucratic politics literatures. In those contexts it usually refers to an individual within an organization who alerts principals to malfeasance.[20] We are referring to parties or groups of party elites who, as part of their standard function, alert voters to foreign policy activities that they consider missteps, failures, or out of step with their preferences.

Institutions and the Flow of Information: Access

Whistleblowers mean little if citizens never receive the information they attempt to relay, or if it diffuses too slowly to allow citizens to engage policy debates *before* leaders have already implemented the policies in question. Absent sufficient media access, citizens are relatively unlikely to receive any messages an opposition whistleblower might send and hence will be unable to hold a leader accountable.

This concern is more than academic. Citizens of different nations vary widely in their access to the mass media and therefore to information about their leaders' activities abroad and whistleblower complaints about those activities. For instance, among democracies from 1965 to 2006, the mean number of televisions per one thousand population is 205, or about one television for every five inhabitants. Greece in 1992 fell very close to this average, at 203 TVs per one thousand people. However, there is enormous variation around this mean. For more than one-third of the democracies in our data, there is at most one television for about every 10 inhabitants. The Philippines in 1993 fell near this level, with, on average, about 101 TVs per one thousand residents. In 1996, TV access was just over half that level in India, at 63 TVs per one thousand residents. This represented a sharp rise from, say, 1985, when Indians had ac-

---

[17] Benson (2009); Moosbrugger (n.d.); Schmitt-Beck (2003); Milner (2002).

[18] Kumlin (2001); Swanson and Mancini (1996).

[19] We recognize that the effects of macro-institutional factors like proportionality or the number of parties in a system on the responsiveness of leaders to citizens in democracies are complex and subject to some debate in the literature. In chapter 2 (both in the text and across several extended footnotes), we address some of these issues and arguments, along with our justifications for employing the party system as an admittedly blunt proxy for the information environment.

[20] E.g., Ting (2008).

cess to only about one television for every 250 residents. The United States and United Kingdom have among the highest levels of TV access among democracies in our data, at 831 (1997) and 850 (1999) TVs per one thousand inhabitants, respectively. While radio access and newspaper access are in some instances higher overall—particularly radio in some developing countries[21]—they exhibit similar variability. The implication is that while press freedom differs relatively little across democracies, *access* to that press varies substantially.

The Keys to Democratic Constraint Are in the Interactions

Cioffi-Revilla and Starr observe that "[p]olitical behavior . . . is caused by two fundamental, necessary conditions: the operational opportunity to act and the willingness to do so."[22] Along these lines, while opposition and access may in some instances and to varying degrees be individually consequential, we argue that each is independently insufficient to constrain the foreign policies of democratically elected leaders. The electorate is unlikely to hear whistleblowers and recognize their messages—that is, it will lack the *knowledge and incentive* to act—without a robust press. At the same time media access and institutions are irrelevant if there is no strong, independent opposition to generate credible information about foreign policy. We will demonstrate that the key factors in determining whether the media will inhibit, embolden, or fail to influence democratic leaders are their propensity to challenge the government's preferred framing of a given policy (which depends on the extent of opposition) as well as the public's likelihood of hearing such a challenge (which depends on access). In short, the effects (on political behavior) of the forces we identify are interactive and interdependent.

In the chapters that follow, we explore these complex interactions in detail. At times this can make for an intricate story about the origins of democratic constraint on foreign policy. However, this intricacy is the source of the important variation in the way foreign policy works within democracies. This makes unpacking it essential for developing and testing our argument.

EFFECTS ON WHAT?

States typically become involved in wars in one of three ways: they *initiate* disputes or conflicts, *reciprocate* in response to challenges from other actors, or *join* with preexisting groups of actors engaged in disputes or conflicts (who may themselves be initiators or reciprocators). We search for evidence for our argument in all three contexts. The first two represent the domains in which the literature has most emphatically argued for distinctive democratic behavior in international conflict. Initiation speaks directly to the democratic peace lit-

---

[21] International Telecommunication Union (2010).
[22] Cioffi-Revilla and Starr (1995: 447).

erature, while reciprocation addresses the substantial literature on domestic audience costs.

The third domain, coalition formation, is a less studied and more current concern. In an era seemingly dominated by multilateral interventions, this is an increasingly important question and allows us to extend our theory to the future as well as to speak to dominant existing debates.

Contextualizing the Relationship: The Role of a Free Press

We have already noted that with respect to conflict behavior our hypothesized interplay between opposition and media access is limited to states with democratic electoral institutions. But there is a second crucial precondition that we should also note from the outset. Simply put, responsiveness is unlikely if a leader can short-circuit the relay of opposition messages through the media by censoring or otherwise limiting the media's independence. Thus, the population of cases to which our theory and hypotheses apply is limited to states with free presses.

A free press is a defining characteristic of liberal democracies. In the United States the press is the only private actor that enjoys specific constitutional protection, via the First Amendment. Many autocracies have elections, legislatures, and the outward trappings of representation, but few tolerate open dissent from the press corps.[23] This near perfect coincidence of democracy and press freedom has obscured the systematic variation in the transmission of information to the public that mediates citizens' capacities to hold their leaders accountable in foreign affairs. This does not, however, mean that the independent effect of press freedom is immaterial. Several scholars have argued that a free press can help account for the democratic peace.[24] Others have argued that it facilitates—via its reputation of being a neutral arbiter uninterested in supporting a particular partisan perspective—the creation of domestic audience costs.[25] Underlying both arguments is the presumed greater credibility to citizens of a free press, relative to an unfree press.

A corollary of our theory, then, is that we should be able to observe our hypothesized relationships between partisan opposition and media access in the context of democracies with free presses, but that they should fade away when these conditions are absent. Throughout the empirical chapters that follow, we assess this corollary and consistently find that our story holds for states with free presses, but not for those without them.

---

[23] For instance, in 2003 (at the outset of the Iraq War), there was nearly an 80 percent correlation between the widely used Polity IV measure of relative democracy and the Reporters Without Borders Press Freedom Index. No country with a Polity score less than 5 (on the −10 to +10 DEMOC-AUTOC scale, where +10 is most democratic) scored higher than eighty-first (Cambodia) in the world in press freedom.

[24] Van Belle (1997, 2000); Choi and James (2006).

[25] Slantchev (2006).

MOVING FORWARD

In the remainder of this volume we develop the notion that media and electoral institutions fundamentally influence the extent of democratic constraint by shaping the flow of information from leaders to citizens. Absent an understanding of these institutions, we are missing essential information that would allow us to comprehend variations in the behavior of democracies in the international system.

In chapter 2 we develop a theory of democratic constraint and derive testable hypotheses. Drawing on literatures ranging from principal-agent theory to political communication to crisis bargaining, we establish expectations about the processes that result in the public actually becoming aware of foreign policy and then responding at the ballot box. We argue that democratic institutions that favor the flow of information between citizens and leaders—most notably those fostering both political opposition that can generate credible information and an independent and accessible media that can transmit it—contribute to constraint. There is, however, enormous heterogeneity among democracies in the extent to which these conditions hold. We develop expectations about how various combinations of these institutional attributes will translate into foreign policy behavior, with a particular eye toward conflict behavior.

In chapter 3, we begin the process of testing our theoretical propositions. We start with the broadest examination of the data in the book, employing a time-series, cross-sectional analysis of conflict initiation in all possible pairs of countries (that is, all dyads) from 1965 to 2006. This analysis demonstrates the interactive relationship between media access and political opposition. Across a variety of indicators of conflict, we show that states with media and political institutions that facilitate the flow of information between leaders and the public are less prone to initiate military conflicts. These findings suggest not only an underlying mechanism that could fuel the democratic peace proposition, but also that not all democracies are likely to be equally peaceful.

Chapter 4 extends the analysis we present in chapter 3 to the thorny question of domestic audience costs. For leaders to generate credibility through audience costs, there must be mechanisms in place that enable citizens to learn about foreign policy failures in a timely and consistent way. The institutional variation among democracies that we identify has important implications for the extent to which citizens can obtain such information. Specifically, we demonstrate that the number of electorally viable political parties in a country, conditional on relatively widespread public access to the mass media, has an important impact on credibility in international interactions. That is, states possessing these attributes fare better—in terms of avoiding reciprocation—when they issue threats or initiate conflicts.

Chapter 5 turns to coalition formation. Here, we examine the validity of our arguments in the context of the lead-ups to the 2003 war in Iraq and the 2001 invasion of Afghanistan. We draw on cross-national data on public support for the wars in Iraq and Afghanistan and the decisions of countries to contribute troops to the coalitions the United States sought to assemble in both conflicts. As expected, we find in both cases that the quality and flow of information from whistleblowers, through the media to citizens, importantly mediates public support for intervention and leaders' responsiveness to public sentiment. Countries with more parties were more likely to have populations opposed to the wars and to contribute fewer troops to the coalitions as their access to mass media increased. In contrast, also as expected, in states with fewer parties we find the opposite relationships: increased media access is associated with *lower* opposition to the wars and *higher* troop contributions.

Chapter 6 takes a step back to assess the validity of a critical assumption underpinning the theory and findings in chapters 2 to 5. This is simply the idea, which we term the "Downsian Premise," that democratic multiparty systems tend to engender political coverage that is more diverse, more policy-centric, and more prone to challenge the government's policy line than coverage in two-party democracies. To test this proposition we conduct content analyses of international media coverage of four recent multinational conflicts (Kosovo 1999, Afghanistan 2001, Iraq 2003, and Libya 2011). Our data range from a minimum of all coverage mentioning Kosovo in about 241 newspapers across twenty-three democracies in 1999 to a maximum of about 1,140 papers mentioning Libya across sixty-five democracies in 2011.[26] We assess the relative emphasis on policy-oriented coverage (as opposed to personality- or human-interest-oriented news), the valence of coverage (that is, the overall average level of support for or opposition to the government's policy), and coverage diversity (measured as the number of distinct topics included in the news). Across these dimensions we find consistent support for the Downsian Premise. Multiparty democracies offer relatively more policy-oriented news, more challenges to the government's policies, and more varied topical coverage than their two-party counterparts. This enhances our confidence in the validity of the theoretical linkages we have drawn between parties, the nature of political information, media access, and public attitudes that are implicit in the statistical analyses of chapters 3 through 5.

Chapter 7 adds context to our statistical findings through more detailed process tracing. We assess the decisions of the United Kingdom, Spain, Germany, and Poland regarding whether they would join with the United States in the coalition of the willing to remove Saddam Hussein from power in Iraq. Among these countries, there was much variation in both key variables we identify as the ingredients of constraint and in the extent to which leaders were responsive to pressure from either their domestic publics or the United States. This deeper, qualitative dive into several representative cases enables

---

[26] These figures include only newspapers that actually covered the respective conflicts. The data sets include additional nondemocracies and many more newspapers. The data are described in detail in the appendix to chapter 6.

us to more fully elaborate the mechanisms that underpin our aggregate data analyses.

Chapter 8 concludes. The theory and findings we present in the book have substantial implications for future academic research in international relations. We argue that insufficient attention to underlying mechanisms has obscured the consistent role of democratic political institutions in conflict processes. Unsurprisingly, the failure to model institutional heterogeneity, most often by modeling democracies dichotomously, has led to ambiguous findings in a number of research domains because scholars have lumped together leaders who face substantial democratic constraint with those who do not. The implication is that not all democracies are alike when it comes to matters of war and peace. In the conclusion, we also draw out the policy implications of our findings and consider the possible roles of the Internet and satellite television— media technologies that had not yet proliferated globally during much of the period under investigation.

Much of what we uncover about the origins on democratic constraint lends itself better to explanation than policy prescription. It is unlikely that countries will rush to change their electoral systems in hopes of spurring the effects that we describe (with the possible exception of a new democracy building its institutions from scratch). More to the point, most leaders do not prefer to reduce their own freedom of action and therefore have little incentive to implement such changes.[27] There are, however, a few policy instruments that influence constraint and are more immediately at the disposal of policy makers in established democracies. Specifically, variations in media ownership structures represent one of the few clear factors influencing media content that are sensitive to policy intervention and that can contribute meaningfully to responsiveness. Ownership regulations are subject to normal legislation, and we consider how the choices that states make about media ownership can independently influence some of the important information processes we describe.

Finally, the insights that we draw out in the context of coalition building and joining are new and relevant to policy makers as well as scholars. These results have clear implications for future efforts at assembling international coalitions for multilateral interventions. From Bosnia to Kosovo to Afghanistan to Iraq to Libya, this has proven an increasingly thorny problem for policy makers. As indicated by the difficulty that the United States had assembling a coalition for Iraq (and echoed at a smaller scale in the French experiences with Libya and Mali), it is also one in which policy makers are clearly operating on a somewhat ad hoc basis, divorced from any general logic of action or notion of best practices. Our findings are the first to provide insight into when leaders are likely to commit to such endeavors in spite of opposition from their publics and when democratic constraint might make for unreliable allies.

---

[27] Baum (2011).

2

Democracies Are Not Created Equal: A Theory of Democratic Constraint

There is an important but underappreciated tension in our understanding of how democracies conduct foreign policy. On its face, it seems that the public should constrain elected leaders' foreign policy activities. Normative theories of democratic accountability require this. Important pillars of international relations research—be it democratic peace or audience cost theory—rest on implicit assumptions about leaders' responsiveness to popular opinion. In practice, however, discrepancies between theory and reality abound. Citizens are generally uninformed about foreign affairs and have little appetite for such information. Leaders, in turn, have both the means and motive to obscure their failings and limit their accountability. Media tend to let them get away with this and, more often than not, behave more like lapdogs than watchdogs.

Does this mean democratic accountability in foreign policy is illusory? Leaders regularly manipulate citizens, whether via claims about weapons of mass destruction in the lead-up to the 2003 Iraq War or about escalation and secret peace plans during the Vietnam War. Yet there is also relatively unambiguous evidence that democracies stand apart from nondemocracies with regard to the most important facets of international conflict. They rarely if ever fight one another,[1] are more credible when they make threats,[2] and win more often when they do fight.[3] It would be surprising if these differences do not originate in some manner from the democratic institutions these states share in common.

Portions of chapter 2 appeared in modified form in "The Relationship between Mass Media, Public Opinion and Foreign Policy: Toward a Theoretical Synthesis" by Matthew Baum and Philip Potter in the *Annual Review of Political Science* 11 (2008): 39–65; and in "The Iraq Coalition of the Willing and (Politically) Able: How Party Systems, the Press and Public Influence on Foreign Policy" by Matthew Baum in the *American Journal of Political Science* 57, no. 2 (2013): 442–58. Reprinted with permission.

[1] Russett and Oneal (2001).
[2] Schultz (2001b).
[3] Reiter and Stam (2002).

How might we square these seemingly disparate observations that democratic constraint often fails when it comes to foreign policy, but that democracies have foreign policies that are distinct from those of other states? The answer lies in recognizing the mistake of comparing aggregate findings on democratic behavior (which suggest that democracies behave differently as a class) and individual cases in which constraint fails (which implies that they are not so distinct after all). Aggregate comparisons across regime types can, of course, reveal a distinction even if constraint is only sporadic. This raises an important question: when are elected leaders subject to democratic constraint on their foreign policy actions, and when are they more or less free to do as they please?

As we prefaced in the introduction, constraint arises from the complex interplay among the electorate's knowledge, political institutions, and the media. These forces shape the flow of information through the political system. Information in turn begets constraint. In this chapter, we lay out these theoretical relationships in detail.

INFORMATION, ACCOUNTABILITY, AND PRINCIPAL-AGENT PROBLEMS

The crux of this book is the argument that information is the key to accountability and constraint in democracies. When it flows freely among leaders, elites, and the public, the principal-agent problem inherent in representative governance is minimized. This allows electoral institutions to function efficiently.

The relationship between a democratic public and their elected leaders closely adheres to what Miller calls "Weber's asymmetry," which describes the difference in power and information between principal and agent: the principal holds authority but the agent—that is, the actor to whom the principal delegates the power necessary to implement the principal's preferences—has the informational advantage.[4] As such, representative government creates a classic principal-agent problem, with elected officials as the often unruly agents of citizens. Downs and Rocke, for example, develop this logic in the context of the decision to go to war.[5] The chief executive is likely to possess far more information than typical citizens, who employ the war's outcome as a basis for evaluating the chief's competence after the fact via elections. More generally, the principal-agent dilemma between representative government and citizens is one of accountability. Elected officials must be held accountable for their actions and those of their government, and citizens must use their voting power to keep good governments in place and to dismiss those that perform poorly. The asymmetry in information, however, creates an inefficiency in which citizens cannot easily differentiate between those officials who act with good strat-

---

[4] Miller (2005).
[5] Downs and Rocke (1994).

egy and intentions but achieve unlucky results and those whose intentions may be contrary to the best interests of the citizenry or focused on personal gain, but whose policies nonetheless produce fortuitous positive outcomes.[6]

Information helps alleviate this problem.[7] Holmstrom suggests that an increase in monitoring leads to increased information, which can enhance principal control. In this view, the ideal solution would be total monitoring—that is, citizens directly observing all of their leaders' actions and motives.[8] Total monitoring would also, assuming an adequate enforcement mechanism (that is, an ability to efficiently replace poorly performing leaders), optimize risk sharing between principal and agent.[9] In some contexts it is possible to employ such solutions. For example, automobile insurers now have the monitoring technology to greatly reduce moral hazard among the insured. However, monitoring is a much thornier prospect in political contexts. The run-up to the 2003 Iraq invasion demonstrates the implausibility of complete monitoring in the political arena and the difficulty of solving this particular version of the principal-agent problem.[10] The case reveals that unambiguous majorities of citizens in countries like the United Kingdom, Italy, and Spain were unable to constrain the foreign policies of their democratically elected leaders when they conflicted with their own.

Information, however, can also come in the form of output. Put differently, the results of a policy can serve as a cognitive shortcut that enables citizens to judge the performance of their elected representatives even in the absence of complete information. Citizens may not have access to the range of information available to elected officials, but they do know when government fails to provide promised or critical services. McCubbins and Schwartz refer to this process as "fire alarm oversight," in which principals rely upon third parties to notify them, or pull the fire alarm, when a problem emerges.[11] In addition, "a meaningful discussion between principal and agent" may promote enough sharing of information to approach equilibrium.[12] Scholz argues that such cooperation could move both parties away from the suboptimal outcomes of a one-shot game and closer to true efficiency.[13] In other words, it moves the parties to a position where both benefit from such cooperation, thereby minimizing the problem of slippage between citizens' preferences and policy outcomes in the absence of complete information.

---

[6] Downs and Rocke (1994).

[7] The most basic principal-agent problem is known as agency slippage. This occurs when, due to imperfect monitoring or asymmetric information, an agent is able to act contrary to the interests of the principal without consequence.

[8] Holmstrom (1979).

[9] Holmstrom (1979).

[10] Miller (2005).

[11] McCubbins and Schwartz (1984).

[12] Miller (2005).

[13] Scholz (1991).

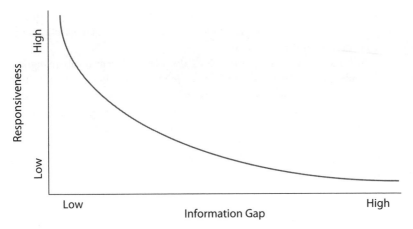

Figure 2.1. Information and responsiveness

As we will demonstrate, similar issues arise in the extent to which citizens can constrain elected officials in foreign policy. In this context, however, electoral and media institutions, rather than "fire alarms" and "meaningful discussion," are the keys to generating and transmitting information that in turn either solves or exacerbates the principal-agent problem inherent in representative government. In effect, the public can constrain foreign policies only when it is aware of them and their outcomes and punishes leaders at the ballot box for failures. At the extremes, if there is no flow of foreign policy information, leaders can do whatever they please without electoral consequence. Conversely, with perfect information elected leaders will adhere completely to the public's preferences (assuming Mayhew's simplification that these leaders care exclusively about reelection).

Figure 2.1 visually illustrates this very simple relationship and indicates that as the size of the information gap increases, responsiveness recedes. Constraint, and with it responsiveness, is virtually nonexistent when the information gap is largest. As the gap narrows, responsiveness rises until, when the gap is at its lowest level, responsiveness is essentially perfect. Of course, the extremes of perfect and zero information are unlikely to occur.[14] We can, however, gain insight into the middle ground by considering what citizens know about foreign policy and how they know it. In our view, political elites lie at the center of this story.

A substantial body of research suggests that typical individuals look to trusted opinion leaders who share their preferences for information about how their electoral representatives are performing. In democracies, this typically

---

[14] The curve in figure 2.1 is thus concave in order to reflect the fact that situations of perfect or zero information, or perfect or zero responsiveness, are unlikely to arise.

takes the form of fellow partisan elites.[15] Thus, in the face of a significant informational disadvantage vis-à-vis elected leaders, the public uses these elite positions as a critical cognitive shortcut.[16]

In addition to dictating positions, elites also play an integral role in signaling to the public when it should engage with the foreign policy process. In this sense, elite signals are akin to McCubbins and Schwartz's aforementioned conception of fire alarms as a means of ameliorating principal-agent problems.[17] The mass public is not consistently looking for cues from elites and updating accordingly. Indeed, as we will discuss in detail, democratic citizens are frequently uninterested in foreign affairs. Instead, they rely primarily on elite discord as a heuristic that signals when their delegation of policy to their elected agents may have gone awry. Zaller notes that elite discord can also produce a "polarization effect" by sparking more critical media coverage.[18] This in turn further heightens attention from the public. Through these mechanisms, political elites—especially opposition partisans—can act as whistleblowers, informing citizens when leaders are diverging sharply from their preferences.

But when does elite discord emerge and when are people able to hear it? The broad brushstrokes of reliance on partisan elites for information about incumbent performance are consistent across democracies. Yet, the extent to which these processes function sporadically or seamlessly depends on electoral and media institutions that actually vary widely. We believe that this institutional variation is the primary explanation for differences in responsiveness between democracies. To establish this, we begin by outlining the natural informational asymmetries that exist between leaders and the publics to whom they are accountable. We then identify how electoral institutions—specifically those that give rise to a larger number of parties and hence a higher potential for elite discord—produce whistleblowers in the form of political opposition, and with them responsiveness. We then turn to variations in media institutions that can either magnify or muffle opposition messages, thereby rendering them either easily heard by the mass public or largely ineffectual.

Drawing on these insights, we derive hypotheses about how these institutional features might influence three key aspects of conflict-related foreign policy decision making in which democracies are widely believed to differ

[15] Rahn (1993); Lupia and McCubbins (1998); Baum and Groeling (2010).

[16] Popkin (1993).

[17] We rely on the McCubbins and Schwartz (1984) fire alarm analogy throughout this volume because it so clearly invokes the theoretical mechanism that we believe drives the importance of independent opposition. However, there are important distinctions between their conception of this process and ours. Specifically, they describe fire alarms as something that principals intentionally set up in order to efficiently delegate to agents. While the nature and role of opposition is something that institutional framers may consider at the time of writing democratic constitutions, this may not always be the case. In other words, we are agnostic on the extent to which this role for opposition in the foreign policy process is intentional or accidental.

[18] Zaller (1994).

as a class in their behavior: conflict initiation, reciprocation, and coalition formation.

AN UNINFORMED, INATTENTIVE ELECTORATE

If an informed public is crucial to foreign policy constraint, it is important to understand the baseline ebb and flow of the public's attentiveness to and knowledge about foreign policy. Unfortunately for democratic idealists, the inertial state of public attention to foreign policy is typically apathy and ignorance.

On its face, this ignorance is worrisome. The capacities of citizens to gather and retain information and to use it to formulate coherent opinions are arguably indispensible to a properly functioning democracy.[19] It is certainly crucial if they, as principals, are to exert even a modicum of control over their elected agents. While Madison, Hamilton, and other like-minded federalists were suspicious of the mass public's capacity to contribute constructively to political decision making, especially in foreign policy, an even older liberal tradition—with origins in the work of Kant, Rousseau, Bentham, and Mill, and more recently manifested in the vast literature on the democratic peace[20]—views citizen engagement as crucial to well-considered policy and peaceful international relations. Contemporary democratic theorists, such as Habermas, also consider responsiveness to the public a cornerstone of democratic governance.[21] Despite the theoretical importance generally placed on the public's engagement with politics and foreign policy, however, social scientists have struggled to consistently characterize the public's actual role in the foreign policy process.

The prevailing scholarly consensus in this area has steadily evolved. Scholars have long questioned the capacity of democratic citizens to gather and process information or manifest consistent opinions,[22] especially with respect to foreign affairs.[23] Early research suggested that public opinion was volatile and lacked a coherent structure,[24] or that the public naïvely followed elite leadership.[25] Sniderman aptly summarizes this view of the public—which Holsti labeled the "Almond-Lippmann consensus"—as "muddle-headed (lacking constraint) or empty-headed (lacking genuine attitudes), or both."[26] An uninformed public, this argument goes, is incapable of independently or critically evaluating a leader's claims. Presumably, such citizens would be almost terminally ill equipped to constrain a leader's foreign policy actions, since they would be

[19] Clawson and Oxley (2008); Dahl (1961); Patterson (1994).
[20] E.g., Doyle (1986); Russett and Oneal (2001).
[21] Habermas (1996).
[22] Campbell et al. (1960); Zaller (1992).
[23] Holsti (2004); Rosenau (1962).
[24] Lippmann and Merz (1920); Almond (1950).
[25] Lipset (1966); Verba et al. (1967).
[26] Sniderman (1993: 219); Holsti (1992).

unable to either identify the truth or know what to think about it even if they could. Moreover, no amount of improvement in the transmission of information would likely solve the problem.

Over time, however, a rebuttal emerged from scholars who, while recognizing that typical individuals do not know very much about politics or foreign policy most of the time, argued that the public's individual and collective behaviors are nonetheless rational, specifically because they are efficient.[27] These scholars argued that, when necessary, citizens overcome their informational limitations through reliance on informational shortcuts.[28] The most notable such shortcuts are the aforementioned opinions of trusted political elites, primarily as reflected in the mass media.[29]

Even with this notion that the public could sometimes rationally and productively engage with foreign policy, a widespread perception persisted that these were exceptions to the general rule that the public was incidental to the foreign policy process.[30] More recently, however, some scholars have begun to characterize public opinion on foreign policy as a relatively stable and consistent counterweight that policy makers must, or at least *should*, take into consideration.[31] In this revisionist view the role of public opinion in foreign policy resembles the presidential veto—rarely used, but always lurking behind strategic calculations of other actors. So long as elected agents roughly adhere to public preferences, citizens need only infrequently engage with the foreign policy process. When elected officials stray too far, a well-functioning system of democratic constraint would alert citizens to the situation and spur them to action. All democracies, however, do not function equally well in this regard.

What institutional factors prompt citizens to perk up, pay attention, and apply curbs on their elected representatives, and when do these mechanisms fail? It is to these questions that we now turn.

---

[27] Popkin (1994); Page and Shapiro (1992); Jentleson (1992). One reason for the public's "rational ignorance" regarding most aspects of foreign policy is, to borrow from Lowi's (1972) typology of government policies, that with the exceptions of some aspects of international trade and protectionism, foreign policy is generally not redistributive in nature and so has ambiguous direct implications for typical citizens.

[28] Popkin (1993); Sniderman, Brody, and Tetlock (1991).

[29] Iyengar and Kinder (1987); Krosnick and Kinder (1990); Larson (2000). A few scholars go even further, arguing that the public can and does remain informed and active in the foreign policy arena, though this never became more than a minority view (Aldrich, Sullivan, and Borgida 1989; Destler 2001).

[30] Holsti and Rosenau (1984); Holsti (2004); Mueller (1973).

[31] Page and Bouton (2006). For more on this point, see Aldrich et al. (2006), who assess the overall scholarly understanding of public opinion in the context of foreign policy in hopes of resolving the debate concerning public competence. They conclude that a new consensus has emerged that the public is able to develop and hold coherent views on foreign policy, that citizens can and do apply their attitudes to their electoral decisions, and that this leads politicians to consider the electoral implications of their overseas activities.

POLITICAL OPPOSITION AS WHISTLEBLOWERS

Leaders, both democratic and autocratic, have clear incentives to hide their foreign policy actions when they conflict with either the latent or the expressed preferences of the public. To minimize their capacity to obscure, there must be heterogeneous and autonomous political elites in positions of power that have independent access to foreign policy information and the incentive to reliably alert the public when leaders stray too far from their preferred policies. We argue that opposition political parties are the most obvious candidates to fill this role in democracies and that the larger the number of consequential opposition parties, the more efficient this mechanism becomes.[32]

Parties as Opposition

Relying on the number of parties as an operationalization is, by design, a significant simplification of the complex relationships between electoral institutions and democratic responsiveness. One can imagine several potential confounds. For instance, the responsiveness-enhancing effects of multiple parties may be muted in systems, like that governing the Netherlands, that tend to reproduce stable, oversized, or grand governing coalitions over long periods of time.[33] Such coalitions could effectively subsume parties that might otherwise serve as credible sources of opposition information.[34]

The basic point is that not all nongoverning parties are necessarily equivalent. Some are likely to be oppositional because they are cut from a different ideological cloth. Others, though outside government, may be ideologically consonant with the governing party or parties and as such less likely to provide discordant information. Alternatively, some parties that hope to enter coalitions with existing incumbent governments may hesitate to blow the whistle, out of fear of losing their opportunity to join the government in the future.[35] Several of these scenarios would at minimum add noise to a measure of the count of parties as an indicator of robust opposition.

We nonetheless focus on the number of opposition parties as our primary operationalization of elite opposition for several reasons. First, doing so is con-

---

[32] Schultz (2001a) also notes the central theoretical role for opposition parties in the audience cost story, but does not model it statistically. Also see Ramsey (2004) for a formal model of the role of opposition in crisis bargaining.

[33] Timmermans and Moury (2006).

[34] The logic behind oversized coalitions made up (mainly) of parties from one side of the political spectrum (assuming there are just two sides) would presumably be different from a "grand coalition," enjoying the same number of legislative seats but made up of parties from across the political spectrum. A grand coalition would seem less likely to produce flows of information that challenge the governing coalition.

[35] Kunicova and Rose-Ackerman (2005).

sistent with the canonical theoretical and empirical literature in this area.[36] While some recent studies (several of which we cite in this chapter) call this linkage into question, the counterevidence is at best uncertain, primarily derived from small- or medium-N studies focused on a relatively narrow group of advanced, mostly European countries. Second, our simplified operationalization of the robustness of political opposition provides tractability. Given the scope and variety of our empirical investigations across both space and time, this consideration looms large. Third, our theoretical logic linking the number of parties (or "nongoverning opposition parties") to responsiveness—that is, more political opposition means more actors with an incentive to blow the whistle on governmental policy failures—is both narrower than and arguably in some respects orthogonal to the prevailing revisionist arguments in the literature on democratic institutions.[37]

Perhaps most important, we marshal considerable empirical evidence across a large number of countries, broad time periods, and multiple ways of measuring conflict in support of our contention that more parties, combined with widespread media access, tend to facilitate greater democratic constraint. Finally, it is worth noting that, for the aforementioned reasons, we likely underestimate the size of the effects of nongoverning opposition parties. Consequently, our results strongly support the theory despite the imperfections in our operationalization of one of the core underlying concepts.

Why More Is Better

Why is a single opposition party sometimes insufficient to blow the whistle on the executive's foreign policy miscues? Downs links the number of political parties to the nature of political debate, arguing that a small number of political parties produces pathologies such as ineffective government in the absence of consensus among voters and ambiguous platforms and positions.[38] More relevant to our argument, he shows via a spatial model that as the number of parties increases, each party must compete over a smaller ideological space and do so through more concrete policy positions. The result is greater granularity in policy positions and more robust opposition to the government. This, in turn, makes it more likely that elite discord will emerge when foreign policy becomes potentially controversial, and by extension that the public will engage with the process.

A hypothetical example illustrates the disadvantages—at least with respect to responsiveness—of the restricted granularity in foreign policy positions introduced by limited opposition. Suppose that President Obama had been caught in a foreign policy misstep in the midst of his 2012 reelection campaign.

---

[36] E.g., Lijphart (1999); Powell (2000); Downs (1957).

[37] E.g., Anderson (2000); Green-Pederson (2006, 2007).

[38] Downs (1957).

It is unlikely that many of his supporters would have abandoned him in favor of his Republican opponent, Mitt Romney, because the two candidates differed so substantially on so many policy dimensions.

A similar logic underpins the lack of any noteworthy voter response to the September 11, 2012, attack on the American embassy in Benghazi, Libya, that killed four US diplomats. In the immediate aftermath of the attack, Obama's average lead over Romney in the various tracking polls catalogued by Real-ClearPolitics.com fell by a statistically insignificant 0.1 percentage points. It then proceeded to rise (statistically significantly) by about 1.5 points during the second half of September. While this lack of an electoral or public opinion reaction to the Benghazi "scandal" was a source of great consternation for some conservative commentators, it is relatively easy to explain when considered within the framework we propose here. The reason, presumably, is that for voters to change candidates, they would have had to also accept changes in their preferred candidates' positions on financial regulation, taxes, health care, gay marriage, abortion, and so on. In contrast, were Israeli Prime Minister Benjamin Netanyahu—whose legislature in 2013 included thirteen parties holding seats—caught in the same situation, he presumably would be more susceptible to defections from centrist and far right religious parties. The higher density of parties across the ideological spectrum in Israel means that these parties are more ideologically proximate to the marginal Likud voter.

In addition, politicians in systems with fewer parties have incentives to offer more vague policy stances in order to appeal to the median voter, which in turn waters down the quality of the information in the system. As Downs observes, "[V]oters in multiparty systems are much more likely to be swayed by doctrinal considerations—matters of ideology and policy—than are voters in two-party systems. The latter voters are massed in the moderate range where both ideologies lie; hence they are likely to view personality, or technical competence, or some other nonideological factor as decisive. . . . Voters in multiparty systems, however, are given a wide range of ideological choice, with parties emphasizing rather than soft-pedaling their doctrinal differences."[39] More recent findings confirm the Downsian notion of a positive relationship between the number of parties and the tendency for such parties to "emphasize doctrinal differences."[40] Along similar lines, Lijphart demonstrates a positive relationship between the effective number of parties in a democracy and the num-

[39] Downs (1957: 126–27).

[40] E.g., Cox (1990); Dow (2001); Swanson and Mancini (1996). That said, Green-Pederson (2006, 2007) finds that in recent years in some smaller Western European multiparty democracies (e.g., Denmark, Norway), parties have increasingly distinguished themselves by emphasizing issue positions over traditional left-right ideological conflict. Some additional research (Ezrow 2008), in turn, provides evidence that parties in proportional systems, and in systems with larger numbers of parties, do not necessarily hold more extreme ideological positions. It is, however, worth noting that in this case, as with Green-Pederson's studies, Ezrow's findings are based on a much smaller number of cases and narrower time frame than our study: eighteen European nations during the 1980s.

ber of issue dimensions over which elections are fought.[41] At its core, the link between the number of opposition parties and costs is based on an electoral logic. Opposition parties are likely to point out the blunders of a sitting president or prime minister because this will, at the margin, weaken the sitting government and perhaps help them at the ballot box down the line.[42] Supporting this logic, Jones finds that less competitive elections lead to reduced accountability of legislators in the US Congress.[43]

To an important extent, variation in opposition (and with it responsiveness) is an intentional consequence of the institutional designs of democracies. It is widely recognized, for example, that consensual systems are built to be more responsive and to feature more parties than majoritarian systems.[44] In consensual systems, leaders frequently face the possibility of a no-confidence vote in the legislature and the resulting loss of power at any time. A foreign policy failure presumably increases the likelihood of such an occurrence, particularly if the executive sits atop a coalition. Consequently, leaders in multiparty systems may be more concerned about public opinion irrespective of the information environment. The implication is that the number of parties alone may drive all of these relationships. If so, once we have accounted for the party system we should find no independent or interactive effects of media access and institutions. As we shall see, we in fact do find consistent evidence of such effects throughout our empirical investigations. This strongly suggests that while it may be *necessary* to account for the party system in order to explain successful democratic constraint, doing so is most likely insufficient.

It is nonetheless important to acknowledge that, for some of the previously noted reasons, the linkage between electoral institutions and democratic responsiveness is not uncontested in the literature. For instance, some recent research finds an ambiguous or inverse relationship between proportionality or extreme party fragmentation, on the one hand, and democratic responsiveness on the other.[45] These studies tend to argue that such factors inhibit citizens

[41] Lijphart (1999); Laakso and Taagepera (1979). (We define "effective number of parties" in chapter 3.)

[42] Some might worry that the proposed relationship between the number of parties in a democratic system and responsiveness is in fact spurious, generated by shared culture. Some of the highest profile, major power democracies—the United States and the United Kingdom, for example—are essentially two-party systems, but they also have a shared Anglo-Saxon heritage. The concern is that this background might be associated with both two-party systems and particular patterns of conflict behavior. However, we find little evidence that this is in fact the case, or at least that it is a primary driver of the effects that we observe in the chapters that follow. As we have noted, our findings are surprisingly consistent and robust, including when we exclude particular states or groups of states such as the United States and the United Kingdom.

[43] Jones (2013).

[44] Powell (2000); Lijphart (1999).

[45] On the ambiguous relationship, see Wlezien and Soroka (2012). On the inverse relationship, see, e.g., Kunicova and Rose-Ackerman (2005), Belchior (2012), and Tavits (2007). On extreme party fragmentation, see Anderson (2000). See also Powell and Whitten (1993) on the role of clarity of responsibility in democratic elections.

from ascribing responsibility for policy outcomes to individual politicians or parties. While others have challenged the empirical evidence underlying some of these revisionist arguments,[46] we would nonetheless stipulate that, at the extremes, such factors might at least potentially work counter to the general Downsian pattern we emphasize in our theory. That said, we maintain—and empirically demonstrate in later chapters—that across democracies and over time, party competition tends, on average, to be positively associated with democratic constraint.

Moreover, it is also worth noting that the "clarity of responsibility" literature has largely focused on holding governments accountable for *economic* rather than *foreign* policies. In most democracies, chief executives dominate foreign policy—especially matters of war and peace—to a far greater extent than economic policy. It is not an exaggeration to say that in wartime, a democracy's president or prime minister typically becomes the face of the nation's policy. Consequently, citizens are likely better situated to hold leaders accountable in foreign than in economic policy, all else equal. Nevertheless, in the appendix to chapter 5 we explicitly account for the possible influence of clarity of responsibility in a series of robustness tests employing the widest set of countries for which appropriate data are available—thirty-four OECD member states.

It is possible to visualize the relationship between the extent of political opposition and typical citizens' political knowledge implicit in Downs's theory. Cross-national surveys measuring citizen political knowledge are unfortunately relatively few and far between. The OECD, however, did conduct a 2007 survey on economic knowledge that included twenty-nine member states.[47] The survey asked respondents in each country to estimate their own nation's growth rate during the prior and current year, as well as the unemployment and inflation rates. From this information, we generate two economic knowledge indicators. The first measures the absolute value of the distance between the average estimate among respondents from each nation and the true values of each economic indicator for that nation, with the various elements summed together to form a single scale (where higher values indicate *lower* accuracy in responses). The second employs the percentages of respondents unable to offer a response (that is, those selecting "don't know") to each question. To create an aggregate knowledge indicator we normalized the two individual elements to 0 to 1 interval scales and added them together. This indicator runs from 0 to 2, where 0 represents maximum and 2 represents minimum economic knowledge.

As additional tests of the relationship between parties and knowledge, we create scales from six factual knowledge questions (per survey) posed to citizens in two surveys: (1) a survey of twenty-five EU member states in November 2004 about the then upcoming European constitutional referendum and (2)

[46] Royed, Leyden, and Borrelli (2000).
[47] European Commission (2008).

the October 2009 European Election Study (EES), which included twenty-six EU member states.[48]

We assess the distinction in economic and political knowledge, as measured by these indicators, between democracies that have an above average effective number of parties and those having a below average value (figure 2.2).[49] The results from a difference of means test indicate that countries with a more diverse political opposition scored 0.56 standard deviations higher on the economic knowledge scale than their lower party counterparts ($p < .05$). For the 2004 EU political knowledge test, the comparison between states with above and below average effective numbers of parties demonstrates that respondents in states with higher numbers of political parties scored 0.96 standard deviations higher on average on the EU referendum knowledge scale ($p < .05$). Finally, for the 2009 EES political knowledge test, states with more than the mean number of parties scored 0.85 standard deviations higher on the political knowledge scale than their counterparts from states with fewer than the mean number of parties ($p < .05$).

In short, citizens in democracies with relatively high numbers of parties ought to—and in these simple tests *do*—score higher on basic measures of political and economic knowledge than their counterparts in democracies with fewer parties.[50]

---

[48] All statements from both surveys were in true-false format. In 2004, they were as follows: (1) "The position of a Foreign Affairs Minister of the European Union will be created," (2) "At least one million citizens of the European Union can request the adoption of a European law," (3) "The President of the European Council is directly elected by European citizens," (4) "A direct European tax will be created," (5) "National citizenship will disappear," and (6) "A member State can leave the European Union if it wishes to do so." For each statement, we recorded the average percentage offering the correct response for each member country. We then added the six statements together to form a six-item scale. The 2009 EES survey lists seven true-false factual knowledge items, with the correct answers provided in the codebook for only six of the seven statements. Of these six statements, four concern the EU and are identical across all countries, while two are identified in the codebook as "country specific." The four universal statements are the following: (1) "Switzerland is a member of the EU," (2) "The European Union has 25 member states," (3) "Every country in the EU elects the same number of representatives to the European Parliament," and (4) "Every six months, a different Member State becomes president of the Council of the European Union." We cannot list all country-specific statements in one footnote. By way of example, the two country-specific statements for the United Kingdom for which correct answers are provided in the codebook are (1) "The British Secretary of State for Children, Schools and Families is Ed Balls" and (2) "There are 969 members of the British House of Commons." As before, we added the six statements together to form a six-item scale. In this case, the data are at the individual respondent level. The scale runs from 0 to 6, with participants receiving one point for each correct response.

[49] To assess the number of parties we relied on Bormann and Golder's (2013) measure of effective number of parliamentary parties (ENPP), which we discuss in detail in chapter 3.

[50] One possible critique of this analysis might be that countries with relatively high numbers of parties might share in common other characteristics—perhaps small, open economies that are especially EU-oriented, as in Scandinavia—that are associated with higher levels of political engagement, and hence higher political knowledge. If so, this would call the hypothesized linkage between party systems and political knowledge into question. We can indirectly test this alternative in the one case where we have individual-level data, the 2009 EES. In that data set, as predicted and as

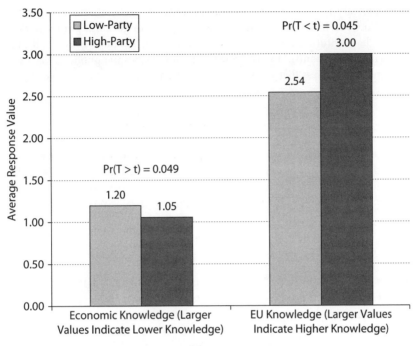

Figure 2.2. Parties and political knowledge
Source: European Election Study (2009) and European Commission (2008).

We thus argue that the extent of political opposition is crucial to the information environment within a democracy. In the immediate term, it translates into more poles of power and opinion. This increases the probability that some among the political elite will find it advantageous to alert the public when foreign policy begins to depart from citizens' underlying preferences. The effect, however, does not stop there. Over the longer term, a diverse opposition changes both the baseline political knowledge and engagement of the citizenry as well as the structure and behavior of the media (which we turn to in the next section). This leaves citizens in countries with more extensive political opposition much better situated to defend their interests.

That said, opposition elites and whistleblowing remain necessary but insufficient for reliably generating electoral accountability and democratic constraint. They will have a minimal impact on actual outcomes if no one, or too

figure 2.2 shows, political knowledge is positively correlated (+.13) with having more than the mean effective number of parliamentary parties (ENPP). However, ENPP is weakly (and negatively) correlated with interest in politics (–.08) and interest in the European election (–.04), even as it is strongly positively correlated with voter turnout in the 2009 EU election (+.34). Hence, there is no evidence in these data that some latent, unaccounted for factor associated with both the party system and interest in politics or the EU explains the observed positive relationship between ENPP and EU-related political knowledge (or participation).

few, can hear them. Quality information entails both generation and transmission. Thus, electoral institutions play a major role in generating information, but media institutions, which we have thus far touched upon only briefly, are the primary mechanism by which information reaches the public. It is to this transmission process that we next turn our attention.

MEDIA INSTITUTIONS AND THE TRANSMISSION OF INFORMATION

The political science literature traditionally has treated the media as an accommodating conduit for leaders' messages.[51] The most well-known variant of this perspective holds that the media index their coverage to elite rhetoric in Washington.[52] For example, reporters who spend many years as White House correspondents can be captured by the institution and become beholden to the administration for the high levels of access granted to them. More recent observers have noted the media's reliance on packaged news, particularly in the form of pictures or video footage, that the White House Press Office is uniquely able to provide and thereby "spin."[53] The implication of the indexing hypothesis is that the media do not—despite a widely held belief in the mission to inform[54]—independently remedy the information inequities between leaders and the public. Rather, without the intervention of opposition elites, they tend to exacerbate the advantages of the executive.

Some research, however, suggests that the media may be more proactive than indexing theories suggest. For example, the political communication "gatekeeper" literature shows how journalists filter elite rhetoric by determining the newsworthiness of stories, implying that what actually gets through to consumers is an unrepresentative sample of elite positions.[55] Extending this research to foreign policy, Baum and Groeling find that common journalistic criteria for newsworthiness (novelty, conflict, balance, and authority) result in a biased representation in the media of elite rhetoric regarding foreign policy crises and wars.[56] This includes systematic overrepresentations of criticism of the president by his own party and support from the opposition party, as well as underrepresentation of support for the president from his fellow partisans.[57]

However, Baum and Groeling further argue that any discrepancies between actual conflict events and their representations in the media will likely recede

[51] Bloch and Lehman-Wilzig (2002); Brody (1992). For an exception, see Baum and Groeling (2010).

[52] Bennett (1990); Bennett, Lawrence, and Livingston (2006); Hallin (1986).

[53] Graber (2002); Iyengar and Reeves (1997).

[54] E.g., Bennett (1997).

[55] Galtung and Ruge (1965); White (1950); Patterson (1998).

[56] Baum and Groeling (2010).

[57] See also Groeling (2010).

over time, as a conflict drags on. The reason is that with time journalists are increasingly able to identify independent sources of information from beyond Washington in general, and the White House in particular. They can then use these independent sources to assess the veracity of information provided by the White House. Baum and Groeling refer to this pattern as a shrinking of the "elasticity of reality."[58]

For our purposes, the key implication is that sooner or later, media in low-party systems will tend to catch up and perform at least some semblance of a watchdog function. This appears to have been the case in the United States vis-à-vis Iraq, where the tenor of media coverage shifted dramatically over time, from initial disproportionate support for the war to disproportionate criticism of the Bush administration's handling of it.[59] Arguably, the end result was the Democratic takeover of the House of Representatives in the 2006 midterm congressional election. The implication is that if a conflict drags on long enough, even relatively unconstrained democratic leaders are eventually likely to feel at least some constraining pressure from their electorate. However, such pressure is likely to arise more gradually in a low- relative to a high-party system, where, due to media indexing, earlier and more frequent challenges to the government are likely to appear in the press.

Such caveats and exceptions aside, the indexing hypothesis has proven durable in part because media do frequently transmit elite messages with largely intact frames.[60] As we have already noted, the public typically is ill informed and hence unmotivated to object. Unless the situation is egregious enough to induce the political opposition to blow the whistle, the public is likely to remain unengaged with the process. Thus, the information equilibrium tends to favor the executive most of the time, and the media typically have incentives to be more responsive to leaders' preferences than to the public as consumers of information.[61]

But to what exactly are the media indexing? Because much of this literature was developed in the context of the United States, where one party holds the presidency (the primary source of indexing) and a single party sits in opposition, scholars have given relatively little consideration to differences in the extent of opposition. What work there is, however, indicates that the greater ideological diversity of multiparty systems tends to translate into

---

[58] See also Baum and Potter (2008).

[59] Baum and Groeling (2010).

[60] It is worth noting that the argument we make here—that media primarily relay leaders' frames or the frames of elite opposition when they contradict the leaders' preferred frame—stands in contrast to the widely held belief that the media in a democracy *should* fulfill a watchdog function (Patterson 2000). Whether or not the media *ought* to be a watchdog of democracy, their *capacity* to meet this normatively lofty standard is subject to debate, with most scholars arguing that the media's reliance on official sources undermines the watchdog function (Cohen 1963; Hamilton 2003; Baum 2003).

[61] Baum and Potter (2008).

more diverse media discussion (in terms of numbers of sources and frames that a given outlet will cover) and consequently a more politically knowledgeable and engaged citizenry (as substantiated, at least suggestively, by the aforementioned survey data).[62]

For instance, research has shown that because they index to a wider array of individual parties, media outlets in multiparty electoral systems tend to attract smaller and ideologically narrower audiences and report in more depth on a wider range of policy issues than their counterparts in two-party systems.[63] These outlets also tend to offer less personality-centric coverage of politics,[64] and more mainstream coverage of ideologically diverse and oppositional viewpoints.[65] In other words, media in multiparty systems tend to deliver more diverse and higher quality political information, where quality is defined as "information voters can use to inform party choices across contests (local, state, and federal) and across time."[66] Citizens in multiparty systems are thus more likely to consume media that have access to, and hence make available to them, competing frames—including alternatives to the government's preferred frame[67]—when leaders engage in foreign policy activities. The implication is that media coverage (or an important subset of it) is likely to be more *functionally* independent from the executive in multiparty democracies than in their two-party counterparts.

The higher quality information environment produced by the media of multiparty democracies leads to long-term advantages for the citizens of these states, at least when it comes to holding their elected representatives to account for their foreign policy decisions. Those advantages, as noted, translate into more a politically knowledgeable public,[68] and by extension a more politically sophisticated electorate.[69] Citizens exposed to a greater range of information thus operate on a day-to-day basis in a richer information environment that will tend to highlight a leader's foreign policy blunders. Such policy debate makes citizens better able to recognize and use ideological cues than their counterparts in two-party democracies. Evidence suggests that such citizens are also, all else equal, better able to incorporate new information into their belief systems.[70] This leaves them better equipped to hold their leaders accountable, relative to citizens in two-party democracies.

---

[62] Greater diversity of frames across media outlets does not, however, necessarily imply any particular degree of ideological balance within or across media outlets in a given country.

[63] E.g., Moosbrugger (n.d.); Benson (2009).

[64] Stromback and Dimitrova (2006).

[65] Sheafer and Wolfsfeld (2009).

[66] Moosbrugger (n.d.: 13).

[67] Sheafer and Wolfsfeld (2009).

[68] Pennings (1998); Powell (1982).

[69] Schmitt-Beck (2003); Kumlin (2001); Bennett (1995).

[70] Kumlin (2001); Milner (2002); Gordon and Segura (1997).

Additional research shows that the effect of a frame on an individual's position tends to be strongest if no competing frame is available to counter it.[71] Given that media in multiparty states are more likely to offer diverse perspectives, this suggests that media coverage is more likely to diverge from the government line in such systems. Consequently, citizens are relatively less likely—given greater access to competing frames—to accept the government's preferred frame. It also suggests that citizens in multiparty states are more likely than their counterparts in two-party states to view the media as credible. Hence, leaders of multiparty democracies ought, all else equal, to be more concerned than their counterparts in two-party democracies with the prospect of public scrutiny of their foreign policy activities.

Finally, these effects can be surprisingly durable. Even relatively attentive and well-informed citizens tend to rapidly forget why they supported or opposed a policy as it fades from the public spotlight. Having engaged with it once, however, they are considerably more likely to remember their prior position—if not necessarily their reasons for holding that position—if a political entrepreneur (perhaps a member of an opposition party) later primes the issue.[72] Criticisms of a leader's foreign policy by her political opponents are therefore more likely to resonate over the long term with a public that is attentive in the short term. Hence, such criticism is more politically effective if the public is attentive to a given issue than if it is largely uninterested.

One empirical implication of these relationships is that as the number of electoral parties in a state increases, we should observe relatively more policy-oriented and less personality- or human-interest-oriented news coverage, as well as less support for government policy and a wider range of frames pertaining to a given policy appearing in the news. More diversity in frames means more alternatives to the government's preferred frame and by extension the possibility of decreased support for it. We term this the "Downsian Premise." We treat this premise as an assumption—that is, our own extension of Downs's core prediction that multipartism will be positively associated with ideology- or policy-centric political discourse—in our tests in chapters 3 to 5. This notion has some preexisting support in the extant comparative institutions literature. Schuck et al., for example, find that the extent of partisan contestation drives the relative salience of elections for the media.[73] Interestingly, they find a threshold effect in which, beyond a certain point, media take notice when they otherwise are much less likely to do so. Along similar lines, evidence suggests that electoral systems fundamentally shape the way the media frame election coverage, with media in higher opposition systems tending toward more nuanced, policy-centric coverage.[74] Nonetheless, in

[71] Druckman (2004).
[72] Lodge, Steenbergen, and Brau (1995).
[73] Schuck et al. (2011).
[74] Schuck et al. (2013).

chapter 6 we return to the task of empirically substantiating this assumption's plausibility.

HEARING THE WHISTLEBLOWERS— THE IMPORTANCE OF THE PRESS

Thus far we have assumed that when the media transmit a message, whatever it is, it reaches the public. In other words, the public has perfect access to the media. However, in reality media access is far from ubiquitous.

Research on the role of the media in conflict processes has largely ignored the implications of variation in the capacity of democratic citizens to *receive* information transmitted via even the freest media. If citizens lack access to the media, most will lack sufficient credible information to assess their leader's foreign policy activities. Even if diverse opposition politicians interested in exposing an incumbent leader's failures *do* have access to press outlets that are inclined to transmit their critiques, absent widespread media access they will have a limited capacity to reach the public. In other words, if citizens lack access to the media and so cannot hear any opposition critiques, it becomes largely irrelevant whether the transmitted information is of low or high quality.

In contemporary mass democracies, the media are typically leaders' primary vehicles for communicating to citizens. This means that, all else equal, in countries where large proportions of the public have ready access to the press, citizens are more likely to be listening when their leaders call. Such leaders are, for better or worse, more constrained, contingent on the quality of information the media offer. They face greater potential risks from acting contrary to the preferences of their citizens, especially if they face an opposition likely to challenge their preferred foreign policy frame. The extent of public access to reliable political information via the media ought therefore to influence leaders' willingness to pursue potentially risky foreign policy actions. After all, absent access to the media, citizens will lack sufficient credible information to evaluate a leader's foreign policy performance, at least in the short run (that is, until the longer-term consequences are apparent).

Some might voice the concern that media access is simply a proxy measure of nations' relative levels of economic development. That is, greater access may simply result from wealth. If so, wealth, rather than media access, would account for any observed effect on responsiveness. We have three responses to this concern.

First, development and media access do not move in lockstep. For example, in 2003, Botswana's per capita GDP of $5,221 was extremely similar to Lithuania's $5,360 per capita, yet television access in Lithuania was more than eleven times higher than in Botswana: 500 televisions per one thousand people, compared to 44 in Botswana. Similarly, also in 2003, Iceland and the United States had nearly identical per capita GDPs of $37,700 and $37,600, respectively, yet

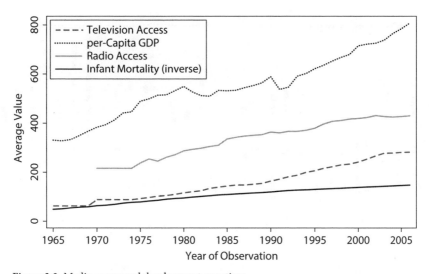

Figure 2.3. Media access and development over time.
Per capita GDP is scaled in hundreds of US dollars so that it can appear alongside the other measures. Television and radio access are measured as devices per 1,000 population. Infant mortality is per 1,000 live births and inverted to aid visual comparison (we do not use the inverse in the regressions that follow). The scaling of these variables is by necessity arbitrary, so the purpose of this figure is not to compare the magnitudes of the measures relative to one another, but rather to compare the trends within and between measures.

the United States had 2.5 times more TVs per one thousand residents: 882 versus 350.[75]

Even when aggregated across states and compared over time, it is clear that overlapping but empirically distinguishable mechanisms drive media access and development. Figure 2.3 shows the relationships among aggregate measures (rescaled for comparison) of television access, radio access, infant mortality, and per capita GDP.

While per capita GDP and both measures of media access are increasing over time, the media measures appear to increase at different rates. For the purpose of figure 2.3 we have taken the inverse of our other measure of development, infant mortality, because it generally moves in the opposite direction from our other development and media indicators. Notably, the trend for infant mortality is somewhat shallower than for our media access indicators.

---

[75] Such differences are not limited to television. In the same year, Haiti, with a per capita GDP of about $334, had, on average, 61 Internet users per one thousand people, while Cambodia, with a modestly higher per capita GDP of about $350, had only about 3 Internet users per one thousand people. At the higher end of the GDP ladder, both New Zealand and Greece in 2003 had per capita GDPs of roughly $20,000, but New Zealand had roughly three times more Internet users per one thousand people: 526 vs. 178.

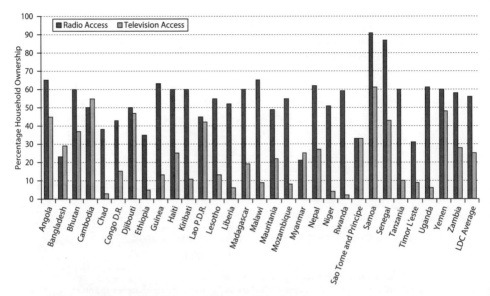

Figure 2.4. Radio and television access among LDCs (2008).
Source: International Telecommunication Union (2013).

Moreover, even among the closely correlated variables there is independent (that is, uncorrelated) shorter-term variation. For instance, the downward trend in infant mortality is considerably more linear than the upward trends in TV and radio access.[76]

More important, our actual models do not employ aggregate measures of development and media access collapsed by year (as is the case for figure 2.3). The above points aside, these trends are, overall, somewhat collinear. Instead, we rely on the substantial variation in media access across states at even relatively similar levels of development. Figure 2.4 demonstrates these variations in television and radio access among thirty-four least developed countries (LDCs) for which we have both radio and television access data.

---

[76] When we transform the trends in figure 2.3 into annual percentage changes in development and media access, we find no meaningful relationships among the "de-trended" variables. For instance, the prior year's changes in both per capita GDP and infant mortality are essentially uncorrelated with changes in television ownership in the subsequent year (with correlations of less than .01 and .06, respectively). If variations in wealth directly caused changes in TV ownership rates, one would expect to see more people buying TVs—and hence increasing TV access—during periods of heightened economic growth, and fewer people buying TVs during recessions. In the latter case, as the existing stock of TVs wears out, the effect should be a decline in replacements, and hence in overall TV access. Yet, both within the same year and with lagged development variables, there is no evidence that marginal changes in development are in any way associated with marginal changes in television access.

Among this group of states with similar levels of economic development, some have substantial radio and television access. Others have comparatively higher television than radio access (or vice versa), and still others have relatively low penetration of both media. The same is true across developed states. Moreover, the figure demonstrates the relatively high penetration of radios in even the least developed countries, which supports our use of this measure in our empirical chapters as a robustness check aimed at alleviating concerns over relative levels of development.

The point is that development and media access do not directly move together. That is, marginal increases in development do not tend to correspond in a clean way with marginal increases in media access. Indeed, there is a great deal of heterogeneity between countries on this dimension that we are able to leverage in order to assess media access independently of any overlap with development. For example, to briefly return to the cases of LDCs, evidence gathered by AudienceScapes in several such countries suggests that there is a relationship between income and television ownership.[77] However, in many instances (for example, Tanzania) it is only the wealthiest citizens who stand apart; everyone else across the income spectrum is fairly similar. That is, the correlation between income and television ownership in these surveys appears largely attributable to a substantial increase in ownership among the wealthiest residents (the top quartile in these data). The differences in rates of TV ownership across the bottom three income quartiles are far less pronounced. Once again, however, radio appears to be the great equalizer, as there is almost no systematic correlation between income and radio usage in the AudienceScapes data.

There is also distinct regional variation in the data that undercuts the idea that there is anything approaching a linear relationship between development and media access. For example, the pattern in Latin America is very different from that in Africa. In Colombia, 99 percent of urban residents (whose per capita GDP of $11,189 is 26 percent below the global average) have television access,[78] while in Pakistan (a much poorer country with a per capita GDP of just $3,149, which ranks it 140th in the world), there is a much less notable urban-rural divide.[79] The implication is that the picture is very complicated. It appears that the relationship between wealth and television access is probably strongest in the very poorest of countries (where primarily the wealthiest residents have televisions), but is less strong among countries that are poor but not destitute.

[77] http://www.audiencescapes.org/ (accessed June 5, 2014).

[78] Colombia's per capita GDP is from 2013 IMF data. According to these data, the global average in 2013 was $15,212. http://www.audiencescapes.org/country-profiles/urban-colombia/urban-colombia/communication-profile-162 (accessed June 5, 2014).

[79] http://www.audiencescapes.org/country-profiles-pakistan-pakistan-communications-profile-research (accessed June 5, 2014).

This brings us to our second retort, which is that because the relationship between media access and development is far from absolute and automatic we can in large part address any remaining concerns by including basic measures of development in our empirical analyses.

A skeptic might counter that the apparent relationship between access and responsiveness is still simply the result of residual correlation. To this critique we offer our third, and arguably most important reply, which is simply that we can think of no theoretically compelling reason why wealth, independent of its relationship with the variables we identify, should causally influence responsiveness. Moreover, even if it does so, it is unclear why such influence would move in opposing directions—as we will argue is the case with media access—depending on a state's party system.

Concerns about the potential role of development aside, if a country lacks basic media freedoms and this lack of freedom stems from the executive, access will become essentially irrelevant and media will fail to index to opposition in the way we have described. To the extent that the executive's political opponents are able to voice their objections in such a system, the media may be forbidden to transmit their critiques to the public, particularly in high-salience foreign policy situations. In a state with few parties and an unfree press, the leader's message will have even less credibility due to her ability to minimize any residual independence of the media's message. Thus, as we noted in chapter 1, press freedom is an essential scope condition, bounding the universe of cases to which our theory should reasonably apply.

The general lack of scholarly scrutiny of press freedom in conflict processes stems in large part from a practical limitation. That is, democracy and media freedom are substantially collinear, making any effects of media freedom difficult to differentiate from the more prevalent arguments about regime type. Nonetheless, recall from chapter 1 that several scholars have noted the centrality of a free press to conflict processes. In each instance, the hypothesized causal mechanism involves the enhanced credibility to citizens of information provided by a press free from government influence. Van Belle argues that this facilitates peaceful conflict resolution among democracies by raising the domestic political risks of war for leaders on both sides of a dispute.[80] Slantchev, in turn, argues that this credibility boost enhances the capacities of leaders to credibly signal resolve to potential adversaries by generating domestic audience costs.[81]

All that said, it is important to recognize that there are some instances in which a free press may not be absolutely required. For instance, Stein asserts that even in societies where journalists risk punishment for challenging the government line, they may, under some circumstances, be willing to do so. Stein argues that when media elites conclude that, for whatever reason, the

---

[80] Van Belle (1997, 2000); see also Choi and James (2006).
[81] Slantchev (2006).

government cannot or will not punish them, they may risk criticizing it. Citizens, in turn, will view the informational content of such criticism as highly credible. They will also see it as a signal that it is safe to protest against government actions.[82]

One noteworthy, albeit short-lived, example of such a pattern took place during the earliest stages of the 1989 student-led democracy movement in Tiananmen Square in China. During the first two days of the protest movement, the government-controlled Chinese media reported events as they occurred, free from government censorship. This may have prompted more Chinese citizens to take to the streets, believing that the government's failure to crack down on the media indicated a lack of either capacity or will to repress the prodemocracy movement. On the third day, however, the Chinese government reasserted control over the media, and soon thereafter violently repressed the protest movement. The implication is that under some limited circumstances, it may be the *absence* of press freedom that makes criticism of the government costly, and hence especially credible.

Conversely, even a free press may be insufficient to produce a pacifying effect of media coverage in democracies. After all, the media in many democracies tend to index their coverage of foreign policy to the most authoritative sources in government—typically the chief executive and her underlings. Consequently, democratic leaders may be able to count on public support in many instances, at least in the short run, even if the media are institutionally independent from government.[83] The implication is that while a free press may be a necessary prerequisite for democratic constraint, it is not, by itself, a sufficient condition.

These caveats aside, a free press remains by far the most common institutional route toward the free flow of information between leaders and the mass public. The alternative scenario we described is an exception to this general rule and certainly not a process one would want to rely upon to provide consistent democratic constraint.

BRINGING TOGETHER INFORMATION GENERATION AND TRANSMISSION

As we noted at the outset to this chapter, information gaps between elected agents (that is, leaders) and citizen principals are pervasive in the foreign policies of democracies, and these gaps have a potentially substantial impact on democratic foreign policy. In prior work we have discussed the role of infor-

---

[82] Stein (2007, 2013). Stockmann (2012), in turn, argues that commercialization may offer another path to credibility for media in authoritarian states. She finds that privately owned media in China enjoy greater credibility with typical citizens than their government-controlled counterparts, in part because the authoritarian regime allows them substantial latitude in their coverage of issues that are not deemed sensitive.

[83] Entman (2003).

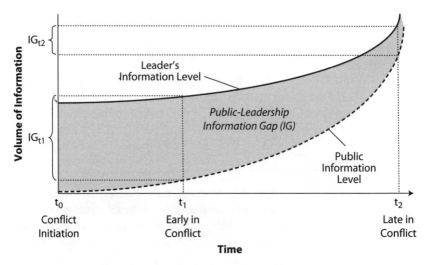

Figure 2.5. Information gap between leadership and the public

mation gaps as a way of understanding changes in democratic responsiveness over the course of a conflict, and by extension within an individual country.[84] Responsiveness generally increases with time and salience precisely because this information gap tends to close over time. Related to the argument we propose here, leadership initially holds a substantial advantage over the public, but this advantage diminishes over time as cues (e.g., casualties) emerge that attract attention from opposition partisans, the media, and the public (figure 2.5).

Leaders enjoy such a substantial initial informational advantage at the outset of a conflict because the baseline state of public attention to foreign policy (and hence demand for foreign policy news) is so low (though we argue that baseline is lower in two-party democracies relative to those with more diversified opposition). In figure 2.5, IG_{t1} represents that relatively large information gap at time t_1 (a hypothetical point in time early in the conflict). However, several factors—including elite discord—can prompt the public to increase its demand for information from the media as well as the amount of authoritative source material available for the media to transmit, thereby narrowing the information gap. This effect becomes more pronounced if a conflict drags on and so allows additional opposition voices to join the fray, represented in figure 2.5 by the smaller information gap (IG_{t2}) at time t_2 (a hypothetical time period later in the conflict).[85]

---

[84] Baum and Potter (2008); Baum and Groeling (2010).

[85] Certainly, policy makers are well aware of the window of opportunity presented by these information asymmetries, and they increasingly look for tools that will allow them to extend their informational and messaging advantages. As Bryan G. Whitman, deputy assistant secretary of de-

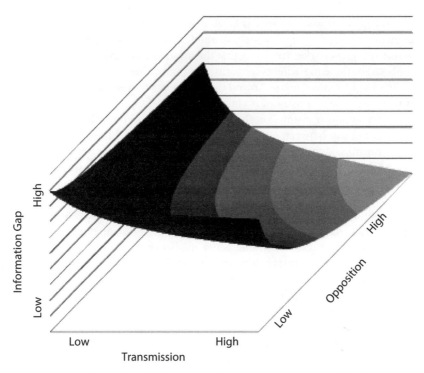

Figure 2.6. Theoretical relationships among information, transmission, and opposition

Our primary concern, however, is not with the narrowing of information asymmetries over time within conflicts, but rather with comparing these gaps across states with varying institutional structures. We posit that both the initial gap at time t_0 (at the outset of the conflict) in figure 2.5 and the speed with which it closes vary with the media and electoral institutions that differ across democracies. Thus, the same basic logic holds within and between democratic states. The addition of dissenting voices in the form of opposition elites reduces the information gap between elected executive agents and citizen principals and increases the speed with which it closes. The effectiveness of these whistle-blowers, however, is mediated by the effectiveness of media transmission in terms of both freedom and access. Figure 2.6 presents the stylized relationship among the size of the information gap, the extent of opposition, and media transmission).

In figure 2.6, the shading progresses from darker (indicating larger informa-tion gaps) to lighter (smaller information gaps). The lightest region and the

---

fense for media operations, observed with respect to the Pentagon's policy of embedding reporters within US combat units in Iraq in 2003, "Our goal was to dominate the information market" (Carr 2003).

lowest informational disparity is located at the right side of the figure in the domain representing high opposition and high information transmission. The gradations grow darker (meaning that the information gap increases) as either (or both) of these ingredients for constraint diminishes.

The implication of figure 2.6 and the arguments that we have made thus far is that democratic constraint is elusive and fragile. Opposition without effective information transmission through the media will do little to narrow the information gap between elected officials (or agents) and their citizen principals. Transmission without opposition is no better. One needs both the generation and transmission of information for the system to work. As we have noted (and illustrated in figure 2.1), as the information reaching citizens improves, so too do responsiveness and democratic constraint. In other words, the fire alarm must sound and citizens must hear it before democracies are likely to behave in meaningfully different ways from autocracies in their foreign policies.

How might this process of interactive mediation actually work? Figure 2.7 summarizes the mechanics behind our argument. The influence of each causal variable can be *ex ante* (indicated by dotted lines), via the leader's *expectations* concerning the likely influence of each variable on the political costs and benefits associated with the policy. This depends in part on expectations regarding news coverage, which the party system influences. It also depends on the likelihood that the public will receive the media's messages and ultimately support the policy, as well as on the leader's political vulnerability, which the party system also helps determine. Influence can also be *ex post* (indicated by solid lines) via leaders' responses to *actual expressed* public opinion. News content, in turn, directly influences public opinion, while simultaneously being influenced by the party system. Finally, the extent of access to news content also influences expressed public opinion.

In the figure, the box around the party system and news coverage represents our theoretical proposition that the latter (the nature and extent of news coverage) is preceded by and depends in significant measure upon the former (the party system). This is, of course, an oversimplification of reality. Research has shown that a variety of factors influence news content, some of which—like the newsworthiness standards of journalists—do not systematically vary across party systems.[86] For our purposes, however, this is a necessary, and we think conceptually justifiable, simplification.

Viewed in this light, it is unsurprising that a somewhat muddled picture of democratic distinctiveness in the realm of foreign policy emerges from the literature. While there are certainly mechanisms by which democracies can resolve their informational problems, they are by no means automatic, and actually vary a great deal between democracies. The failure to model this heterogeneity (typically by modeling states dichotomously, as either democratic or

---

[86] E.g., Baum and Groeling (2010); Entman (2003); Bennett (1990); Patterson (1998); Hallin (1986).

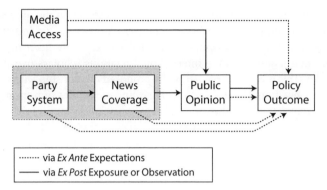

Figure 2.7. Illustration of processes by which media access, party systems, and news coverage influence foreign policy decision making

autocratic) has led to ambiguous findings because it lumps leaders who are relatively constrained together with those who are not.

FOREIGN POLICY RESPONSIVENESS AND INTERNATIONAL CONFLICT BEHAVIOR

In order to test this argument about the centrality of information generation and transmission in democratic constraint, we turn to three key moments in international conflicts: initiation, reciprocation, and the assembly of coalitions. The first and second of these relate closely to debates that have dominated international relations research for the past two decades. The third, coalition behavior, addresses an increasingly important concern in the post–Cold War era.

By beginning with initiation we arguably address the starting point and most basic element of conflict behavior and tap into one of the few seemingly established truths in international relations—the proposition that democracies do not fight one another. Levy argues that the empirical observation of an absence of conflict among democracies is the closest thing we have to a "law" in international relations.[87] But if we are correct that some democracies are considerably more constrained than others in their foreign policies, then this law may need refining. It might not be democracy per se that matters, but rather a particular constellation of democratic institutions. Regardless, by establishing our findings in this context we are able to identify an important element of the mechanism underpinning the democratic peace and link this area of inquiry with other segments of the literature that, to date, scholars have largely treated as distinct.

---

[87] Levy (1989). There are, of course, critiques of this view. See, for example, Owen (1994) and Rosato (2003).

Once a state initiates a conflict, the inevitable next step in the process is the target state's decision to reciprocate or acquiesce. Moreover, after initiation, reciprocation (of threats or dispute initiations) has arguably been the second most common fixation among international relations scholars over the past two decades. This is due in large part to its proposed relationship with the audience cost proposition.[88] Our assertions regarding the origins of responsiveness have clear implications for the idea that democratic constraint might make democracies more credible in their international commitments. If we are correct about the nature of variations in democratic constraint, it would be reasonable to expect that we should be able to find empirical manifestations of such variations in reciprocation as the primary empirical domain for testing the audience cost proposition.

Though newer, the emerging literature on coalitions explores an equally important, and arguably more pressing, issue in international politics. As the assembly of the coalition of the willing for the 2003 conflict in Iraq demonstrated, it can be difficult to predict which states are likely to join with a potentially (or actually) unpopular multilateral endeavor and which will judge the costs to be too high. Popular opinion (and variations in leaders' abilities to withstand it) appears integral to explaining states' decisions to join or eschew controversial or difficult-to-assemble coalitions, like those formed in response to the post–Cold War conflicts in Bosnia, Kosovo, Afghanistan, Iraq, Libya, and Syria. It seems highly probable that it will be necessary in the coming years to revisit such processes for multinational interventions elsewhere in the world. When such a need arises, it would be helpful to better understand which states are likely to contribute and which are more likely to remain on the sidelines.

By unpacking the role of opposition and information within democracies, we bring these questions of initiation, reciprocation, and coalition formation together in a unified framework that has been absent from prior work on the behavior of democracies in international conflict. An additional advantage of exploring the question of constraint in multiple domains and through numerous diverse analyses is that doing so provides a comprehensive and challenging regimen of tests for our theory. In the chapters that follow, we identify consistent findings despite substantial variation in periods of analysis, data, models, and analytic techniques. This increases our confidence in the validity and generalizability of our core arguments. It also alleviates the concerns that would potentially arise if we leaned too heavily on any one data set or empirical context. In particular, the well-traveled conflict-events data that underpin the empirical findings on the democratic peace and domestic audience costs have their detractors.[89] By extending our analysis into novel data on coalitions, we establish that neither the potential deficiencies of these data sets nor the idiosyncrasies of any particular data set drive our findings.

---

[88] Fearon (1994); Schultz (2001a).
[89] E.g., Downes and Sechser (2012).

Each of these conflict domains—initiation, reciprocation, and coalition formation—maps to our theory slightly differently and therefore implies a distinct set of hypotheses. We develop these hypotheses, which guide the remainder of the book, in the three sections that follow.

INITIATION AND THE DEMOCRATIC PEACE

When and how do domestic publics deter their own leaders from initiating conflicts? Despite the voluminous literature on the democratic peace, this remains an open question. That literature suggests that democracies do not typically initiate conflicts against one another, but precisely how this process works remains opaque.

Understanding the origin of the recent literature on the democratic peace helps to explain the relative dearth of theory about the mechanism underlying it. Scholars regularly trace the idea of peace between democracies to Kant.[90] However, the lineage of the current literature is more appropriately traced to the echoes of the behavioral revolution that fundamentally shifted empirical research in international relations in the 1960s and 1970s. Drawing on the first broad data sets of international conflict, a number of scholars observed the absence of conflict between democratic states in their statistical models.[91] However, this legacy has meant that the democratic peace has had difficulty progressing—so much so that some have described it as an empirical pattern in search of an explanation.[92] Indeed, the mechanisms identified by this literature largely consist of post hoc explanations for empirical findings.

For instance, in one of the most influential studies in this domain, Maoz and Russett consider the possible mechanisms that could account for the seeming absence of wars between democracies.[93] In the end they settle on shared norms as the most likely explanation. However, theory plays a quite different role in their examination than it does here. Where they primarily are seeking a plausible story that could account for their findings, we seek to develop a more robust, deductive theory of democratic constraint that will yield testable hypotheses about the data generating mechanism. Consequently, our theory is considerably more precise than the majority of work in this area. It clearly delineates a causal process and by doing so tells us something about the "why" and "how" between important phenomena such as the democratic peace and democratic credibility. As we have noted, in our view this process is less about shared norms than it is about the electoral and media institutions that tie democracies together as a class but nonetheless vary among them.

90 Kant ([1795] 1983).
91 E.g., Rummel (1979); Babst (1972); Singer and Small (1972).
92 Ray (2000).
93 Maoz and Russett (1993).

Certainly, democratic leaders contemplating a military activity abroad have good reason to weigh the potential domestic political costs and benefits of doing so. After all, war is risky. Research has shown that leaders—especially in democracies—who lose military conflicts pay a substantial political price at home, sometimes including removal from office.[94] We argue that, for the previously discussed reasons, the downside risks of conflict initiation are systematically greater for leaders of multiparty democracies where citizens have ready access to the media, relative to their counterparts in democracies without these attributes. Since the domestic political risks associated with foreign policy failure tend to exceed the potential benefits of success,[95] democratic leaders—especially in democracies where the costs are both potentially higher and more likely to be imposed—typically have more to lose than to gain by engaging in risky foreign conflicts.

The conditional nature of our arguments means that we have less clear expectations about the unconditional ("naïve") relationship between the number of parties and conflict since such expectations do not directly follow from our theory. We nevertheless pose these arguments and assess them along the way for two reasons. First, if we fail to reject them, this suggests that our proposed conditional mechanism misses some part of the overall story, with the residual captured by the unconditional coefficients. Such a finding would be a clear invitation to future work. Second, other authors have proposed and investigated versions of these simpler relationships, and we wish to engage that research on its own terms. For example, Reiter and Tillman investigate whether the number of parties, by itself, decreases the incidence of conflict by increasing constraint on leadership (they find that it does not).[96] Palmer, London, and Regan also find that the number of parties in a ruling coalition has no influence on likelihood of dispute initiation or escalation.[97] However, Leblang and Chan find that proportional representation (PR) systems are less likely than their majoritarian counterparts to fight wars.[98] With respect to audience costs and our investigation of reciprocation, Prins and Sprecher find that coalition governments (i.e., those with more parties in power) are more likely than single-party governments to militarily reciprocate crises.[99] The point is that while our theory does not generate clear expectations for the independent effect of partisan structures, others in the literature do.

Public scrutiny raises both the potential domestic political risks and rewards associated with a conflict. For instance, citizens are likely to punish their leader less severely for acting contrary to their preferences if they are inatten-

---

[94] Bueno de Mesquita and Siverson (1995); Smith (1996); Downs and Rocke (1994).
[95] Baum (2004a, 2004b).
[96] Reiter and Tillman (2002).
[97] Palmer, London, and Regan (2004).
[98] Leblang and Chan (2003).
[99] Prins and Sprecher (1999).

tive and uninformed than if they are highly engaged, all else equal.[100] Consequently, given the aforementioned disproportionate increase in costs given failure, relative to benefits given success, all else equal and to the extent possible, leaders are likely to prefer to risk employing military force abroad relatively free from public scrutiny. This in turn implies that public scrutiny may, under at least some circumstances, deter leaders from using military force by disproportionately raising the expected political costs of doing so, given a bad outcome. Given that the mass media represent the primary source of public information about foreign policy, this further implies that greater public access to mass media, especially in multiparty systems where such media are free from government censorship, is likely to be associated with more risk-averse foreign policy behavior by democratic leaders.

This pattern, of course, assumes that citizens are less prowar than their leaders. Yet it is certainly possible that citizens might support a given fight more than their government, and hence perhaps pressure a leader to enter a conflict and punish her politically if she fails to do so. For instance, Layne identifies several cases—such as the 1861 Anglo-American crisis known as the Trent Affair and the 1898 Anglo-French Fashoda crisis—where democratic citizens appear to have pushed their leaders to the brink of war against other democracies.[101] In such a circumstance, greater media access and more parties might *raise*, rather than lower, the likelihood of going to war. However, if one accepts our assumption that using military force typically attracts greater public attention than *not* doing so, then it follows from our prior assumptions regarding the relative costs versus benefits of war, leader's preferences regarding public scrutiny, and the relatively greater likelihood of public scrutiny in multiparty democracies, that such cases are likely to be the exception, rather than the rule.[102]

Consequently, in cases where we are unable to measure the state of public opinion—as in the time-series, cross-sectional analyses of initiation and reciprocation—we assume that citizens are, on average, less prowar than leadership, all else equal. However, in our tests of coalition formation in chapter 5 we have

[100]   Baum (2004a).

[101]   Layne (1994).

[102]   To cite an extreme example, even as Nazi Germany was sweeping across Europe in the late 1930s and early 1940s, strong domestic antiwar opinion constrained President Roosevelt from entering World War II until *after* the direct attack on the United States at Pearl Harbor (Baum and Kernell 2001). UK Prime Minister Neville Chamberlain, in turn, infamously appeased Hitler at Munich in 1938. While this conciliation historically is viewed in a negative light, at the time as many as 83 percent of British citizens in one poll supported Chamberlain's policy (http://www.historylearningsite.co.uk/public_opinion_and_appeasement_i.htm, accessed May 29, 2014). More recently, an average of 56 percent of respondents (in both cases) across nineteen and sixty-three countries, respectively, *opposed* the multinational interventions in Kosovo in 1999 and Afghanistan in 2001 (excluding the United States and United Kingdom; these figures rise to nearly 60 percent in each case). As previously noted, in turn, an average of two-thirds of survey respondents across sixty-two countries opposed the war in Iraq in 2003.

sufficient cross-national public opinion data on two conflicts (in Iraq and Afghanistan) to characterize the extent of public support for, or opposition to, coalition involvement for a large cross section of democracies. Hence, in these instances we relax this assumption. Instead, we assume that public opinion in democracies theoretically can either *push* leaders toward conflict or *pull* them away from it.

Consistent with the observation that the number of parties tends to be positively correlated with the extent of democratic constraint, previous studies have found that widespread public access to free media can by itself constrain public officials. Shi and Svensson, for example, demonstrate that media access is associated with a decline in expropriation of public resources for private gain because it leads to an increase in the public's level of information about government performance.[103] Along similar lines Besley, Burgess, and Prat show that media access can lead to an increase in governmental responsiveness to food shortages through much the same mechanism.[104] These findings arguably suggest that an unconditional media prediction may not be entirely "naïve."

Nonetheless, in the context of our argument, we remain primarily concerned with the contingent nature of party and media access effects. The reason is that, unlike the above research, our theory accounts for both the responsiveness-enhancing effects of increased media access in some circumstances (that is, high-party systems), as well as for additional cases (that is, low-party systems) where media access *inhibits* rather than enhances responsiveness.

Indeed, the core of our theory holds that the effects of opposition and media access on constraint are conditional. We therefore anticipate the full constraining effect only when both conditions are present. In other words, information generation matters only if that information is successfully transmitted to citizens. Transmission to citizens, in turn, can succeed in producing democratic constraint only if the necessary information is available for transmitting. In fact, when partisan opposition is low, increased media access is less likely to introduce constraint than to facilitate rally effects that favor independent executive action. Of course, even in low-party states, opposition parties presumably retain the incentive to criticize the incumbent government. Yet media institutions are less likely than their counterparts in high-party states to allow them to effectively do so, instead amplifying the government's perspective via indexing. This leads to our two conflict initiation hypotheses. These conditional hypotheses represent the critical tests of our theoretical argument as it

---

[103] Shi and Svensson (2006).

[104] Besley, Burgess, and Prat (2002); see also Besley and Burgess (2001). Shi and Svensson operationalize media access as "radios per capita," while Besley and Burgess employ newspaper circulation. For reasons we discuss in the next chapter, we believe television ownership represents a superior indicator of media access. However, as we also discuss in chapter 3, as robustness tests we replicate our key models using combined measures of television and radio access. Insufficient data on newspaper circulation were available for our statistical analyses in chapters 3 to 5, though we do employ newspaper data in our content analyses in chapter 6.

applies to conflict initiation and, hence, are where it will be falsified should it prove invalid.

H1a: Initiation hypothesis—For higher party states, as media access increases, the probability of conflict initiation will decline. As the number of parties declines, this relationship will weaken, and for low-party states will reverse, with increased media access associated with a higher probability of conflict initiation.

H1b: Low-access initiation hypothesis—At lower levels of public media access in the initiator state, variation in the number of parties will not significantly affect the likelihood of conflict initiation.

RECIPROCATION AND AUDIENCE COSTS

The ability of leaders to generate credibility through audience costs is also contingent on the presence of independent political parties, conditioned on the extent of public access to an independent media that can bridge the gap between political elites and citizens. Overlooking these contingencies may cause researchers to wrongly conclude that no relationship exists between regime type and credibility. The reason is that in some democracies—those with predominantly two-party electoral competition and limited media access—the hypothesized link is likely to be tenuous at best. Conversely, in others—particularly multiparty systems with high levels of public access to mass media—we anticipate a strong audience cost effect. Grouping all such democracies together introduces a great deal of error into the model, thereby reducing the efficiency of estimates of democracy's effect on dispute behavior. The consequence can be a false negative result (that is, a Type II error). Only by unpacking democracy to investigate the effects of variations *within* democracies can we expect to rediscover the audience cost signal hidden within the noise introduced by conflating appropriate and inappropriate cases.

While audience cost arguments play an integral role in rationalist theories of war and peace, uncovering empirical support for them has proven challenging. The very nature of audience costs makes them difficult to detect. Leaders who successfully generate credibility do not incur costs, leading to potential bias stemming from partial observability.[105] The solution that Schultz and others employ is to explore reciprocation as a secondary implication of the audience cost argument.[106] The logic is that the decision to reciprocate a dispute indicates the extent to which the targeted state finds the initiator credible. We follow this logic by exploring the relationship between the institutional variables we have identified and both dispute and threat reciprocation.

The existing scholarship on audience costs shares an implicit assumption about the nature of democracies. This is simply that the actions and statements

---

[105] Schultz (2001b).
[106] E.g., Weeks (2008); Downes and Sechser (2012).

of democratically elected leaders are immediately transparent to the voting public. This expectation, however, is at odds with our argument concerning the integral role of opposition elites and media in the transmission of information. Since the internal logic of the audience cost argument directly implies that democratic leaders have strong incentives to obscure their failings, these remedies to informational asymmetries are crucial if the system is to effectively generate credibility. That is, while nothing in the audience cost argument requires the public to be perfectly informed, the theory does rest on the assumption that citizens engage with foreign policy enough to be aware of the commitments and failures of their elected representatives.

It therefore follows that opposition parties play a key role in informing the public when leaders are not performing, including when leaders' foreign policy bluffs are called. This possibility meshes closely with the received wisdom about the role of elite discord in the formation of public opinion about foreign policy. For instance, recall from our earlier discussion that in studies of the US media, scholars have found that news content, especially in times of war, tends to reflect the tone of policy debate in Washington.[107] This suggests that as the number of parties increases in the initiator state, the probability of reciprocation by the target state will decrease.

Access to mass media is integral to the process of generating audience costs because when access is limited, the public has a diminished capacity to reliably identify foreign policy failures. In such a setting, the leaders in power, regardless of how they gained office, can control the flow of information in a way that renders hollow the threat of electoral sanction. Even if there are opposition politicians with an interest in exposing the failure of an incumbent leader, absent broad media access their ability to communicate with the public is constrained. An additional "naïve" expectation—which we again note in order to establish a baseline and speak more directly to the extant literature—follows. This is simply that as media access increases in the initiator state the probability of reciprocation by the target state should decrease.

That said, as was the case for our assessment of the democratic peace proposition, the key test of our theory lies in the interaction between party systems and media access. We expect the strongest credibility-enhancing effects to emerge in the presence of an extensive and vocal opposition and a public able to hear them. Unlike the initiation predictions, however, we do not anticipate a full reversal in valence of the effects of media access as the party system varies. The reason stems from our assumptions concerning the differences in media content in different party systems. If, as we argue, media in low-party systems are especially likely to index coverage to the executive, then greater access to media will not raise audience costs and the credibility that they provide,

---

[107] For the general case, see Bennett (1990). For more specific arguments about media indexing in times of war, see Zaller and Chiu (2000); Entman (2003); and Baum and Groeling (2010).

thereby reducing reciprocation. Rather, in low-party systems the executive will have at best a limited capacity to generate audience costs regardless of media access. Consequently, in such systems, and unlike high-party systems, we expect no meaningful relationship between media access and reciprocation. This logic leads to our reciprocation hypotheses:

H2a: Reciprocation hypothesis—For higher party states, as media access increases, the probability of reciprocation by target states will decline. As the number of parties declines, this relationship will weaken, and for low-party states there will be no significant effect on the likelihood of reciprocation by target states.

H2b: Low-access reciprocation hypothesis—At lower levels of public media access in the initiator state, variations in the number of parties will not significantly affect the likelihood of reciprocation by target states.

COALITION FORMATION

Scholarly concern with the formation of multilateral coalitions is relatively new, and hence the literature immediately addressing it is correspondingly sparse. However, the question is closely related to the long-standing scholarly concern with third-party interventions in ongoing conflicts.[108] In early work on the topic, Yamamoto and Bremer point out that major powers intervene as third parties only after carefully considering the likely actions of other major powers. Others have sought to extend the logic underpinning third-party intervention in conflict.[109] Drawing primarily on formal models, Altfeld and Bueno de Mesquita as well as Kim argue that joining behavior is mostly driven by balance-of-power considerations,[110] while Corbetta draws on network analysis to argue that preexisting ties with the disputants dictate whether a state is likely to join a conflict.[111]

There are important distinctions between these early arguments and our theory. Like the majority of those working in international relations at the time, Bremer and others investigating these issues primarily emphasized international strategic considerations rather than domestic institutions. Moreover, intervening in an ongoing conflict is a somewhat different calculation than the decidedly more modern problem of whether or not to join a multilateral coalition.

That said, some scholars have considered domestic variables closer to those we are concerned with here. Werner and Lemke, for example, look at regime and economic similarities as a way of understanding the side on which an in-

---

[108] E.g., Bremer (1992).
[109] Yamamoto and Bremer (1980).
[110] Altfeld and Bueno de Mesquita (1979); Kim (1991).
[111] Corbetta (2010).

tervener will likely enter a conflict.[112] Balch-Lindsay and Enterline, in turn, argue that states are more likely to intervene on behalf of other states with similar domestic political institutions.[113] While related, this is a somewhat different claim than our assertion that a state's own political and media institutions matter most.

The more politically sophisticated citizenry that we argue accompanies multiparty democracy and the more diverse media it engenders are particularly important in the context of coalition formation, as the public may have a very limited period of time in which to mobilize for or against a leader's proposed intervention. Because media in multiparty democracies tend to expose citizens to more varied policy frames than their counterparts in two-party democracies, citizens in multiparty democracies are less likely to accept the government's preferred frame. They are therefore more likely to challenge a leader who attempts to manipulate opinion in favor of joining an international coalition. Such citizens will also have a reduced propensity to rally behind leaders in times of conflict. Hence, leaders of multiparty democracies ought, all else equal, to be more concerned than their counterparts in two-party democracies with the prospect of public scrutiny of their decisions to join a multilateral coalition. Two hypotheses concerning public support for, and states' decisions regarding, joining military coalitions follow:[114]

H3: Coalition support hypothesis—For higher party states, as media access increases, public support for joining a military coalition will decline. As the number of parties declines, this relationship will weaken, and for low-party states will reverse, with increased media access associated with higher public support for joining a military coalition.

H4: Coalition joining hypothesis—For higher party states, as media access increases, the likelihood of joining a coalition will decline. As the number of parties declines, this relationship will weaken, and for lower party states will reverse, with increased media access associated with higher likelihood of joining a military coalition.

To varying degrees, leaders interpret variations in contemporaneous public support for an issue as evidence of the likely strength of potential support over the longer term. Indeed, election-minded leaders are particularly responsive to anticipated *future* (that is, longer-term) public opinion.[115] The closer the link between the two, the greater the influence of contemporaneous opinion on a leader's decision making. This link, in turn, is likely to be tightest in multiparty

[112] Werner and Lemke (1997).

[113] Balch-Lindsay and Enterline (2000).

[114] As previously discussed, our coalition support and joining hypotheses assume that, on average, citizens are likely to be less prowar than are leaders. However, where we explicitly measure the effects of public opinion on decision making, as in our conditional low- and high-party opinion effects hypotheses, we relax this assumption.

[115] Zaller (1994); Rosenau (1961).

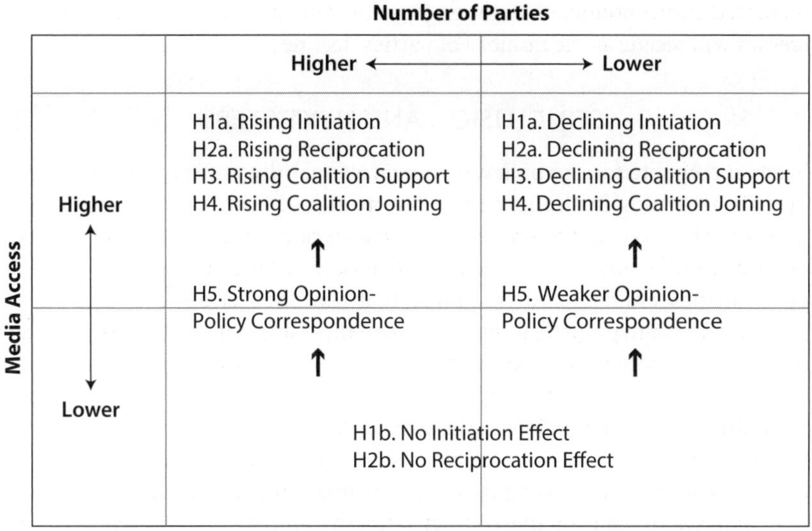

Number of Parties

		Higher ←————————→ Lower	
Media Access	**Higher** ↑ ↓ **Lower**	H1a. Rising Initiation H2a. Rising Reciprocation H3. Rising Coalition Support H4. Rising Coalition Joining ↑ H5. Strong Opinion- Policy Correspondence ↑	H1a. Declining Initiation H2a. Declining Reciprocation H3. Declining Coalition Support H4. Declining Coalition Joining ↑ H5. Weaker Opinion- Policy Correspondence ↑
		H1b. No Initiation Effect H2b. No Reciprocation Effect	

Figure 2.8. Hypothesized effects on conflict initiation and reciprocation, coalition support and joining, and opinion-policy correspondence as number of parties and media access vary

systems, due to the prevalence of more politically sophisticated citizens, whistleblowing elites, and watchdog-oriented media. Our final hypothesis follows:

H5: Parties and opinion-policy correspondence hypothesis—For high-party states, greater public access to the media will be associated with increased correspondence between governments' decisions regarding coalition joining and public opinion. As the number of parties declines, greater public access to the media will have a weaker influence on the correspondence between governments' decisions regarding coalition joining and public opinion.

Figure 2.8 summarizes our seven hypotheses. It presents the predicted effects on initiation, reciprocation, coalition support, coalition joining, and the degree of correspondence between public opinion and policy, depending on the constellation of our two key causal variables, media access and the number of parties.

Because our predictions are dynamic, the two-by-two matrix presented in figure 2.8 differs from typical such tables in its emphasis on *changes* in our dependent variables as media access and the number of parties vary (depicted by arrows) from lower to higher levels. For instance, the upward-facing arrow associated with H5 in the higher parties region indicates that given a relatively high-party system, we should see relatively stronger opinion-policy correspondence as media access increases. Conversely, the downward-facing arrow associated with H5 in the lower parties region indicates that the magnitude of

increased correspondence between opinion and policy as media access increases will recede as the number of parties declines.

CONCLUSION AND NEXT STEPS

When it comes to foreign policy, democracies vary dramatically in the capacity of their governing institutions to resolve principal-agent problems. Information is the key. When it flows freely due to a vibrant opposition and an accessible press, leaders are constrained and democracies are able to reap the dividends of peacefulness and credibility that theorists have ascribed to them. However, at the hypothetical extreme where these attributes are entirely absent, their foreign-policy behavior will be observationally equivalent to that of autocracies.

In the chapters that follow, we assess our seven hypotheses in hopes of convincingly substantiating our core assertion about the tenuous nature of democratic constraint. The book employs three primary research methods, quantitative analyses of each of the conflict domains and hypotheses we have just described, media content analysis aimed at assessing the Downsian Premise, and qualitative analyses of the lead-up to the 2003 war in Iraq. This mixed-methods approach enables us to balance generalizability and the need to speak to the extant literature on the one hand, and more careful process tracing that isolates and fleshes out our proposed causal mechanisms on the other.

3

Democratic Constraint, the Democratic Peace, and Conflict Initiation

Democracy promotion has long been a staple of US foreign policy. Woodrow Wilson famously declared that World War I was fought to "make the world safe for democracy." More than half a century later, Clinton's *National Security Strategy of Engagement and Enlargement* argued that promoting democracy was in the strategic interest of the United States because "democracies create free markets that offer economic opportunity, make for more reliable trading partners, and are far less likely to wage war on one another."[1]

During the George W. Bush administration, however, the policy morphed from one of democracy promotion to active democratization, culminating in its explicit use as a rationale for the 2003 invasion of Iraq. Key figures in the Bush administration, including National Security Advisor Condoleezza Rice, based their policies on firsthand knowledge of academic literatures associating democracy with international behaviors that are advantageous for the United States as a global hegemon, particularly the diminution of both international conflict and terrorism. The following exchange with Rice, during a 2008 interview on CNN, is a case in point:

QUESTION: Do you regret your role in the Iraq war?
RICE: I absolutely am so proud that we liberated Iraq.
QUESTION: Really?
RICE: Absolutely. And I'm especially, *as a political scientist*, not as Secretary of State, not as National Security Advisor, but as somebody who knows that structurally it matters that a geostrategically important country like Iraq is not Saddam Hussein's Iraq . . . that this different Iraq under

Elements of chapter 3 appeared in "Looking for Audience Costs in All the Wrong Places: Electoral Institutions, Media Access and Democratic Constraint" by Philip Potter and Matthew Baum, in the *Journal of Politics* 76, no. 1 (2014): 167–81; as well as in "Media, Audience Costs and the Democratic Peace" by Philip Potter and Matthew Baum in *Political Communication* 27, no. 4 (2010): 453. Reprinted with permission.

[1] Clinton (1995: 2).

> *democratic* leadership . . . is well on its way to being a multiethnic, multiconfessional democracy.[2]

This level of policy influence should have been among the greatest triumphs of international relations theory and academic political science in the post–Cold War period.[3] However, a substantial number of international relations scholars, including some of those who worked most directly with the democratic peace as an academic proposition, objected vociferously to the Bush administration's use of it.[4] Those in this camp argued that the Bush administration's application of democratic peace theory mistakenly conflated the effects of external imposition of new democracy with those of consolidated, indigenously developed democracy. As Mansfield and Snyder note, during the initial phases of democratization countries can actually become more aggressive and war-prone, not less so.[5]

Based in part on such concerns, academic opinion diverged strongly from general public opinion on the war in Iraq (figure 3.1). Comparing scholarly opinion with the attitudes of the general public in the United States reveals substantial gaps between scholars and typical citizens across the ideological spectrum, with academics consistently less supportive of the war effort.[6]

The ivory tower's retort that new democracies tend to be unstable or that there is something different about imposed democracy, however, actually exacerbates rather than resolves the underlying problem. Because most of our knowledge about democratic behavior in foreign affairs derives inductively from observation (i.e., the observation that democracies generally don't fight one another, or that relatively new ones tend to fight often) rather than theory, we actually know very little about why or how democracy matters. Consequently, we are essentially flying blind when it comes to applying this theory to practice, as the Bush administration did in Iraq. Policy makers can promote democracy in the hopes of getting the desirable outcomes we have observed in the aggregate data. But given the vagaries of international politics and the number of confounding variables at play, there is no reason to be particularly hopeful that this will work in any individual case. The point is that absent a clear understanding of *why* that desirable outcome has emerged, promoting democracy means behaving a bit like laboratory rats who learn that they get a treat when they press a button. They keep pressing as long as they continue to

[2] Official transcript available at http://2001–2009.state.gov/secretary/rm/2008/12/113304.htm (accessed May 26, 2014), emphasis added.

[3] We say post–Cold War because of the notable impact of ideas like deterrence theory, mutually assured destruction, and assured second strike, which had their origins in the work of academics such as Thomas Schelling and became integral to Cold War strategic thinking.

[4] Thirty-three of them went so far as to place a signed advertisement on the *New York Times* op-ed page (on September 26, 2002) voicing their objections.

[5] Mansfield and Snyder (2007).

[6] Peterson, Tierney, and Maliniak (2005).

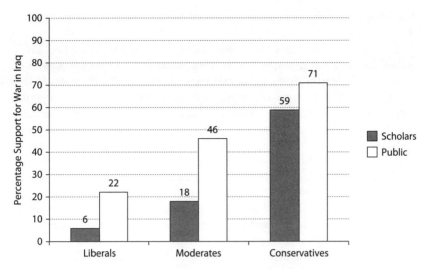

Figure 3.1. Scholarly versus public opinion on the 2003 war in Iraq.
Source: Peterson, Tierney, and Maliniak (2005).

get the outcome they want, but if the button ceases to yield treats, they know neither why nor what they can do about it. Clearly, it would be far better to understand and test the mechanism, thereby tracing the process by which democracies (or some subset of them) are associated with certain international behaviors.

How then might democracy lead to more peaceful behavior? Doyle, whom scholars often credit with reigniting interest in the democratic peace proposition, points to the Kantian notion that the unique norms and political values adopted by the citizens of democratic nations drive the process.[7] This is one possible mechanism, but it has proven persistently difficult to pin down and measure. Alternatively, it could simply be a matter of maturity as Mansfield and Snyder imply.[8] But, if that is right, how and why does consolidation pacify?[9]

Nearly from the start, an institutional variant of the democratic peace has counterbalanced this normative explanation. For example, Bueno de Mesquita and colleagues argue that democratic leaders, when faced with war, are more inclined than autocrats to shift resources to the war effort because of the electoral repercussions of failure.[10] This translates into a military advantage, makes

---

[7] Doyle (1983); Encarnacion (2006).

[8] Mansfield and Snyder (2007).

[9] Mansfield and Snyder (2007) argue that, among other things, the consolidation process tends to incentivize nationalist appeals that can fuel regional conflict, but tests of this mechanism are elusive.

[10] Bueno de Mesquita et al. (1999).

democracies unattractive targets, and makes them more selective in their choices of targets.

As we outlined in detail in the previous chapter, we make a related but finer-grained institutional argument. In our view, states start to reap the benefits of democracy (at least with respect to constraint on executive preferences in foreign policy) when electoral and media institutions support a political opposition that is vibrant and audible to voters. These forces combine to place meaningful popular constraints on the executive's foreign policy preferences. In chapter 2 we argued that two such factors mediate the willingness of leaders to risk engaging in military disputes. These are, first, the extent to which the state's electoral institutions give rise to an extensive opposition in the form of multiple political parties and, second, the extent to which the media are widely accessible to the public and therefore able to relay the information the political opposition generates. Absent the former condition, information about foreign policy missteps will be unavailable to the media and hence to citizens, who will therefore be poorly equipped to punish the leader should the policy prove ill conceived. Absent the latter, the extent and credibility of the opposition and mass media will matter little, as the public will fail to receive any information at all.

To refresh, in chapter 2 we outlined our expectation that the conditional relationship between the extent of partisan opposition and media access will produce the most consequential effects on conflict initiation. We describe these effects as our initiation and low-access initiation hypotheses (H1a and H1b, respectively). We posit that while at low levels of public media access the number of parties matters little (H1b), the relationship between parties and initiation comes into focus at higher levels of media access (H1a). In this chapter we test these predictions.

It is worth emphasizing that these hypotheses imply a monadic democratic peace (i.e., democracy with the attributes we identify fight less overall) rather than a dyadic peace (i.e., democracies don't fight each other). This is a substantial departure from the existing literature, which has generally found empirical evidence only for the more limited dyadic proposition. That we find strong support for our key predictions underlines the potential importance of these arguments for academics and policy makers alike.

PERIOD AND STRUCTURE OF ANALYSIS

To assess our hypotheses we explore a period spanning 1965 to 2006. This period of analysis is substantially shorter than those prevalent in the democratic peace literature, which often reach back to the nineteenth century. However, the truncation is necessary to incorporate the media element of our argument. Specifically, we constrain the period to correspond with the television age because access to television serves as one of our primary measures of media access and because global data on media access prior to the mid-1960s are spotty at best.

An additional consideration is that this period largely predates the global emergence of the Internet and satellite television as major mechanisms for mass communication. We discuss the importance of the Internet at length in appendix 2 to this chapter and of both technologies in chapter 8. The Internet in particular functions through a quite different mechanism—making it arguably at least somewhat orthogonal to our story—and holds the potential to drive consumers to less domestically based content.[11] However, as we discuss in the appendix to this chapter and in chapter 8, to date in practice it largely mirrors traditional media in the most critical respects for our theory.

Moreover, as of this writing television remains *by far* the most important source of news and information about politics for the vast majority of the world's population. That said, in all the models that follow we control for Internet penetration rates using data from the International Telecommunication Union.[12]

The time series does, however, introduce unavoidable challenges that are less easily addressed. Foremost, this is a period dominated by either the bipolar system that characterized the Cold War (1965–88) or overwhelming US dominance (1989–2006). Where possible, we have assessed whether this transition meaningfully alters our results and find that it does not. It also raises questions about the generalizability of our findings to the present and future. It is, for example, possible that aspects of our story hold differently in the increasingly multipolar world we inhabit than they did in the bipolar and unipolar periods we explored when developing and testing our theory. We dig more deeply into these concerns in the conclusion, and argue that the essential mechanisms still hold even as some of the means adapt over time.

Since this is the first empirical chapter of the book we begin by introducing the key variables from which we derive our findings. In subsequent chapters we will simply refer back to these descriptions wherever possible in order to avoid interrupting the flow of the discussion with excessive technical details.

[11] Satellite television potentially could also direct consumers away from domestically sourced content. Unfortunately, the necessary data for a systematic analysis of the effects of satellite TV access—distinct from overall TV access—are unavailable. We nonetheless also discuss the possible impact of satellite television in more detail in chapter 8. To preview that discussion, we find that the potential for a distinct impact primarily occurs in counties with weak media and electoral institutions and therefore falls largely outside the scope of our theory.

[12] We employ Internet access as a control variable because the Internet emerges only toward the tail end of our time series. This makes it impractical to integrate it into our media access indicators that span the entire forty-one-year period of our analysis. We nonetheless tested a media access measure that included all available Internet access data. Most likely for reasons we discuss in chapter 8, the results differ hardly at all from those reported in this and subsequent chapters.

MEASURING CONFLICT INITIATION

As is the standard practice in this literature, our unit of analysis is the "directed dyad" or pair of states. In keeping with recent work in this area, we include all dyads in the analysis. However, the findings hold (see appendix 1 to this chapter) when the sample is limited to "politically relevant dyads" that include a major power or two states separated by no more than twelve miles of water.[13] Following Russett and Oneal and others who have built on their work on the democratic peace, our dependent variable is binary, coded one whenever state A initiates a military dispute against state B in the directed dyad in a given year.[14]

For data on dispute initiation, we begin with the Militarized Interstate Dispute (MID) 4.0 data set, which codes one on the first year of a MID within a dyad and zero otherwise. The Correlates of War (COW) project describes a MID as a series of interactions between states that include the threat, display, or use of military force.[15] In short, the COW project defines MIDs as ranging from any overt threat to use military force on the low end, to a full-scale war involving one thousand or more battle deaths at the high end.

As a stricter test of the relationship with militarized disputes, we restrict some models to fatal MIDs, or disputes entailing at least one battle-related casualty. Since the vast majority of MIDs involve no violence at all, it is worth establishing whether the findings hold at this threshold or are driven by the less consequential MIDs.

The tests on MIDs are the obvious starting point given their prevalence in the literature. However, ideally we would expand the inquiry beyond one data collection effort, thereby allowing us to assess the robustness of our theory of democratic constraint across different data environments. Every data set has idiosyncrasies and detractors, and it is therefore important to establish that any theory holds outside the confines any single empirical context. Put more simply, by testing our models in multiple domains we can enhance confidence in the validity of our findings.

To accomplish this, we also test the robustness of our findings against an entirely distinct formulation of the dependent variable—"international crises" from the International Crisis Behavior (ICB) Project. The ICB Project specifies two defining conditions for an international crisis: (1) a change in type and/or an increase in intensity of hostile verbal or physical interactions between two or more states, with a heightened probability of military hostilities; that, in turn, results in a (2) destabilization of their relationship and a challenge to the structure of an international system—global, dominant, or subsystem.[16] We

---

[13] We presented the results for politically relevant dyads in table 3.A1.3 and figure 3.A1.1.

[14] Russett and Oneal (2001).

[15] Gochman and Maoz (1984: 587).

[16] Brecher and Ben-Yehuda (1985).

thus create a second dependent variable, coded one if state A initiates an international crisis against state B in a given year.

MEASURING THE EXTENT OF OPPOSITION WITH POLITICAL PARTIES

We operationalize the extent of political opposition in two ways. We begin with Golder's measure of the effective number of parliamentary parties (ENPP).[17] This indicator is essentially a measure of parties with parliamentary representation—it weights each party by its seat share in the legislature and as a result excludes any parties that fail to win seats (regardless of their overall activity or share of the vote). To further establish the robustness of our findings, we turn to a second operationalization of the extent of political opposition, specifically Golder's measure of the effective number of elective parties (ENEP).[18] This latter indicator is based on the total number of parties in the electoral system, weighted by their *vote* share, and thus includes those that do not win enough votes to gain seats in the legislature. To illustrate, Germany has a 5 percent threshold to gain a seat in parliament. Should a party receive 4 percent of the popular vote it will count toward ENEP but not ENPP. In general, we consider ENPP to be the better measure of the domestic political environment. It more closely relates to our theory because it captures the number of parties *actually serving in the legislature* and therefore best situated to have independent access to the sort of information that could facilitate meaningful public constraint on the executive. However, because reasonable critics might disagree with that assessment, we replicate all models using both party measures.[19]

---

[17] Golder (2005) defines ENPP based on the following formula, from Laakso and Taagepera (1979): $\frac{1}{\sum s_i^2}$ where s_i is the percentage of seats won by the *ith* party, with independents or "others" coded as a single party.

[18] Golder (2005) defines ENEP, in turn, with the following formula, which like the measure of ENPP is taken from Laakso and Taagepera (1979): $\frac{1}{\sum v_i^2}$ where v_i is the percentage of votes won by the *ith* party (as opposed to the seat share).

[19] ENPP and ENEP correlate at .86. The distinction between them arises primarily because some parties fail to win sufficient numbers of votes to gain legislative seats. One might argue that ENEP does a better job of excluding a second possible, internal, path to democratic constraint. That is, as the number of parties within the legislature increases, the potential arises that more of them may find themselves in positions—inside a governing coalition—where they can serve as veto players, or checks on the government (Tsebelis 2002). Notably, this effect is independent of the relationship between the party system and public scrutiny of elected officials. That said, the relationship between the number of parties in the legislature (ENPP) and the size of governing coalitions varies widely across countries. (For instance, a correlation analysis based on thirty-four OECD member countries indicated that at the outset of the Iraq War in March 2003, ENPP and the number of parties in the governing cabinet correlated at about .46, indicating that while they are clearly related, they are by no means equivalent.) Perhaps more important, the vast majority of our models do not meaningfully differ across these alternative specifications of opposition. We replicate all of our key analyses using both measures, and note the instances in which this is or is not the case.

The effective number of parties is deliberately constructed to underweight extreme outliers (that is, countries with unusually high numbers of small, or fringe, parties). It is thus ill suited for capturing factors like high-party fragmentation or oversize coalitions that could, at least at the extremes—per the clarity of responsibility argument introduced in chapter 2—potentially weaken or reverse the predicted relationship between parties and constraint. However, we argue that it is the most appropriate and best available indicator for measuring the predominant relationship between typical party systems and democratic constraint worldwide. Moreover, it is the *only* such indicator available across a wide range of democracies (beyond EU member states and a few other OECD members) and over significant spans of time. All that said, as mentioned in chapter 2, in the appendix to chapter 5 we employ available data on thirty-four OECD countries to estimate the size and durability of governing coalitions at the outset of the Iraq War in March 2003. This allows us to assess to at least a limited degree whether or not these factors mitigate or otherwise mediate the effects of the effective number of parties on troop contributions to the 2003 Iraq War coalition.

Finally, in order to include nondemocracies in the analysis, which is necessary for engaging with existing work on the democratic peace, we assume that there is just one "effective political party" in these states. However, since we are primarily concerned with distinctions *within* democracies (rather than between democracies and autocracies) we restrict most of our models to democracies only and therefore also exclude the standard dichotomous measure of democracy/autocracy.

MEASURING MEDIA ACCESS

We also operationalize media access in multiple ways. The simplest of these measures is the number of televisions per one thousand people. Throughout this book we primarily focus on television access for two reasons, one conceptual and one practical. Beginning with the latter, far more (and more reliable) data are available on television access than for other mass media. More significantly, however, television has been and remains by far the most important form of media worldwide for presenting political information to *mass* audiences. According to a 2009 Pew Center survey of twenty-five countries—spanning nearly every region of the globe and level of economic development—an average of 72 percent of respondents named television as their primary source of news about national and international affairs.[20] Newspapers came in second at less than 10 percent, while the Internet took fourth place on the list, at 7.9

---

[20] The countries included in the survey were Canada, the United States, Argentina, Brazil, Mexico, Britain, France, Germany, Spain, Poland, Russia, Egypt, Israel, Jordan, Lebanon, Palestinian territories, Turkey, China, India, Indonesia, Japan, Pakistan, South Korea, Kenya, and Nigeria.

percent. It is reasonable to anticipate that the dominance of television during much of our period of analysis was at least as high as in 2009, and likely much higher.

Nevertheless, to broaden the analysis we also explore a combined measure of TV and radio access, which we arrive at by calculating the sum of televisions per one thousand people (normalized to a 0–1 scale) and radios per one thousand people (also normalized to a 0–1 scale). This measure allows us to address the uneven development among the countries in our analysis. In some developing countries televisions are harder to come by and radios remain relatively important information sources, particularly among poorer segments of the populations. This is partly attributable to radios being less reliant than televisions on regular access to electricity. Consequently, households in some less developed nations are relatively more likely to own a radio than a television. For instance, in a 2010 study by the International Telecommunication Union, out of thirty-seven least developed countries (LDCs) for which data were available, households in all but four countries had more radios than televisions.[21]

Including this combined indicator is particularly helpful in the early years of our data set when citizens in developing nations had much greater access to radios than to televisions.[22] Because radio is an older technology than television, it became a low-cost consumer product—and hence proliferated around the world—earlier in the twentieth century. Consequently, radio penetration had peaked in most parts of the world by the late 1960s, while TV ownership increased over the course of the ensuing decades covered in our data.

We primarily rely on the television access measure rather than the combined measure both because of the closer link between television and our theoretical mechanism and because the data on radio access in the 1960s are too sparse to be reliably included in the models. As a result, the combined measure of television and radio access sacrifices five years of our time series, restricting it to 1970 to 2006. It is therefore more appropriate for a secondary test of our hypotheses.

MEASURING PRESS FREEDOM

As we noted in chapter 2, we include press freedom in some models to test a secondary implication of our theory. That is, if the mechanism we propose is indeed driving our findings, then our hypothesized relationships should emerge only in states with free presses.

The long-standing concern with including press freedom in models of the liberal peace is the extent to which it covaries with democracy, both mathemat-

---

[21] International Telecommunication Union (2010).

[22] To illustrate this point, among democracies the correlation between time and our TV access indicator is .28, indicating a relatively strong increase in TV access over time.

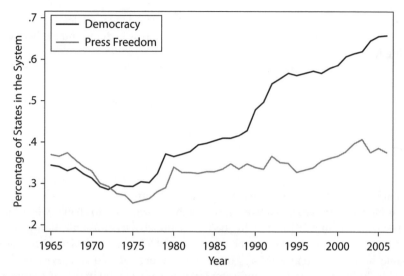

Figure 3.2. Democracy and press freedom, 1965–2006

ically and, to an important extent, conceptually. Many autocracies have some of the institutional trappings of democracy, such as nominal "opposition" parties and rubber-stamp legislatures, but few tolerate open dissent from the press corps. In contrast, there are few examples of heavily restricted media among established democracies outside wartime. There is, however, some relatively minor variance in press freedom among established democracies. For example, in contrast to the almost ironclad First Amendment protections afforded to the American press, libel laws are far stronger in the United Kingdom and free speech in Germany does not extend to certain statements surrounding Nazism.

The extent of the collinearity between democracy and press freedom is visible in figure 3.2, which plots the mean values of our measures of press freedom and democracy over time.[23] The values on the left-hand axis are percentages of total states, with the darker line representing the percentage of democracies and the lighter line representing those with free presses.

Overall, democracy and press freedom correlate at approximately .70, but the distinction between the two trends stems largely from a clear divergence

---

[23] Data on regime type are from the Polity IV data set (available at http://www.systemicpeace .org/polity/polity4.htm, accessed June 2, 2014). Data on press freedom are based on a combination of Van Belle's Global Press Freedom data set (1965–94) and Freedom House's Freedom of the Press data set (1980–2006). Later in this section we discuss the combined variable in greater detail, including how we dealt with the overlapping years. To be clear, this figure represents a substantial simplification of the dyadic data that we employ in the actual analyses.

(essentially a slope shift) in 1989. This, of course, coincides with the fall of the Soviet Union, which led to the breakaway of numerous former republics and the reassertion of functional independence by states formerly within the Soviet sphere. In the rush of state formation that accompanied this process, many states quickly installed democratic electoral institutions, which led them to be classified as democracies. Press independence, however, was slower to follow. This is unsurprising given that such independence is largely predicated on norms of noninterference that had little precedent in these countries prior to 1989.[24]

That said, as we have noted, our primary interest is in variation among democracies rather than between democracies and autocracies, and among democracies press freedom is near universal despite minor variation over time resulting from the exceptions among unconsolidated democracies. For this reason, in most models we do not include a measure of press freedom, both because it is conceptually redundant and because of its overall collinearity with democratic institutions.

In initial models, however, where we also consider autocracies, we do include measures of press freedom. This serves as an indirect test of our theory. The reason is that the informational mechanisms we have outlined should primarily, if not exclusively, function in the context of a free press, since an unfree press would allow the executive to short-circuit the link between an independent opposition and the public.

To avoid issues with collinearity we do not simultaneously include the initiator's status as a democracy and the extent of its press freedom in the same model. Instead, to directly account for the most robustly supported formulation of the democratic peace proposition, we include a control for joint democracy.[25] In models limited to democratic initiators, we simply account for the democratic status of the target state.

Where we do include a measure of press freedom, we rely on two data sources. For the 1965 to 1979 period, we employ Van Belle's global Press Freedom data set.[26] For the period 1995 to 2006, we rely on Freedom House's Press Freedom Index, which measures "the degree to which each country permits

---

[24] This also offers a hint as to an additional mechanism that might underpin Mansfield and Snyder's (2007) finding that unconsolidated democracies do not share in the democratic peace—they routinely lack robust media institutions that can transmit information in the way we argue is necessary to generate democratic constraint.

[25] To generate this measure, we turn to the most widely employed indicator in the political science literature, the Polity democracy score. The convention in the literature is to subtract a state's score on the 10-point Polity autocracy scale from its score on the 10-point democracy scale. We then count the dyad as jointly democratic if both states received scores of 6 or above.

[26] Van Belle (1997) provides a four-category scale, where 1 = free, 2 = somewhat free (but compromised by unofficial government influence or corruption), 3 = somewhat controlled by the government, and 4 = directly controlled by the government. He recommends dichotomizing the indicator, so that scores of 1–2 = free, and 3–4 = not free. We employ this coding in our data.

the free flow of information."[27] For the years in which both indicators are available (1980–94), we code media as free only if both indicators do so.

ADDITIONAL CONTROLS

There are a number of confounding factors that are likely correlated with both the explanatory variables we have just outlined and the incidence of conflict. As such, we must account for them or they could potentially bias our findings and undermine any conclusions that we might draw from them.

For example, numerous scholars have argued that power differentials between adversaries influence the emergence of conflict. However, the precise nature of this relationship remains the subject of considerable debate. Some have suggested that points at or near parity are unstable (particularly when a transition is expected).[28] Others have argued that a strong preponderance of power provides an opportunity for violence or that declining power can motivate conflict.[29] We are agnostic on these questions, at least as they relate to the argument we make here. But to address the potential for bias, control for the initiator's relative share of total capabilities within the dyad, utilizing data adapted from the COW National Material Capabilities (NMC) data set.[30]

The literature has widely defined the relationship between trade and conflict as a key element of the "Kantian tripod," along with democracy and international organizations.[31] Trade may also be related to the institutional variables we identify. To differentiate between these effects, we rely on Gleditsch's trade data.[32] We generate values for each state from the ratio of bilateral trade and GDP. This captures the degree to which trade is important relative to the overall size of the economy. Following convention, we then assess the lower of the two trade-dependence scores.

Major powers are, by definition, states with significant capabilities and wide-ranging interests in the international system. It follows that dyads con-

---

[27] Freedom House scores all countries on a 0–100 scale—based on the legal, economic, and political environment—where 0 = most free and 100 = least free. Freedom House provides recommended cut points to divide states into three categories: free, partly free, and not free. Following these cut points, we code all "free" states as one and partly or not free states as zero. (This coding correlates better with Van Belle's recommended dichotomous coding than an alternative specification moving "partly free" states to the "free" category.) The Freedom House data are available at http://www.freedomhouse.org/report-types/freedom-press#.U3y711hdVKo (accessed May 16, 2014).

[28] Organski (1958); Tammen (2000); Organski and Kugler (1977).

[29] Levy (1987).

[30] The NMC data set contains annual values for total population, urban population, iron and steel production, energy consumption, military personnel, and military expenditures (Singer 1972, 1987).

[31] Russett and Oneal (2001).

[32] Gleditsch (2002).

taining at least one major power are likely to differ in their conflict behavior in important ways from those that do not. To address these issues, we account for the presence in a dyad of any of the five states coded by the COW project as major powers during our period of analysis: the United States, United Kingdom, Soviet Union/Russia, China, and France.[33]

For conflict to occur, states must have an issue of contention, but they must also be geographically proximate enough (relative to their abilities to project power) for hostilities to actually take place. To address this spatial dimension of conflict and mobility, we control for the log of the capital-to-capital distance (in kilometers), as well as for whether the states in a dyad are contiguous.[34]

As with capabilities, the literature is replete with contradictory arguments about the implications of a standing alliance in a relationship between two states. The orthodox view is that states with formal alliance relationships are less likely to fight, and therefore any assessment of likely conflict must account for alliances.[35] Others, however, have credited alliances with both preventing and provoking international violence. Bueno de Mesquita and Lalman argue that the relative tightness or polarization of alliances at a global level has an important relationship with international conflict and violence.[36] Still others, drawing on examples such as World War I, suggest that rigid alliances can draw states into conflicts that they might otherwise avoid. Regardless, all of these authors share the view that standing alliances are correlated in one way or another with conflict, and it seems plausible that they might also influence our key explanatory variables. Therefore, to address this potential source of bias, we account for the alliance portfolio similarity of the states in the dyad.

We include an additional control variable that is not typical in models of conflict initiation: infant mortality. We do so to account for each country's relative level of development.[37] This variable reduces the likelihood that our media access variables will pick up any development effect that might then be collinear with media exposure, the object of our theoretical interest. This is important because some development research has employed our key indicator of media access—television ownership—as a proxy for standard of living.[38] At the same time, development may be associated with increased demands for politi-

---

[33] This results in dummy variables assessing whether states in the dyad are major powers: major/major, major/minor, and minor/major. Minor/minor is the reference category.

[34] Gleditsch and Singer (1975); Henderson (1997); Schampel (1993). We take the logarithm of the capital-to-capital distance to account for the rapid decay of the ability to project power and influence as distance increases. For contiguity, we employ a six-category scale coded 1 = land contiguity, 2 = contiguous across up to 12 miles of water, 3 = contiguous across 13–24 miles of water, 4 = contiguous across 25–150 miles of water, 5 = contiguous across 151–400 miles of water, 6 = not contiguous.

[35] Singer (1966).

[36] Bueno de Mesquita and Lalman (1988).

[37] Lake and Baum (2001).

[38] E.g., Guo and Grummer-Strawn (1993); Montgomery et al. (2000).

cal responsiveness and, through this mechanism, have a relationship with our dependent variable. While we also employ other measures of development— such as wealth, growth, and education—in subsequent chapters, we primarily rely on infant mortality because it has the most complete data and is more sensitive to the bottom end of the income spectrum (which is where our most serious concerns about the role of development lie) than other available measures, such as per capita GDP.[39]

That said, we also include the per capita GDP of the initiating state in most models.[40] Aside from the potential relationship with media access, which we believe is better accounted for with the measure of infant mortality, scholars have attributed to economic development several, potentially contradictory, effects on conflict propensity. Some have argued that conflict is an increasingly inefficient way for rich states to obtain resources, relative to trade, enticement, and co-optation.[41] At the other end of the spectrum, poor states may not be able to project power beyond their borders.

Another critical factor is the extent to which pairs of states have a history of conflict with one another. The extensive body of work on enduring rivalries has shown that one of the best predictors of a state's involvement in a conflict with another state is a recent prior conflict with the same state.[42] This is in part because it is easier to generate public support for a conflict when the public is already familiar with and negatively disposed toward the adversary. A case in point is the United States and Iraq. Following the 1991 Persian Gulf War, the United States and its allies (particularly Great Britain) engaged in a decade-long campaign of vilifying Iraqi leader Saddam Hussein. They also undertook numerous military actions against the Iraqi regime, ranging from enforcing a no-fly zone in northern Iraq to launching a four-day aerial bombing campaign in 1998, termed Operation Desert Fox. Throughout the decade, they warned of dire consequences should Hussein succeed in acquiring weapons of mass destruction. Consequently, when President George W. Bush began his public campaign to justify war against Iraq following 9/11, the American public was primed by a decade of American policy to accept the basic premise that Saddam Hussein represented a grave threat to US national security. We follow Carter and Signorino's advice for dealing with this potential source of bias.[43]

---

[39] We address remaining concerns about the relationship with development with the aforementioned measure that includes radio access, which is less correlated with cross-national differences in development. More fundamentally, however, as noted previously, we can think of no clear logical argument for why development would influence conflict behavior in opposing manners depending on the number of parties in a given state. Absent such a logic, it is unclear how development could be driving our results.

[40] Data come from the World Bank.

[41] Rosecrance (1986).

[42] Goertz and Diehl (1992).

[43] Carter and Signorino (2010). Specifically, this involves accounting for the number of peace years between observations of conflict by including a set of cubic spline variables derived from that

Finally, as we discussed earlier in this chapter, we control for Internet penetration rates in order to account for the Internet's potential effect on the relationship between our informational mechanism and conflict initiation.

RESULTS

To provide a sense of the structure of our analysis but avoid overburdening the reader, we provide just one regression table (table 3.1) in the text of this chapter (and none in those that follow). While many more regressions underpin our findings, we have relegated all subsequent tables of coefficients to appendices in order to avoid interrupting the flow of the chapters.

We begin with the most general analysis possible in which we include autocracies (by making the aforementioned assumption that they have no effective electoral opposition, that is, ENPP = 1) and the measure of press freedom to account for this important distinction between autocracies and democracies.

Model 1 presents the bare-bones specification with no additional covariates, which we provide to demonstrate that the key findings do not depend on the presence of the numerous control variables. This parsimonious model also allows us to maintain the maximum available data, thereby increasing our confidence that the observed effect of the interaction between partisan opposition and media access is not a function of bias generated by missing data in the covariates.

That said, as we have noted, numerous factors are potentially correlated with variables on both sides of our equations, and we must therefore account for this possibility if we are to avoid potential bias. Model 2 incorporates the basic controls found throughout most of the literature on the liberal peace. In model 3 we add infant mortality to control for development as well as per capita GDP. Model 4 presents the same model with the alternative measure of partisan opposition (ENEP), while model 5 replaces our standard measure of television access with the combined measure of radio and television access.

The problem of rare events is endemic to large, dyadic, time-series, cross-sectional conflict data sets. This is simply because the chances are remote that there will be a conflict between any two states in a given year. In our data set, out of roughly 900,000 total dyad years, there were only 1,397 MID initiations (fatal MIDs and crises are even rarer). In other words, the likelihood of a use of force between a randomly selected pair of states in a given year is extremely remote, less than one fifth of one percent. To address this issue, model 6 presents a log-log model, which is specifically designed to correct for the bias introduced by rare positive occurrences.[44]

---

variable. Available evidence indicates that this solves the problem. The Durban-Watson d-statistic goes from approximately 0.2 without the correction to approximately 3, indicating no autocorrelation in the residuals. As an alternative, we also explored the corrections suggested by Beck, Katz, and Tucker (1998) and obtained nearly identical results.

[44] To some extent, our additional checks on politically relevant dyads, rather than all dyads,

Table 3.1. Models of Democratic Constraint and Conflict Initiation, All States

	No Controls	Traditional Controls	Development Controls	ENEP	TV & Radio Access	Log Log Model
	1	2	3	4	5	6
Parties	-0.1174***	0.0325	-0.0094	0.0159	0.0441	-0.0089
	(0.036)	(0.054)	(0.059)	(0.034)	(0.061)	(0.057)
Access	0.0001	0.0006	-0.0009	0.0000	0.0729	-0.0008
	(0.000)	(0.001)	(0.001)	(0.001)	(0.436)	(0.001)
Parties × access	0.0000	-0.0003	-0.0001	-0.0000	-0.2296	-0.0001
	(0.000)	(0.000)	(0.000)	(0.000)	(0.141)	(0.000)
Press freedom	-1.3377***	-0.4558	-0.9067*	-0.7192*	-1.4361**	-0.8668*
	(0.148)	(0.366)	(0.425)	(0.304)	(0.510)	(0.418)
Parties × press freedom	0.1753***	-0.0597	-0.0051	0.0256	0.0425	-0.0099
	(0.046)	(0.122)	(0.135)	(0.070)	(0.153)	(0.134)
Access × press freedom	0.0038***	0.0020*	0.0038**	0.0029***	2.1940***	0.0036**
	(0.001)	(0.001)	(0.001)	(0.001)	(0.649)	(0.001)
Press freedom × parties × access	-0.0008***	-0.0004	-0.0006	-0.0006*	-0.1796	-0.0006
	(0.000)	(0.000)	(0.000)	(0.000)	(0.227)	(0.000)
Joint democracy	—	-0.3536**	-0.3555**	-0.3522**	-0.4060**	-0.3484**
		(0.132)	(0.131)	(0.134)	(0.138)	(0.129)
Alliance	—	-0.1381***	-0.1443***	-0.1368***	-0.1772***	-0.1352***
		(0.031)	(0.031)	(0.031)	(0.034)	(0.029)
Side A's proportion of capabilities	—	1.2191***	1.1420***	1.1807***	0.9169***	1.1474***
		(0.157)	(0.158)	(0.159)	(0.165)	(0.155)
Trade dependence	—	0.0364***	0.0370***	0.0352***	0.0395***	0.0351***
		(0.008)	(0.008)	(0.008)	(0.008)	(0.007)
Major/major power	—	3.3265***	3.3005***	3.4801***	2.8042***	3.1601***
		(0.270)	(0.268)	(0.259)	(0.285)	(0.247)
Minor/major power	—	1.4938***	1.4276***	1.4764***	1.3076***	1.4023***
		(0.275)	(0.274)	(0.274)	(0.296)	(0.270)
Major/minor power	—	1.2225***	1.1957***	1.3554***	1.0931***	1.1442***
		(0.128)	(0.125)	(0.124)	(0.143)	(0.121)
Contiguity	—	2.7306***	2.7717***	2.6877***	2.6117***	2.7506***
		(0.138)	(0.138)	(0.136)	(0.152)	(0.133)
Distance	—	-0.6129***	-0.6040***	-0.6302***	-0.7373***	-0.5773***
		(0.043)	(0.043)	(0.043)	(0.053)	(0.038)
Internet penetration	—	0.0032	0.0066	0.0025	0.0061	0.0059
		(0.006)	(0.006)	(0.006)	(0.006)	(0.006)
Infant mortality	—	—	-0.0042***	—	-0.0048***	-0.0041***
			(0.001)		(0.001)	(0.001)
GDP per capita (× 1,000)	—	—	-0.0104	—	-0.0329***	-0.0102
			(0.0071)		(0.0085)	(0.0070)
Observations	923,534	360,008	355,333	356,843	332,966	355,333

Robust standard errors in parentheses. *p < .05. **p < .01. ***p < .001.
Note: In this and other tables reported throughout the book, in order to limit the number of displayed decimal places, we multiplied select coefficients by some number (indicated below the variable label by, for instance, " × 1,000" or "× 100," etc.).

To begin, we note that the key coefficients that relate to our hypotheses are relatively consistent across all model specifications. This is notable given the significant changes to the controls, dependent variables, and modeling techniques across specifications. It suggests that while many of the controls do appear to influence states' conflict propensities, their relationships with the dependent variable appear, in these data, largely distinct from those of our key independent variables. This robustness further suggests that the results from the fully specified models are unlikely to be artifacts of model specification.

Interpreting the substantive magnitudes of the effects of our key causal variables (media access and opposition) and their conditional relationships with the dependent variable (conflict initiation), however, is not intuitive in these maximum-likelihood models (another reason why we relegate the other coefficient tables that underpin our analyses to the appendices). Furthermore, the correct hypothesis test is not the difference between the coefficient estimates and zero, but rather whether variations across access and opposition are distinguishable from one another. The point is that the statistical significance or insignificance of the coefficients actually tells us fairly little about the validity of our hypotheses, and particularly our key interactive hypotheses (H1a and H1b).

To address these issues, we calculate predicted probabilities of conflict initiation for key combinations of media access, partisan opposition, and press freedom with all other covariates held constant. This procedure makes it possible to investigate both the magnitude and statistical significance of the effects on the dependent variable caused by variations in the key causal variables in interaction with one another. In this instance, we assess the effects of increasing television access and media access (that is, television plus radio) from zero to two standard deviations above the mean in high- and low-party states, while holding the control variables constant at their mean values. For this analysis, we define low-party states as those in which ENPP is 2, while we define high-party states as ENPP equal to 5 (that is, from approximately a half standard deviation below the mean for democracies to a half standard deviation above the mean for democracies). Throughout chapters 3 and 4, when assessing ENEP in other figures, we use the same thresholds for low and high in order to facilitate comparison (ENEP has a similar distribution).

The first column of figure 3.3 shows the relationship in free press states, while the second column focuses on states without press freedom. Several notable findings emerge. Foremost, as anticipated by our initiation hypothesis (H1a), among states with press freedom, at higher levels of television or media access high-opposition states are considerably less likely to initiate conflicts than are their low-opposition counterparts. Consistent with our low-access

---

further assuage the rare events concern. We also obtain similar results when we employ Tomz, King, and Zeng's (1999) RELOGIT procedure.

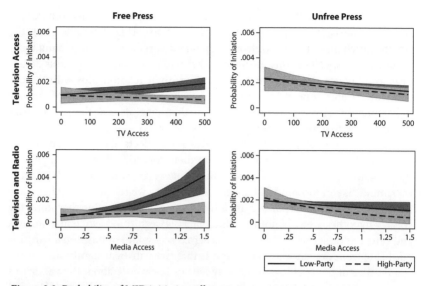

Figure 3.3. Probability of MID initiation, all states.
Television access represents the number of televisions per one thousand population. Media access represents the number of TVs and radios per thousand population, each normalized to 0–1 intervals and then summed.

initiation hypothesis (H1b), in turn, the difference between low- and high-party states becomes statistically significant beginning at about 275 televisions per one thousand population (which is approximately a half standard deviation above the global mean). For our media access measure, the distinction becomes statistically significant at about 0.75, which is approximately a standard deviation above the global mean.

Increased media access is associated with declining probabilities of conflict initiation in high-party states with free presses. However, these declines are not statistically significant at the .05 level. The opposing pattern prevails in low-party states with free presses, where we see a notable and statistically significant increase in the probability of conflict initiation (in keeping with H1a). The likely explanation for this rising rate of initiation among low-party states as media access increases is that minimal opposition, in conjunction with a credible (i.e., free) and highly accessible press, is the perfect recipe for a substantial rally-round-the-flag effect—that is, a short-term spike in support for the leader at the outset of a military conflict.[45]

---

[45] Mueller (1973); Brody (1992); Baum (2002). As we have noted, media in low-party states are substantially more compliant with elite (and especially leadership) messaging than their brethren in higher-party systems. Political opposition also tends to be disproportionately less robust, particularly in times of conflict or crisis. The result is the appearance of elite consensus around the leaders' foreign policy preferences, at least at the outset of a conflict, and hence less constraint on the use of force. It is worth noting, however, that the relatively large confidence interval around

Part of the reason for the small absolute decline in probability for high-party states is that the overall predicted probabilities are very low owing to the low overall probability of a MID, particularly in a data set composed of all possible dyads. We can therefore better understand the magnitudes in terms of changes in relative probabilities. Among high-party states, moving from zero to five hundred televisions per one thousand people results in a 42 percent decrease in the likelihood of a MID, though, as noted, this decline is not statistically significant. For low-party states an equivalent increase in access results in an approximate doubling of the probability of a MID ($p < .05$).

As we noted in chapter 2, the linkage that we draw between partisan opposition and media access assumes that the media content relayed through this theoretical mechanism is relatively free from tampering or direct censorship. The fact that our findings collapse absent free media institutions supports that intuition and in doing so bolsters the validity of the mechanism we propose rather than some unknown alternative mechanism.

Comparing the top panels with those on the bottom, it is clear that the findings are robust to either formulation of the media measure. As we have discussed, this resolves some concern over the extent to which development is driving the underlying findings. Given this equivalence, we primarily report the results from our analyses focused on television access because of the superior coverage of this measure.[46]

DEMOCRATIC CONSTRAINT AMONG DEMOCRACIES

As we have noted, examining the interaction between media and electoral institutions across all states in the system requires significant assumptions about the way in which these institutions function in autocracies. This is a particular problem when it comes to measuring the extent of political opposition, which we approximate by assuming that nondemocracies have one effective political party (Golder, from whom we obtained these data, does not code nondemocracies at all). While this is for the most part a reasonable approximation of the partisan structure of these states, it is likely that in some cases it fails to capture the true extent of political opposition. Others, for example, have pointed out that such opposition can arise from within ruling coalitions.[47] Underscoring the point that all autocracies are not created equal in this regard, Weeks indicates that there are important institutional distinctions within the broader class of autocracies that substantially influence their propensity to initiate conflicts.[48]

---

low-party, high-access, free press states stems from the small number of observations meeting this description.

[46] Additional models with the combined measure are available in appendix 1 to this chapter.

[47] Peceny and Butler (2004); Bueno de Mesquita et al. (2003).

[48] Weeks (2012).

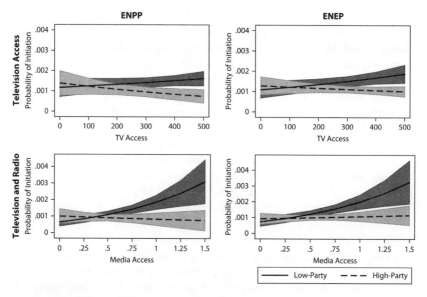

Figure 3.4. Probability of MID initiation, democracies only

That said, variations in democratic institutions—specifically partisan and media institutions—drive the mechanisms that we describe in chapter 2. Developing a parallel story about the origins of *nondemocratic* constraint, beyond the relatively brief discussion in chapter 2, is beyond the scope of this book (moreover, to a substantial extent this is what Weeks has already addressed). It therefore makes sense to replicate the findings that we generated for all states in the system (figure 3.3) for only the subset that are democracies. In this way we can show that neither the omission of autocracies nor the substantial assumptions required in order to incorporate them into the analysis are driving our results.[49] Figure 3.4 illustrates the substantive results for our key variables.

The most notable feature of figure 3.4 is how closely it replicates the left-hand portion of figure 3.3 that focuses on free press states. This is particularly so among low-party states where the probability of initiation increases with media access, indicating the extent to which substantial opposition is a necessary condition for constraint. In all cases, as predicted by the low-access initiation hypothesis (H1b), the high-opposition states become statistically distinguishable from their low-opposition counterparts at higher levels of media access. As indicated by the right-hand side of the figure, these findings also hold for ENEP as an alternative measure of the extent of opposition. In addi-

---

[49] We present the coefficients from these estimates in table 3.A1.1.

tion, as predicted by our initiation hypothesis (H1a), the slopes for high- and low-party states generally move in opposite directions as media access increases, with initiation becoming less likely in high-opposition states (albeit insignificantly so in most cases) and more likely in low-opposition ones.

ALTERNATIVE MEASURES OF CONFLICT

Other analysts have complained that the MID data set is littered with fishing disputes and minor border incursions that are neither politically important nor within the control of leaders, the opposition, or the public.[50] In response to such concerns we assess the robustness of our findings by testing our models across multiple indicators of conflict. We begin by limiting the analysis to MIDs involving fatalities (with a binary dependent variable coded one for MIDs involving at least one fatality and zero otherwise). We expect that these are, all else equal, a higher-salience subset of the broader class of MIDs. If our theory is accurate, insofar as it applies to conflict initiation, it should not be exclusively driven by lower-level nonviolent events.

As we have noted, however, a still better robustness test would rely on an entirely distinct data collection effort for a measure of conflict initiation. For this, we turn to the previously introduced crisis data from the ICB Project. Crises presumably are subject to the same theoretical relationships that we are interested in testing, but they are both conceptually distinct and immune to some of the specific critiques that scholars have lodged against the MID data (though they are certainly subject to their own). The point is not that this is a superior measure to the MID data (or vice versa), but rather that the relative strengths and weaknesses of the two data sets are distinct and we should therefore be reassured if the proposed relationships emerge in both contexts.

Figure 3.5 presents the substantive relationship from our key interaction for fatal MIDs and international crises with all other right-hand-side variables held constant.[51] Again, the key takeaway is the similarity between these findings and those derived from the prior MID analyses. At higher levels of media access high-opposition states are statistically significantly (for ENEP only) and substantially less likely to initiate both crises and fatal militarized disputes than are their low-opposition counterparts. Notably, however, this is one of the few instances where the ENPP findings are not statically significant at the .95 level (though they are nearly so). While the interactions in the ENPP models are significant and produce graphed probabilities comparable in appearance and magnitude to the ENEP results, the slightly larger error terms result in insignificant differences between high- and low-party states over the span in the data that we assess. The lessened stability of the findings

---

[50] E.g., Downes and Sechser (2012).
[51] See table 3.2 for the statistical models underlying figure 3.5.

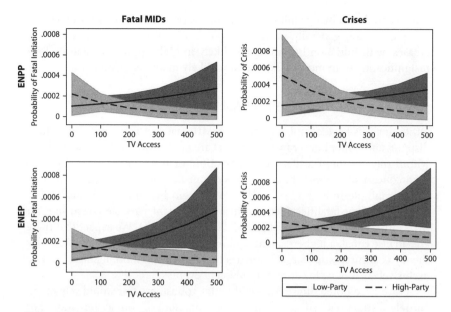

Figure 3.5. Fatal MIDs and crises

on crises and fatal MIDs is unsurprising given that these events are even more infrequent than the already relatively rare occurrences of MIDs. The greater scarcity of fatal MIDs and international crises, relative to all MIDs, is also apparent in the wider confidence intervals in figure 3.5. Among low-party states in the fatal MIDs data, there are sufficiently few high media access observations that the confidence interval expands rapidly, crossing that of the high-party states.

THE INDEPENDENT EFFECTS OF OPPOSITION AND ACCESS

Because the key conditional findings represent the crux of our theory, we have thus far not addressed the independent effects of the constituent parts of the interaction term. Figure 3.6 presents the predicted probabilities of MIDs as parties and media vary (with all covariates held constant).[52]

The first panel of figure 3.6 provides limited evidence in support of a relationship between the level of opposition—that is, the number of parties—and conflict initiation in addition to the conditional relationship that has been our focus. The decrease in the probability of initiation does not approach standard

---

[52] The statistical model that gives rise to figure 3.6 can be found in table 3.1—in the same model that underpins figure 3.3.

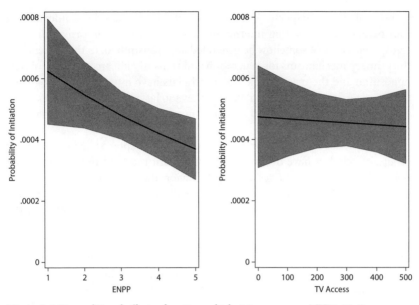

Figure 3.6. Unconditional effects of parties and television access on MID initiation

levels of significance but is suggestive of an independent negative relationship consistent with extant research in this area.[53] This tepid finding, however, indicates that the constraining effect of opposition operates largely through the conditional relationships with media access. For television access (the right side of figure 3.6) there appears to be no independent relationship at all with conflict initiation outside the conditional relationship. The key insight is that *both* factors—opposition and access to the press—need to be in place to consistently yield constraint.

CONCLUSION

As we noted in the introductory chapter, scholars of international conflict have, with few exceptions, shown little interest in the role of the mass media or electoral institutions as either a potential inhibitor or a facilitator of international conflict. At the same time, rationalist theories of war view information failure as a primary cause of interstate conflict, while democratic peace theorists consider the accountability of democratic leaders to their electorates as important for leaders seeking to project credibility in international disputes by, for instance, generating domestic audience costs.

---

[53]   E.g., Reiter and Tillman (2002).

Both of these perspectives share an emphasis on the role of information transparency in mitigating international conflict. Yet, for information to be transparent, it must somehow be generated and transmitted. In the current era, the primary mechanisms for generation and transmission are a robust political opposition and the mass media. Media scholars have more readily recognized the importance of transmission, though they too largely view the media as having *at most* an infrequent and (usually) marginal influence on international affairs.

The evidence that we have presented in this chapter suggests that both groups of scholars have overlooked an important mechanism through which the media do influence states' conflict behavior: the mediation of leaders' risk assessments. Our findings support our conditional hypotheses and indicate that parties and the media do, in combination, play important roles. In the presence of robust political opposition, mass access to the media raises leaders' perceptions of political risk associated with using military force. This makes them more hesitant to initiate military disputes. However, absent robust opposition, the relationship *reverses*, as leaders confident in their ability to control the framing of their policies are emboldened, rather than inhibited, by enhanced access to the public eye. Since these effects move in opposing directions, when researchers lump all democracies together the average effect of media access on dispute initiation approximates zero. The implication, as we argued in chapter 2, is that reducing regime variation to a binary value—either democracy or not—obscures some of the key mechanisms underlying democratic conflict behavior.

Once we recognize the diversity of democratic institutions, we find that we can easily reconcile the general dearth of evidence of uniquely pacific democratic conflict behavior at the monadic level with the recurrent finding of a dyadic democratic peace. More specifically, we find that robust political opposition, mass access to media, and the credibility-enhancing effects of a free press can, in tandem, go a long way toward accounting for the long-standing empirical observation that democracies rarely go to war against one another.

The arguments we present and test here suggest the need for more finely honed policies that move beyond a single-minded focus on democratization. Specifically, our findings indicate that those looking to institute executive constraint and the positive international externalities that come with it should promote specific institutional attributes rather than democracy in any form. This means a much more mundane promotion of robust media and pluralistic electoral institutions. While such policies may be less dramatic than images of ink-stained thumbs raised in the air signifying a nation's first free election, they may prove more effective in producing the very pacific foreign policy behavior that democratic leaders—especially US presidents—routinely cite as a primary justification for promoting democracy abroad.

It is nonetheless worth noting that while policy makers rarely cite factors like the number of parties or media access in speeches about promoting democracy, when the proverbial rubber meets the road, they often advocate that new democracies choose consociational constitutions. A case in point is Iraq. While American leaders publicly focused on the triumph of free elections, they more quietly pushed Iraq to adopt a multiparty, consociational system. They did so not in anticipation of any additional pacifying effect on Iraqi foreign policy owing to multipartism (as per our argument here). Rather, they viewed consociationalism as necessary to create sufficient domestic political buy-in among the disparate stakeholders in Iraq. In other words, the United States advocated a multiparty system for domestic political purposes. Yet our findings suggest that this choice may potentially produce an important, albeit perhaps unintended, foreign policy externality: greater democratic constraint. Nonetheless, US advocacy of a multiparty system is perhaps surprising and arguably ironic, since the United States is itself the archetypal majoritarian two-party democracy. Such a system, if successfully institutionalized, could produce the very sort of robust political opposition that we argue underpins, along with mass access to media, the pacific behavior of *some* democracies. Of course, it remains an open question whether Iraq will successfully institutionalize its nascent democratic institutions. As of this writing, even the state's territorial integrity is seemingly under siege.

All that said, as is always the case with time-series, cross-sectional analyses, the evidence presented in this chapter represents the proverbial view from thirty thousand feet. The indicators are aggregate and most of the micro-level details necessarily assumed away (that is, relegated to the error term). Our task in three of four subsequent empirical chapters (chapters 5–7) is to drill down to the micro level, by investigating individual conflicts and the behavior of specific countries and leaders during those conflicts. We will thus seek to determine whether states behave in particular conflict situations in ways consistent with our theory (chapter 7), whether media cover conflict as our theory anticipates (chapter 6), and whether our key variables can help account for other types of conflict behavior, including coalition joining (chapter 5) and reciprocation (chapter 4).

APPENDIX 1: STATISTICAL TABLES AND ROBUSTNESS TESTS

Table 3.A1.1 presents the coefficients for models limited to just democracies. These models are identical in all respects to the models in table 3.1 except that they exclude autocracies and hence also press freedom. As we have noted, the findings that emerge are very similar.

Table 3.A1.2 provides the coefficients for the models that assess the robustness of the findings to alternative dependent variables—fatal militarized inter-

Table 3.A1.1. Models of Democratic Constraint and Conflict Initiation, Democracies Only

	No Controls	Traditional Controls	Develop- ment Controls	ENEP	TV & Radio Access	Log Log Model
	1	2	3	4	5	6
Parties	0.0482***	0.0641	0.0469	0.0768*	0.1386^	0.0392
	(0.012)	(0.075)	(0.073)	(0.037)	(0.074)	(0.072)
Access	0.0029***	0.0025**	0.0020*	1.6307***	1.9187***	0.0018*
	(0.000)	(0.001)	(0.001)	(0.325)	(0.411)	(0.001)
Parties × access	−0.0005***	−0.0007**	−0.0006*	−0.2859***	−0.4062**	−0.0006*
	(0.000)	(0.000)	(0.000)	(0.073)	(0.129)	(0.000)
Joint democracy	—	−0.4105**	−0.4088**	−0.4411**	−0.4476**	−0.3873**
		(0.136)	(0.140)	(0.147)	(0.147)	(0.136)
Alliance	—	−0.0755	−0.0437	−0.0365	−0.0293	−0.0350
		(0.046)	(0.045)	(0.048)	(0.048)	(0.043)
Side A's proportion of capabilities	—	0.9314***	0.8659***	0.6770**	0.7097***	0.8430***
		(0.196)	(0.201)	(0.207)	(0.210)	(0.198)
Trade dependence	—	−0.8683*	−1.5581**	−1.6031**	−1.6381**	−1.5241**
		(0.388)	(0.550)	(0.612)	(0.614)	(0.554)
Major/major power	—	3.7107***	4.0664***	3.5422***	3.3209***	3.8394***
		(0.354)	(0.377)	(0.433)	(0.453)	(0.358)
Minor/major power	—	1.9610***	1.8749***	1.8418***	1.8234***	1.8190***
		(0.298)	(0.322)	(0.344)	(0.347)	(0.316)
Major/minor power	—	1.5274***	1.7682***	1.8635***	1.5836***	1.7554***
		(0.161)	(0.187)	(0.221)	(0.232)	(0.185)
Contiguity	—	3.2340***	3.2641***	3.2157***	3.2390***	3.1737***
		(0.195)	(0.198)	(0.222)	(0.220)	(0.193)
Distance	—	−0.5127***	−0.5363***	−0.6196***	−0.6029***	−0.5332***
		(0.060)	(0.065)	(0.073)	(0.073)	(0.061)
Internet penetration	—	—	0.0047	0.0053	0.0031	0.0047
			(0.007)	(0.007)	(0.007)	(0.007)
Infant mortality	—	—	0.0008	0.0008	0.0011	0.0009
			(0.001)	(0.001)	(0.001)	(0.001)
GDP per capita (× 1,000)	—	—	−0.0019	−0.0259*	−0.0203*	−0.0036
			(0.010)	(0.010)	(0.010)	(0.001)
Observations	539,957	266,098	261,857	244,619	247,678	261,857

Robust standard errors in parentheses. ^$p < .10$. *$p < .05$. **$p < .01$. ***$p < .001$.

state disputes and international crises. Models 1 to 4 focus on fatal MID initiation and replicate the various permutations of ENPP/ENEP and TV access/media access as operationalizations of our key concepts from our core models. Models 5 to 8 repeat the exercise for international crises.

Finally, as an additional check on the validity of our findings we explore whether they hold in the context of politically relevant dyads. Table 3.A1.3 provides the coefficients and standard errors from these specifications.

Table 3.A1.2. Models of Democratic Constraint and Conflict Initiation, Democracies Only, Alternative Dependent Variables

	Fatal Initiation ENPP/TV	Fatal Initiation ENPP/TV & Radio	Fatal Initiation ENEP/TV	Fatal Initiation ENEP/TV & Radio	Crisis ENPP/TV	Crisis ENPP/TV & Radio	Crisis ENEP/TV	Crisis ENEP/TV & Radio
	1	2	3	4	5	6	7	8
Parties	0.2588^ (0.142)	0.4011** (0.150)	0.1769** (0.066)	0.2505** (0.078)	0.4227*** (0.112)	0.5438*** (0.115)	0.1909*** (0.049)	0.2505*** (0.056)
Access	0.0066** (0.002)	4.8018*** (1.099)	0.0073*** (0.002)	4.3567*** (0.943)	0.0059** (0.002)	3.4272*** (0.790)	0.0063*** (0.002)	2.6891*** (0.716)
Parties × access	-0.0023** (0.001)	-1.4251*** (0.407)	-0.0021** (0.000)	-1.2143*** (0.368)	-0.0021*** (0.001)	-1.0966*** (0.290)	-0.0018*** (0.000)	-0.9540*** (0.191)
Joint democracy	-1.4777** (0.558)	-1.6559** (0.587)	-1.3931^ (0.554)	-1.5354** (0.592)	-0.7233^ (0.394)	-0.9158* (0.392)	-0.7253^ (0.388)	-0.9283* (0.390)
Alliance	-0.2498^ (0.152)	-0.3034 (0.187)	-0.2642^ (0.153)	-0.3313^ (0.188)	0.1231 (0.091)	0.1538^ (0.090)	0.1048 (0.091)	0.1419 (0.092)
Side A's proportion of capabilities	1.0700^ (0.572)	0.8063 (0.633)	1.0020^ (0.560)	0.7210 (0.613)	1.2228* (0.622)	0.8353 (0.668)	1.0462^ (0.606)	0.7481 (0.655)
Trade dependence	-0.4015 (0.753)	-0.5687 (1.002)	-0.4471 (0.824)	-0.7165 (1.037)	-2.8837** (1.113)	-3.3864** (1.261)	-2.8840** (1.098)	-3.3095** (1.257)
Major/major power	4.1869** (1.302)	3.4087* (1.371)	4.2552** (1.369)	3.6741** (1.352)	2.1416^ (1.293)	2.3229^ (1.335)	2.3182^ (1.289)	2.8997* (1.326)
Minor/major power	2.5782** (0.871)	2.8082** (0.917)	2.6223** (0.872)	2.8426** (0.923)	2.5434** (0.885)	2.7527** (0.872)	2.7439*** (0.805)	2.8938*** (0.823)
Major/minor power	2.338*** (0.347)	2.5676*** (0.455)	2.7705*** (0.381)	3.3151*** (0.431)	2.7709*** (0.414)	3.0849*** (0.428)	3.1805*** (0.417)	3.8060*** (0.429)
Contiguity	4.2266*** (0.491)	4.2726*** (0.561)	4.2012*** (0.549)	4.3800*** (0.603)	4.0483*** (0.447)	4.0562*** (0.517)	4.0205*** (0.460)	4.0565*** (0.528)
Distance	-0.4390** (0.158)	-0.5786** (0.207)	-0.4956** (0.169)	-0.598** (0.209)	-0.3337* (0.137)	-0.3712* (0.155)	-0.4209** (0.133)	-0.4247** (0.147)
Internet penetration	-0.0039 (0.032)	-0.0012 (0.029)	0.0063 (0.031)	0.0154 (0.029)	0.0252 (0.021)	0.0268 (0.018)	0.0301 (0.019)	0.0347* (0.018)
Infant mortality	-0.0037 (0.004)	-0.0055 (0.005)	-0.0038 (0.004)	-0.0069 (0.005)	0.0049 (0.004)	0.0012 (0.004)	0.0045 (0.003)	0.0002 (0.004)
GDP per capita (× 1,000)	-0.0933* (0.044)	-0.1448*** (0.043)	-0.1177*** (0.034)	-0.1601*** (0.036)	-0.0042 (0.025)	-0.0429 (0.027)	-0.0431^ (0.022)	-0.0529^ (0.027)
Observations	261,857	247,678	258,692	244,619	261,857	247,678	258,692	244,619

Robust standard errors in parentheses. ^p < .10. *p < .05. **p < .01. ***p < .001.

Table 3.A1.3. Democratic Constraint and Conflict Initiation, Democracies and Politically Relevant Dyads

	No Controls	Traditional Controls	Develop-ment Controls	ENEP	TV & Radio Access	Log Log Model
	1	2	3	4	5	6
Parties	0.0482***	0.0641	0.0093	0.0589	0.0838	0.0051
	(0.012)	(0.075)	(0.086)	(0.039)	(0.088)	(0.085)
Access	0.0029***	0.0025**	0.0020^	1.8681***	2.1987***	0.0019^
	(0.000)	(0.001)	(0.001)	(0.395)	(0.504)	(0.001)
Parties × access	−0.0005***	−0.0007**	−0.0009**	−0.3361***	−0.4992**	−0.0009*
	(0.000)	(0.000)	(0.000)	(0.091)	(0.172)	(0.000)
Joint democracy	—	−0.4105**	−0.5681***	−0.6347***	−0.6357***	−0.5399***
		(0.136)	(0.153)	(0.162)	(0.161)	(0.150)
Alliance	—	−0.0755	−0.0516	−0.0384	−0.0308	−0.0509
		(0.046)	(0.046)	(0.050)	(0.050)	(0.045)
Side A's proportion of capabilities	—	0.9314***	0.4977*	0.2229	0.2965	0.4695^
		(0.196)	(0.254)	(0.276)	(0.272)	(0.248)
Trade dependence	—	−0.8683*	−0.8782^	−0.9372^	−0.9070^	−0.8510^
		(0.388)	(0.471)	(0.505)	(0.490)	(0.462)
Major/major power	—	3.7107***	2.3848***	2.5190***	2.1198***	2.2930***
		(0.354)	(0.377)	(0.436)	(0.449)	(0.358)
Minor/major power	—	1.9610***	−0.1232	0.0520	0.0563	−0.1759
		(0.298)	(0.366)	(0.397)	(0.396)	(0.359)
Major/minor power	—	1.5274***	−0.0053	0.6759*	0.2351	0.0030
		(0.161)	(0.273)	(0.343)	(0.323)	(0.267)
Contiguity	—	3.2340***	2.1724***	2.2721***	2.2815***	2.1149***
		(0.195)	(0.203)	(0.222)	(0.222)	(0.193)
Distance	—	−0.5127***	−0.1787**	−0.3163***	−0.2865***	−0.1745**
		(0.060)	(0.069)	(0.080)	(0.080)	(0.067)
Internet penetration	—	—	0.0028	0.0054	0.0018	0.0029
			(0.010)	(0.009)	(0.009)	(0.009)
Infant mortality	—	—	−0.0018	−0.0014	−0.0010	−0.0018
			(0.002)	(0.002)	(0.002)	(0.002)
GDP per capita (× 1,000)	—	—	−0.0028	−0.0598***	−0.0484**	−0.0044
			(0.014)	(0.017)	(0.016)	(0.013)
Observations	539,957	266,098	31,256	28,663	28,836	31,256

Robust standard errors in parentheses. Temporal coefficients are suppressed. ^$p < .10$. *$p < .05$. **$p < .01$. ***$p < .001$.

To better assess the extent to which the key findings carry through in these specifications, we again chart the predicted probabilities. Figure 3.A1.1 thus replicates figure 3.4 in all regards but for the limitation to politically relevant dyads. The findings hold despite the substantial decline in the number of observations, which is fully an order of magnitude less than those in the preceding models of all dyad years.

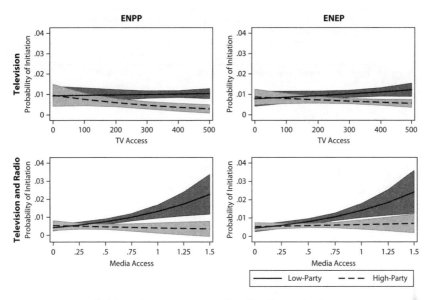

Figure 3.A1.1. Probability of MID initiation, politically relevant dyads

APPENDIX 2: THE ROLE OF THE INTERNET

Where our period of analysis overlaps with the Internet age, the logic underlying our story is far more likely to apply given domestically oriented Internet consumption than in a hypothetical alternative world of truly global information consumers—one that does not yet appear to exist. Indeed, as we will show, evidence suggests that Internet users heavily focus on domestic Internet sources, and almost exclusively so in their news consumption. We argue throughout this book, in turn, that the institutional context in which media produce domestically sourced news strongly influences its content.[54]

Along these lines, recent survey data make possible a suggestive, if far from definitive, investigation into the relative importance of the Internet, and the extent to which, for our relatively narrow theoretical purposes, it functions in ways similar to newspapers and television. The 2009 European Election Study introduced in chapter 2 included a battery of questions asking respondents how often they watched TV programs, read newspapers, or looked at websites

---

[54] If one considers *all* Internet consumption—rather than focusing on news sites (that is, those most pertinent to our argument)—then, by at least one alternate metric, the pattern becomes more varied. For instance, in Europe, circa 2012, network routers located in cities within the region accounted for 70 percent of all international Internet bandwidth, still a quite large figure. However, the corresponding figures for Africa and Latin America were far lower, about 20 percent (http://www.telegeography.com/assets/website/images/maps/global-internet-map-2012/global-internet-map-2012-x.png, accessed May 29, 2014).

Table 3.A2.1. Effect of Media Consumption on Political Knowledge Regarding 2009 European Election

	Coeff./(*Std. Err.*)
How often watch campaign news on TV	−0.172***
	(0.015)
How often read campaign news in newspaper	−0.286***
	(0.015)
How often visit websites for campaign news	−0.0725***
	(0.019)
Male	0.623***
	(0.020)
Ideological self–placement (left to right)	−0.006
	(0.004)
Ideologue	0.0286***
	(0.005)
Age stopped school	0.138***
	(0.006)
Age stopped school^2	−0.002***
	(0.000)
Unemployed	−0.390***
	(0.039)
Social class	0.150***
	(0.011)
Standard of living	0.021*
	(0.010)
Union member	0.081***
	(0.024)
Constant	2.006***
	(0.112)
Observations	23,249
R^2–	.223

Robust standard errors in parentheses. *$p < .05$. ***$p < .001$.

to learn about the 2009 European election. Possible responses included "never," "sometimes," or "often" (coded as 1, 2, and 3, respectively). To investigate the relative influence of each medium, we regressed the same six-question political knowledge scale previously utilized in chapter 2 on these three media consumption questions, along with a series of political and demographic controls (table 3.A2.1).

The results indicate that greater consumption of all three media are positively and statistically significantly ($p < .001$ in all three cases) associated with political knowledge, with the strongest effects for newspaper consumption (OLS coefficient = .29), followed by television (coefficient = .17) and the Internet (coefficient = .07).

These raw figures indicate that increased newspaper consumption is associated with the largest gain in political knowledge. This is unsurprising, given the relatively greater emphasis on election news in newspapers relative to television—with the latter medium's disproportionate emphasis on entertainment—

Table 3.A2.2. Weighted Political Knowledge Effects of Consuming TV, Newspapers, and Websites for Information about 2009 European Election, Low- versus High-Party States

	Low-Party	High-Party	Difference
Television	153.7	167.2	13.5
Newspapers	248.2	280.2	32.0
Internet	17.2	21.6	4.4
Total weighted media consumption effects	419.1	469.0	49.9

We employ ENPP to distinguish low- versus high-party states.

and the Internet, with its virtually infinite variety of content. On another level, however, these figures offer an incomplete picture, as they do not take into consideration frequency of exposure. A better estimate of the total influence of each medium in a given country would also take exposure into account.

To do so as best we could, given the obvious limitations of these quite vague questions, we added together participant responses on a per country basis, assigning respondents 2 points for responses of "often," 1 point for "sometimes," and 0 points for "never." We then multiplied the aforementioned coefficient on each medium by the total score on that medium (that is, the number of people falling into each category). Summing across all individuals' scores for a given medium yields an estimate of the relative total effect of self-reported consumption of that medium on political knowledge. To further test whether political knowledge effects followed the patterns predicted by our Downsian Premise, we then divided countries based on their ENPP score (above or below the overall mean among countries in the data set). Table 3.A2.2 summarizes the results, which we then graphically illustrate in figure 3.A2.1.

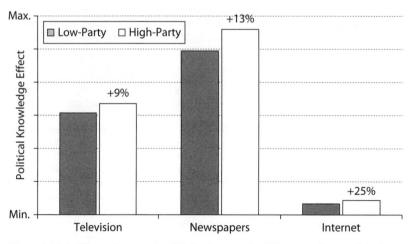

Figure 3.A2.1. Effects of consuming EU election news in different media on political knowledge, low- versus high-party

The raw numbers are difficult to intuitively interpret, and hence we exclude them from figure 3.A2.1. However, the key for our purposes is their relative magnitudes. Figure 3.A2.1 shows that newspapers, in the net, maintain their advantage in terms of their effect on respondents' election-related political knowledge, with television coming in second and the Internet a distant third.

This result must, of course, be interpreted with great caution, as the quite blunt three-category media consumption scales are likely muting substantial differences between the several media. After all, terms like "sometimes" and "often" may mean quite different things for different individuals, or even across different media. For instance, a far larger TV advantage in total consumption emerges when measured by a more extensive and precise battery of questions asking respondents about their consumption of up to eight individual news programs and eight newspapers. The survey queried respondents about three or four specific popular outlets per medium in their countries, and then allowed respondents to offer as many as five additional outlets in open-ended questions. For each outlet, they indicated the number of days in the past week they had watched or read the program or newspaper. From these batteries of questions, we created two scales, adding up the total number of days per week across eight TV programs and eight newspapers.[55] Measured in this manner, respondents report consuming about 90 percent more television news programs than newspapers. Indeed, if we employ those consumption estimates— by weighting the regression coefficients by this latter exposure estimate—TV news clearly eclipses newspapers when it comes to enhancing political knowledge. This latter finding is consistent with a host of surveys, including one cited in chapter 2, that find respondents in countries around the world rating television as their most important news source by wide margins.

Arguably the most important aspects of figure 3.A2.1, at least for our purposes, are the differences between low- and high-party EU member countries, on the one hand, and the importance of Internet consumption, compared to TV news and newspaper consumption, on the other. In the latter case, our results suggest that watching television news contributed roughly eight or nine times more to election-related political knowledge than looking at election-related web pages on the Internet, depending on the party system. The corresponding difference for newspapers is a thirteen- to fifteenfold greater contri-

[55] The TV and newspaper batteries differed in one respect. For TV news, respondents were provided with the names of four outlets, compared to three for newspapers. Respondents were then able to offer up to five additional outlets from each medium. To equalize the scales, we included the top eight outlets for TV news (including those mentioned in the survey and those offered by respondents in open-ended responses). Inspection of the data indicates that respondents generally reported higher consumption of the outlets they themselves mentioned, relative to those named by the interviewer. Moreover, dropping either the fourth TV outlet named by the interviewer or the final outlet named by the respondent produced virtually identical results (as in both cases the level of consumption was extremely low). Consequently, we concluded that the most straightforward strategy was to simply drop the ninth TV outlet for the handful of respondents who answered the final open-ended question.

bution. The implication is that while all three media contributed significantly to political knowledge regarding the 2009 EU election, television news and newspapers vastly outpaced the Internet as news sources for election-related information.

Turning to the party system comparison, here the results support our Downsian Premise across all three media. For television news, newspapers, and the Internet, media consumption in high-party states contributed more to political knowledge than equivalent consumption in low-party states, by 9, 13, and 25 percent, respectively. In addition to lending increased support to the Downsian Premise and further substantiating the theorized linkage between the Downsian Premise and differences in political knowledge, these results also indicate that Internet consumption appears to follow similar patterns as other media. In fact, the low- versus high-party differential is, in these data, proportionately far larger with respect to Internet news consumption than for either television news or newspapers.

One likely explanation for this pattern is the aforementioned domestic orientation of most Internet news consumption. While—notwithstanding the so-called Great Firewall of China—most Internet users have the *potential* to access a global marketplace of information, the vast majority of news-oriented websites typical users visit provide overwhelmingly domestic-oriented content. Regardless, two conclusions emerge from these explorations. First, the Internet does not appear to have fundamentally altered the relationship between domestic institutions and the information environment. Second, while the Internet is clearly increasing in importance as a source of political information, when viewed on a global scale it continues (at least as of this writing in May 2014) to lag far behind traditional news sources—like television, newspapers, and radio—both in terms of public access and in its influence on political knowledge.

4

Looking for Audience Costs in All the Wrong Places: Constraint and Reciprocation

In chapter 3 we identified a relationship between the forces that we argue generate constraint over executive foreign policy preferences (partisan opposition and media access) and the initiation of international conflict. Initiation, however, is just the beginning of the conflict process, and our theory of democratic constraint also has implications for the subsequent stages. Chief among these is the reaction of the other side (i.e., the target) once conflict is initiated or a threat proffered. Does the extent of constraint on the initiator influence how the target perceives and hence responds to these actions?

The answer to this question, of course, is more meaningful to scholars of international relations than a simple explication of the next step of many in the stylized process that leads to war. Schultz and others have tied reciprocation to the substantial body of work on the role of domestic audience costs in international conflict.[1] The idea is that while investigators cannot directly observe audience costs, we should be able to indirectly observe the presence or absence of the credibility they bestow through variation in rates of reciprocation. Put more simply, states with the additional credibility generated by audience costs should see the conflicts they initiate and the threats that they make reciprocated less often than their counterparts whose institutions deny them this extra credibility.

The audience cost argument in general, and this empirical implication of it in particular, however, have recently come under serious and sustained attack. Trachtenberg and Snyder and Borghard explore historical crises and find little evidence that audience costs played a discernible role in any of them.[2] Downes and Sechser question the empirical work on MID reciprocation that underpins

Elements of chapter 4 appeared in "Looking for Audience Costs in All the Wrong Places: Electoral Institutions, Media Access and Democratic Constraint" by Philip Potter and Matthew Baum, in the *Journal of Politics* 76, no. 1 (2014): 167–81; as well as in "Media, Audience Costs and the Democratic Peace" by Philip Potter and Matthew Baum in *Political Communication* 27, no. 4 (2010): 453. Reprinted with permission.

[1] Schultz (2001a).
[2] Trachtenberg (2012); Snyder and Borghard (2011).

most empirical findings on audience costs, arguing that the theory is largely unsubstantiated because most of the previously assessed disputes involved no coercive threat.[3] Moreover, their reanalysis of their own data set of compellent threats (which they argue is the more appropriate test) reveals no evidence that democracies are any better than nondemocracies at making credible threats.

Yet audience costs are crucial to the prevailing scholarly understanding of international conflict. As Schultz puts it, they are the "dark matter" of international relations—hard to observe directly, but central to our theoretical models.[4] Extending that analogy, without audience costs the "equations" describing international interactions become unbalanced and our understanding of conflict behavior unravels along with leading explanations for long-standing empirical observations. While perhaps beyond their purview, the recent spate of articles challenging the audience cost proposition offer nothing with which to replace it. As Schultz notes, this leaves the discipline with important unanswered questions. Moving forward productively, then, requires that we dig more deeply into the processes that might give rise to credibility through audience costs in order to understand the origins of the divergent results that have emerged in the recent literature.[5]

As we introduced in chapter 2, we argue that insufficient attention to the underlying mechanisms and institutional variation obscures the consistent role of domestic political costs in conflict processes. Specifically, there is a dearth of research into the factors mediating the transmission of information from leaders to the ultimate source of audience costs—the public. Thus, we differentiate among democracies, arguing that only a subset are in fact able to generate audience costs and therefore that not all are equally well equipped to credibly signal resolve.[6] The distinctions lie in our theory of democratic constraint, which outlines two central components that democracies need if they are to generate credibility through audience costs: (1) whistleblowers who are positioned to ensure that information about a leader's foreign policy missteps will reliably become public, and (2) public access to that information.

Given the established low baseline of public attention, what prompts the mass public to sometimes pay enough attention to foreign policy matters to impose audience costs? To recap our theory as it applies to reciprocation and the audience cost argument, we argue that voters use heuristics to help them determine both when to engage with foreign policy issues and what to think about them when they do. Research has shown that in many situations citizens are able to make rational decisions with relatively little information by employing informational shortcuts,[7] most notably by relying on the opinions of trusted

[3] Downes and Sechser (2012).
[4] Schultz (2012).
[5] Schultz (2012).
[6] Notably, as was the case in chapter 3, this parallels the work of Weeks (2008) in the context of autocracies.
[7] Sniderman, Brody, and Tetlock (1991); Popkin (1993).

and well-positioned partisan elites.[8] However, in an absolute sense, whistle-blowers with insufficient media access will never reach the public. Similarly, a public with universal media access but without extensive opposition to blow the whistle will rarely hear about foreign policy missteps. The implication is that the risk of whistleblowing will inhibit leaders only when there is a credible threat that the public will hear when the whistle blows.

In chapter 2 we derived our reciprocation and low-access reciprocation hypotheses (H2a and H2b, respectively). These hold that with low levels of public media access in the initiator state, variations in the number of parties will not significantly affect the likelihood of reciprocation by target states (H2b). However, as media access increases, an inverse relationship will emerge between the number of parties and the frequency of reciprocation (H2a). In this chapter we assess these propositions.

RESEARCH DESIGN

Just as the main body of empirical work on the democratic peace tends to have a common ancestor in Russett and Oneal's models, empirical work on audience costs tends to build on Schultz's models of conflict reciprocation.[9] We begin by roughly replicating these models because this approach allows for the most direct comparison with existing work in this area. As we have noted, Schultz's empirical insight is that, all else equal, states that are able to generate audience costs should be more credible to their adversaries and therefore face less reciprocation when they initiate conflicts.[10] He and others who have followed on his work therefore look for evidence in patterns of militarized interstate dispute (MID) reciprocation.[11] Consistent with this work, our primary measure of dispute reciprocation is equal to one when the target state responds militarily (and zero otherwise).

Of course all reciprocation is not equal. In particular, low-level, nonviolent reciprocation may be less subject to variations in initiator credibility in part because it has a lesser chance of leading to uncontrolled escalation. Such tepid reciprocation may in fact represent a hedging strategy from a target state that believes the initiator is indeed credible but is perhaps playing for time and information, or is seeking to minimize the costs from its own domestic audience that might follow immediate acquiescence. In contrast, higher-level reciprocation, including the actual use of violence, is a clearer indication that the target is challenging the initiator's credibility. It may therefore be the case that violent

[8] Larson (2000); Krosnick and Kinder (1990); Iyengar and Kinder (1987). Popkin (1993) terms this process "low information rationality."

[9] Russett and Oneal (2001); Schultz (2001a).

[10] Smith (1998); Schultz (1998).

[11] As in chapter 3, data come from the Correlates of War Project Militarized Interstate Dispute data set (Ghosn, Palmer, and Bremer 2004). MID reciprocation equals one when the hostility index score for the target (the cwhost2 variable) is greater than one.

reciprocation drives any credibility-based effects for overall reciprocation (combining both low- and high-level types).

Consequently, we assess the robustness of the simple MID reciprocation formulation of the dependent variable by splitting reciprocation into a scale ranging from no reciprocation, to nonviolent reciprocation, to violent reciprocation entailing escalation to the actual deployment or employment of military force. We assess these outcomes in ordered and unordered multinomial logit models.

Downes and Sechser challenge the use of MIDs altogether, arguing that many of the disputes in the MID data set are inappropriate for testing the audience cost logic.[12] In response, we replicate our analysis with their reformulated data set of militarized compellent threats. Downes and Sechser consider a threat successful if the target either immediately acquiesces or does so short of a threshold of one hundred military fatalities on the target side. They reverse the coding such that successful threats are coded as zero, rendering the expected signs for our variables of interest the same as those for the models of reciprocation.

Our period of analysis spans the same period we assessed in chapter 3, 1965–2006 (1970–2006 for models that employ our combined TV and radio "media access" measure). As was the case for our replication of models of the democratic peace, this is a much shorter period than is typical in the literature. Hence, when our findings diverge from those in the extant literature, this may, at least in part, be attributable to this truncated time frame. In addition to employing a more limited period of analysis, we make several additional departures from existing models. As has been the case throughout this volume, we are primarily concerned with distinctions within democracies (rather than between democracies and autocracies). Hence, in an attempt to be particularly conservative, we replicate our approach in chapter 3 by largely restricting the models to democracies. These models therefore exclude the standard dichotomous measure of democracy/autocracy found in typical audience cost models. However, as an alternative approach we also test models with a democracy dummy variable, which we interact with our variables of interest.

We maintain the key operationalizations of our theoretically relevant independent variables from our analysis in the preceding chapter. We rely on the same dual operationalization of the extent of political opposition, both Golder's measure of the effective number of parliamentary parties (ENPP) and, as a robustness check, the effective number of elective parties (ENEP).[13] To assess the media environment, we again employ televisions per one thousand population and the combined measure of television and radio access.

Following Schultz and the numerous studies that have built on his work, we control for the power dynamic within the initiator/potential reciprocator dyad, as well as a measure of whether those states are contiguous, whether they are

[12] Downes and Sechser (2012).
[13] Golder (2005).

allies, and the degree of similarity in their alliance portfolios.[14] As we did for conflict initiation, we also control for infant mortality and per capita GDP in order to address the potential relationship between media access and development.

RESULTS

Because it is difficult to substantively interpret log likelihoods and conditional coefficients, we transform the logit coefficients from our models into predicted probabilities of reciprocation as media access and the number of parties vary, with all other controls held constant. Figure 4.1 plots the results.[15]

In chapter 2, we characterized as naïve the expectations that as the number of parties or media access increases, independently of one another, reciprocation by target states will become less frequent. The results in figure 4.1 provide at most partial evidence in favor of these unconditional relationships. Low-opposition states (relative to their high-opposition counterparts) face a higher probability of reciprocation at low levels of media access, but a lower one at high levels of media access. However, the statistically significant ($p < .01$) downward sloping curves are limited to high-party states. As our theory, but *not* the naïve expectation, would anticipate, those for low-opposition states are essentially flat and insignificant across the span of media or television access.

Our theory, however, rests far less on the baseline predictions than on the conditional relationships between party systems and media access, as represented by H2a and H2b. These hypotheses predict that the reciprocation-repressing effects of increased media access ought to heighten as the number of parties rises (H2b), but only beyond some minimum threshold of media access (H2a). As suggested above, this is clearly the case across all four graphics in figure 4.1. In low-party cases, the slopes associated with increased media access are generally relatively shallow and insignificant. In sharp contrast, all the high-party cases are sharply downward sloping and significant ($p < .01$).[16]

The functional form imposed by the logistic maximum likelihood model causes the predicted probability of reciprocation to swing from near one to near zero for high-party states across the explored span of media access. It is therefore helpful to also assess the magnitudes of these effects toward the middle of the curve. The model (illustrated in the top-left graphic in figure 4.1) predicts that a hypothetical high-party state with three hundred televisions per one thousand population will see 30 percent of the conflicts it initiates recipro-

---

[14] Schultz (2001a).

[15] In table 4.A.1 we present the logit models underlying figure 4.1. As in chapter 3, high-party is at ENPP or ENEP = 5, while low-party is set at 2.

[16] Significance levels are based on the full range of TV access. The significance levels remain $p < .01$ when TV access varies from one standard deviation below to one standard deviation above the mean.

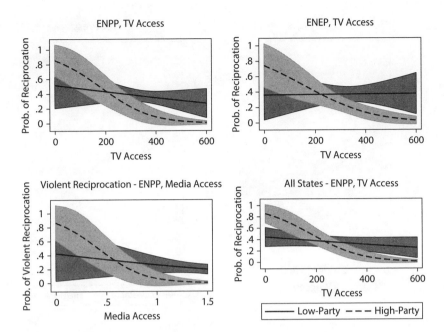

Figure 4.1. Probability of reciprocation

cated. This declines precipitously to approximately 15 percent when television access increases to just four hundred per one thousand population.

In most cases the effects of variations in the number of parties are statistically indistinguishable at the low end of media access (the exception being the bottom right panel of figure 4.1 where it actually reverses). This supports our theory concerning the necessity of access: increased whistleblowing has no statistically identifiable effect on credibility when the mass public is relatively unlikely to get the message. The effects become statistically distinguishable near the overall mean level of television access among democracies in our data of about 350 televisions per one thousand people. For the combined media measure, the corresponding threshold is at about the 50 percent level. Finally, we observed quite similar effects when we focus only on violent reciprocation as when we explore *all* reciprocation.

The similarity across the four panels in figure 4.1 is worth remarking upon since the graphs actually arise from notably distinct model specifications. In particular, the robustness to the restricted MID definition (violent reciprocation, shown in the bottom-left graphic in figure 4.1) begins to assuage some of the concerns regarding the measurement of that indicator. The ENEP replication (top-right graphic in figure 4.1) increases our confidence in the robustness of our findings to different party system measures. Finally, the comparability of the "all states" model (bottom-right graphic in figure 4.1, which has a much

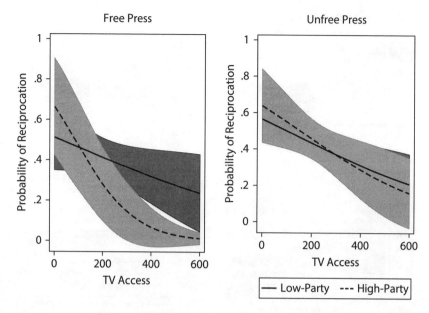

Figure 4.2. Probability of reciprocation, free and unfree presses

larger N and more complex interaction terms) further enhances our confidence in the robustness of our findings.

We next revisit the role of a free press. As was the case for initiation, we anticipate that the mechanism that we have outlined as being integral to reciprocation and credibility primarily should function in the presence of a free press. Without basic press freedoms, numerous whistleblowers and universal access to media would in most circumstances (notwithstanding the possible exceptions discussed in chapter 2) do little to inform the public. To confirm this expectation we assess the three-way interaction among opposition, access, and press freedom. Figure 4.2 presents the results of that model—the first panel is for states *with* and the second is for those *without* a free press.

As was the case for initiation, high-party systems with extensive media access are associated with a decreased rate of dispute reciprocation, but only when there is a free press. Furthermore, as was the case for the preceding models, the distinction between high- and low-party systems comes into focus at higher levels of media access. In contrast, when the press is not free there is no meaningful distinction in reciprocation rates between low- and high-party systems.

UNPACKING MILITARIZED DISPUTES

In the results reported thus far, we cannot isolate the distinctions between movement from nonreciprocation to violent reciprocation, from nonrecipro-

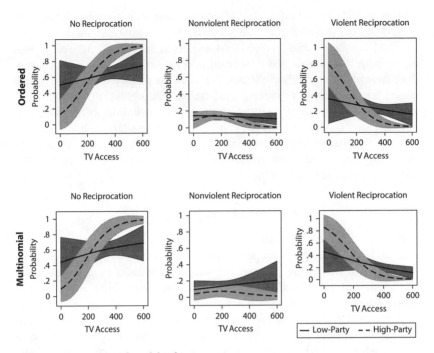

Figure 4.3. Disaggregated models of reciprocation

cation to nonviolent reciprocation, or from nonviolent to violent reciprocation. The reason is that the "all reciprocation" dependent variable treats both violent and nonviolent reciprocation as a positive occurrence, while the "violent reciprocation" dependent variable treats both nonreciprocation and nonviolent reciprocation as a negative occurrence. We have argued that the observed effects on reciprocation of variations in media access and party systems are likely strongest in high-level disputes involving the actual deployment or employment of military force. To determine to what extent higher-level, or violent, reciprocation is in fact driving the observed relationships derived from our combined, dichotomous indicators, we create a single scaled variable where zero equals not reciprocated, one equals reciprocated with maximum of threat, and two equals reciprocated with force deployment or employment. This change requires a shift to an estimator that allows for more than two values on the dependent variable.

At first glance, this reformulated dependent variable appears best suited for an ordered logit analysis. However, statistical testing suggests that the three categories are not entirely distinct, which violates an assumption of that model.[17] Consequently, we also undertake a second analysis employing multinomial logit, which does not require an ordered scale. In figure 4.3 we separately

---

[17] This concern stems from observed overlap in the *tau beta* coefficients, which, given the

plot the probabilities of these levels of reciprocation for both ordered (top three charts) and unordered (bottom three charts) multinomial logit models.

These results essentially replicate those from our prior analyses, in that across both the ordered and unordered models variations in TV access produce large and statistically significant effects, in the predicted directions. These effects are much more prominent (and statistically significant) in high-party systems than in low-party ones (where the results are uniformly insignificant). Furthermore, consistent with our expectations, these alternative models suggest that the interaction of party systems and media access matters far more for nonreciprocation and violent reciprocation than for the more ambiguous category of nonviolent reciprocation.

COMPELLENT THREATS

Our initial hypotheses all address the relationship between democratic institutions and dispute reciprocation as an indirect measure of the ability to generate audience costs. There are, however, substantial drawbacks to reciprocation as an indicator of the presence or absence of a functional audience cost mechanism. Foremost among these is the reality that reciprocation is a second-order implication of the audience cost argument. That is, the domestic calculations that fuel the audience-cost mechanism are assumed rather than tested because leaders who face audience costs have obvious incentives not to incur them. This means that, if nothing else, we are uncovering important variation in dispute reciprocation (driven by a mechanism other than audience costs), which is interesting and important in itself. However, this begs the question of what that alternative data-generating mechanism might be. Our findings add to a growing literature tying reciprocation to the domestic politics of the initiating state, which, when taken together, increasingly crowd out mechanisms other than audience costs.

Reciprocation is difficult to measure. Even if it is a conceptually sound indicator of variations in audience costs, the coding may be substantially flawed. Indeed, scholars such as Downes and Sechser have convincingly documented some coding deficiencies.[18] These concerns aside, models of reciprocation have become standard in this literature in large part because until relatively recently scholars had identified few equally plausible alternatives. Since we are making several novel adaptations to audience cost theory, we began by applying them to the standard measure in order to allow comparability.[19]

---

magnitudes of their standard errors, suggest potential overlap in the first two categories. We present the coefficients underlying figure 4.4 in table 4.A.2, in the appendix to this chapter.

[18] Downes and Sechser (2012).

[19] It is also worth recalling that because our research question necessarily limits our analyses to democracies in the era of broadcast media we are dealing with a somewhat skewed sample of democracies largely in the Cold War period. However, since we are interested in variation within

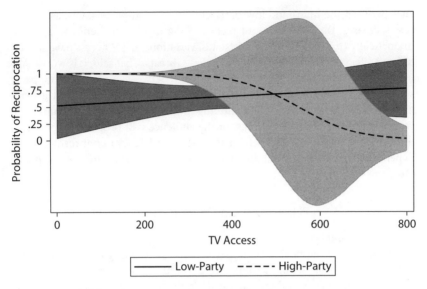

Figure 4.4. Probability of reciprocation (compellent threat)

That said, while there are several reasons why the evidence for audience costs should be recoverable from extant data on reciprocation, it is also the case that it should arise in cases of compellent threats. Given the documented issues with the MID data, it is particularly important that our theory holds up in other contexts. Moreover, this is a particularly revealing test of the robustness of the mechanism that we propose due to the sparseness of the data and the fact that Downes and Sechser report a null finding for the relationship between a simple measure of democracy and threat response.[20]

To address the concerns raised by Downes and Sechser, as well as to confirm that the mechanism we identify applies even to their very strict definition of compellent threat, we respecified the above-described models using their alternative dependent variable. To aid comparisons with their work, we primarily employ Downes and Sechser's control variables (made slightly more parsimonious due to the smaller number of post-1965 observations).[21]

Figure 4.4 reveals a relationship that is similar to those we have presented throughout this chapter, though decreased statistical power, owing to the small sample size, inflates the confidence interval surrounding the high-party curve.[22] However, there is a statistically significant and substantively meaningful differ-

---

democracies, this is less troubling than it is in other studies such as those specifically concerned with the democratic peace.

[20] Downes and Sechser (2012).

[21] The models can be found in table 4.A.3. For an in-depth discussion of the control variables, see Downes and Sechser (2012).

[22] The results from the statistical models can be found in table 4.A.2, and are consistent with

ence between the high- and low-party curves. In high-party states, as TV access increases, the probability of reciprocating to a compellent threat drops dramatically ($p < .01$); in low-party states, variations in TV access have no significant effect on reciprocation to compellent threats. That said, it is worth noting that the statistically significant difference between high- and low-party states emerges at a higher level of television access than is the case in the prior models. Nevertheless, any positive finding in this domain stands in contrast to Downs and Sechser's null findings for the audience cost proposition based on their compellent threats data.[23] In general, the consistency of our results across dependent variables should further increase confidence in the proposed mechanism.[24]

THE PROBLEM OF PERCEPTION

The issue at hand is not simply whether a state can generate audience costs, but rather whether the opposing actor *perceives* this as resulting in increased credibility. While a discussion of subjective perceptions is somewhat beyond the purview of our theory and tests, in our view this issue of the perception of audience costs is insufficiently addressed throughout the audience costs literature. The blind spot likely originates from the original legacy of the audience costs proposition as a stylized theory. However, by introducing a more complex mechanism, we beg the questions of whether and how these variations are perceptible to the other side in an international interaction.

Our empirical investigations can test only implications of this process rather than the process itself. We argue, however, that the answer to this question likely lies in the way that intricate, institutionally based biases in foreign policy behavior coalesce over time into reputations for credibility (or the lack thereof). In this view, there is an important distinction between the question of whether an adversary is bluffing in the immediate term and her reputation for credibility developed over time. Institutions that systematically affect the costs and benefits of bluffing will influence its actual frequency. Though the process itself may be opaque to an adversary in any particular instance, over time it will coalesce into a reputation for credibility that will be more durable and readily apparent to an adversary.

Our theory implies that the combination of a larger number of parties and extensive media access likely decreases the actual propensity of a state to bluff. Having more parties makes bluffing harder for at least two reasons. First, parties in multiparty systems typically face stronger incentives than their counterparts in two-party systems to differentiate themselves from one another on

---

those in table 4.A.1. Figure 4.2 presents the predicted probability of reciprocation for model 2 of table 4.A.2.

[23] Downes and Sechser (2012).

[24] These can be found in table 4.A.2.

policy.[25] The implication is that there is a relatively higher likelihood that one will defect and undermine a bluff. Increased media access, in turn, makes it more likely that defecting parties will be able to reach and hence influence the public. This raises the likelihood that citizens will hold leaders accountable for failed bluffs.

Second, democracies with many parties and accessible media tend to make a great deal of noise when they lack unity, and this noise occurs in a domain where it is readily apparent to adversaries. The result is that bluffs, particularly ambitious ones, are difficult to execute. These same forces make bluffs more costly if they are called. This is simply because they raise the potential for elite discord and increase the availability of political alternatives (i.e., other parties that could potentially take power), implying that states with these attributes are, all else equal, less likely to bluff in marginal circumstances.

Over time, the forces we have described could coalesce into a reputation for credibility and commitment that is knowable to adversaries based on past experiences with the state in question. That said, these processes might be too subtle to be observed by an adversary seeking to judge credibility in a one-off encounter. Such one-off encounters, however, are rare in international politics. Indeed, this reputational effect is particularly important because most threats and conflicts happen within relatively well-worn international relationships. Threats are rarely "bolts from the blue" that originate from countries with which there has been little prior interaction. Most relationships (and threats) are geographically constrained and occur between countries that have long-standing historical experience with one another.[26] The exceptions tend to be global powers like the United States, but these countries loom so large in the international consciousness that their reputations could precede them even when they interject themselves into situations where they have previously been uninvolved. Thus, the basis for the reputation may not be directly observable or known to the adversary, but the fact that prior interactions have consistently reinforced it makes the reputation stronger.

The question then is which signals are more or less likely to break through the fog and contribute to reputations. Our argument is that the set of factors we identify (i.e., party and media systems) are prime candidates because their institutional basis means that they operate over long time frames and are relatively immune to strategic manipulation by leaders. Thus, while we are not able to assess these processes directly in our empirical analyses, it is plausible to hypothesize that states possessing the attributes we identify will see less reciprocation in the disputes and threats that they initiate than their counterparts lacking these attributes. This is what we demonstrate in our empirical analyses.

---

[25] Downs (1957).
[26] Senese (1996, 2005); Tir and Diehl (2002).

CONCLUSION

The ability of leaders to use their citizenry to generate credibility in their international interactions is variable and context dependent. Specifically, electoral institutions that give rise to a whistleblowing opposition, combined with sufficient media access to make it likely that citizens will be aware of any such whistleblowing, facilitate credibility. Put differently, if the domestic institutions in a democracy are such that the public is unlikely to hear about foreign policy blunders, or what they do hear does not challenge the leader's policies, then the leader will face relatively low potential political costs. Without costs, there is no increased credibility.

This study contributes to an emerging literature explicating the domestic nuances of the audience-cost argument.[27] Scholars of international conflict need to take seriously the domestic processes that underpin the audience-costs argument. Since the link between leaders' actions and the public's response is far from automatic, it behooves us to understand the institutions that shape this relationship. This includes the critical intervening role of the mass media as the primary vehicle for transmitting information between leaders and citizens. Failing to account for the implications of differences in media and electoral institutions for information transmission seems likely to perpetuate the seeming disconnect between theoretical propositions and empirical evidence that has bedeviled researchers interested in employing audience cost theory. It also limits scholars' capacities to fully explicate the implications of domestic audience costs in cases when disputes are or are not likely to escalate to war, as well as the role of democratic institutions in generating credibility.

Our findings also address the current debate in political science regarding whether audience costs exist at all and, if so, why they are important, with the views that they either do not, are not, or both, unifying the previously cited work by Snyder and Borghard, Trachtenberg, and Downes and Sechser, as well as motivating a recent special issue of *Security Studies*.[28] That scholarship purports to show that democracies cannot or do not generate meaningful audience costs, and concludes that audience costs, if they exist at all, are politically inconsequential. By demonstrating that, in fact, audience costs matter for democracies only under certain conditions and that this finding holds even in the stricter tests proposed by several of these authors, our analysis helps to resolve some of the primary concerns in that debate.

Finally, our findings contribute to the ongoing debate over the relative merits of alternative data sets for assessing the audience costs proposition. If Downes and Sechser are correct that most MIDs do not involve threats (and we believe that they are), the question remains as to why the existing literature has

---

[27] E.g., Levendusky and Horowitz (2012); Tomz (2007).
[28] Snyder and Borghard (2011); Trachtenberg (2012); Downes and Sechser (2012).

found a relationship between dispute reciprocation and democracy despite the well-documented deficiencies of those data sets.[29] This question is particularly important, since our analyses produced equivalent findings across the MID and compellent threats data sets, suggesting that the original findings drawn from the MIDs data arise from more than fitting the error. We argue that the answer is that at each stage of a conflict—initial threats, initiation, escalation, and full-scale engagement—leaders who are subject to sanction from a domestic audience face higher costs for failure. Thus, it is not the particular form of executive commitment that matters so much as the relatively higher costs of backing down from it.

APPENDIX: STATISTICAL TABLES AND ROBUSTNESS TESTS

Table 4.A.1 presents the results of our primary audience-cost regressions. Model 1 explores the effect on all dispute reciprocation. Model 2 repeats this, but relies on ENEP as an alternative measure of the extent of partisan opposition. Model 3 limits the analysis to violent reciprocation (that is, the actual deployment or employment of military force) and also replaces the standard measure of television access with the alternative combined television and radio indicator in a model otherwise similar to model 1. Model 4 replicates this same analysis but includes *all* states, regardless of regime type, while introducing a dummy variable for democracies, which we interact with ENPP and media access. As we noted in chapter 3, we do not rely exclusively on this formulation of the model because it requires a substantial (but defensible) assumption regarding the number-of-parties data. Specifically, we must treat autocracies (which are otherwise missing values for this variable) as having a single party. This effectively asserts that these states lack independent opposition (which, though we believe it to be a defensible simplifying assumption, is not entirely true in all cases) and forces all the explanatory power for those states to the media and press freedom variables.

A key insight from table 4.A.1 is that the sign (negative) and significance (high) of the key conditional coefficient are equivalent to those found for the interaction term ENPP × television access in table 4.A.1, which presents the models that informed figure 4.1. Indeed, the strong majority of coefficients remain consistent and stable across the models.

Multinomial and Ordered Logit

In addition to the dichotomous tests, we assess the robustness of our findings by delving further into the question of whether violent reciprocation drives the

[29] Downes and Sechser (2012).

Table 4.A.1. Models of Reciprocation

	Core Model	ENEP	Violent Reciprocation/ TV & Radio Access	All States
	1	2	3	4
Parties	0.6820*	0.6694**	0.5279^	0.0586
	(0.310)	(0.248)	(0.280)	(0.118)
Access	0.0045	0.0061^	1.9928^	−0.0018
	(0.004)	(0.003)	(1.031)	(0.001)
Parties × access	−0.0033**	−0.0030***	−1.0324*	−0.0003
	(0.001)	(0.001)	(0.470)	(0.000)
Major/major power	−1.3015	−1.2235	−0.8791	−0.4587
	(1.026)	(1.103)	(1.151)	(0.455)
Minor/major power	1.2869	1.2529	1.0115	0.4936
	(0.789)	(0.915)	(0.856)	(0.349)
Major/minor power	0.1458	−0.2387	−0.2595	0.5058
	(0.730)	(0.778)	(0.774)	(0.355)
Side A's proportion of capabilities	0.0767	−0.1729	−0.2539	0.0388
	(0.704)	(0.700)	(0.708)	(0.304)
Alliance	−0.4393	−0.3913	−0.3371	−0.1817
	(0.448)	(0.484)	(0.441)	(0.192)
Contiguity	1.3202**	1.1894*	1.0172*	0.8070***
	(0.459)	(0.482)	(0.477)	(0.215)
Distance	−0.0203	−0.1272	−0.0213	−0.0189
	(0.211)	(0.230)	(0.250)	(0.097)
Status quo—initiator	−1.0504*	−1.2032*	−0.6560	−0.2257
	(0.528)	(0.586)	(0.482)	(0.285)
Status quo—target	1.9914**	2.2940**	1.8436**	1.0194**
	(0.681)	(0.744)	(0.633)	(0.323)
Revision type—government	1.2812	1.6166	0.9320	0.4313
	(0.958)	(1.078)	(0.901)	(0.558)
Revision type—political	0.6585	0.9073	0.4181	−0.1998
	(0.571)	(0.613)	(0.535)	(0.308)
Infant mortality	−0.0050	−0.0070	−0.0005	0.0014
	(0.005)	(0.005)	(0.005)	(0.002)
GDP per capita (× 1,000)	−0.0003	−0.0167	−0.0240	0.0300
	(0.045)	(0.048)	(0.045)	(0.025)
Internet penetration	−0.0240	−0.0391	−0.0331	0.0027
	(0.029)	(0.033)	(0.028)	(0.015)
Democracy	—	—	—	−1.7611*
				(0.837)
Democracy × parties	—	—	—	0.6679*
				(0.306)
Democracy × access	—	—	—	0.0065*
				(0.003)
Democracy × parties × access	—	—	—	−0.0029**
				(0.001)
Observations	264	263	237	862

Robust standard errors in parentheses. ^p < .10. *p < .05. **p < .01. ***p < .001.

overall relationship. As previously discussed, we accomplish this by converting the multiple dependent variables assessed in the previous analyses into a single scaled variable and retest the hypotheses.

Table 4.A.2 presents the coefficients from our ordered and multinomial logit models.

Table 4.A.2. Models of Reciprocation, Ordered and Multinomial Logit

	Ordered	Multinomial Nonviolent Reciprocation Outcome	Multinomial Violent Reciprocation Outcome
	1	2	3
Parties	0.7317**	0.2931	0.8353*
	(0.275)	(0.426)	(0.342)
Access	0.0047	0.0058	0.0037
	(0.004)	(0.006)	(0.004)
Parties × access	−0.0033**	−0.0026	−0.0036**
	(0.001)	(0.002)	(0.001)
Major/major power	−1.2454	−13.7508***	−0.7586
	(1.012)	(1.462)	(1.075)
Minor/major power	1.2723^	1.2287	1.4798^
	(0.769)	(1.022)	(0.897)
Major/minor power	0.3135	−0.5944	0.6763
	(0.661)	(0.984)	(0.824)
Side A's proportion of capabilities	0.2220	−0.3626	0.5748
	(0.550)	(1.041)	(0.814)
Alliance	−0.5387	0.1577	−0.8289^
	(0.406)	(0.600)	(0.501)
Contiguity	1.3949***	0.7890	1.6008***
	(0.422)	(0.825)	(0.471)
Distance	−0.0317	0.0792	−0.0422
	(0.209)	(0.331)	(0.238)
Status quo—initiator	−1.1443*	−0.6011	−1.2503*
	(0.469)	(0.806)	(0.572)
Status quo—target	1.5650**	2.3856**	1.6889*
	(0.594)	(0.904)	(0.735)
Revision type—government	1.0908	1.3231	0.8472
	(0.839)	(1.356)	(1.302)
Revision type—political	0.7142	−0.0080	0.9446
	(0.538)	(0.974)	(0.635)
Infant mortality	−0.0048	−0.0021	−0.0071
	(0.004)	(0.008)	(0.005)
GDP per capita (× 1,000)	−0.0040	−0.0339	0.0026
	(0.046)	(0.066)	(0.052)
Internet penetration	−0.0233	−0.0564	−0.0106
	(0.031)	(0.052)	(0.037)
Observations	264	264	264

Robust standard errors in parentheses. Nonreciprocation is the base outcome for the multinomial models.
^$p < .10$. *$p < .05$. **$p < .01$. ***$p < .001$.

Compellent Threats

Table 4.A.3 presents the coefficients from our analysis of Downes and Sechser's compellent threat data.[30] Model 1 provides the three-way interaction among opposition, media access, and press freedom, but excludes all control variables. Model 2 adds standard controls, and model 3 includes the measure

[30] Downes and Sechser (2012).

Table 4.A.3. Logit Analyses of Compellent Threats

	No Controls	Standard Controls	Development Controls
	1	2	3
Parties	0.2425	0.0213	−0.1788
	(0.745)	(0.741)	(1.178)
Access	0.0422	0.0292	0.0362*
	(0.033)	(0.030)	(0.017)
Parties × access	−0.0128	−0.0102	−0.0107*
	(0.009)	(0.008)	(0.005)
Press freedom	−4.6345^	−6.2679*	−7.8053
	(2.524)	(2.636)	(5.105)
Press freedom × parties	1.3330	2.4991*	3.7046
	(1.109)	(1.112)	(3.148)
Press freedom × access	−0.0346	−0.0190	−0.0201
	(0.033)	(0.031)	(0.018)
Press freedom × parties × access	0.0102	0.0043	0.0036
	(0.009)	(0.009)	(0.007)
Initiators	—	3.3125	3.0583
		(2.019)	(2.110)
Contiguity	—	−1.7938	−2.6824
		(1.091)	(1.879)
Alliance	—	0.5761	0.2614
		(1.933)	(1.756)
Status quo initiator	—	0.0180	1.3243
		(1.773)	(1.963)
Status quo target	—	−2.4050	−2.6086
		(1.751)	(1.746)
Territorial threat	—	0.6036	−0.0408
		(0.839)	(0.906)
GDP per capita (× 1,000)	—	—	−0.1534
			(0.139)
Infant mortality	—	—	0.0084
			(0.019)
Observations	75	75	59

Robust standard errors in parentheses. ^$p < .10$. *$p < .05$.

of infant mortality to account for the development issue. Because Downes and Sechser's data end in 2001 we do not include a measure of Internet access. In all these models we have been very selective in our choices of control variables due to the low number of observations and corresponding issues with statistical power. This is also why we report models only for all states. Models limited to democracies have similar structures with regard to the shape and signs of the curves, but are insignificant in many cases due to insufficient statistical leverage.

Figure 4.3 is derived from model 3 of table 4.A.3. To reiterate, while the key coefficients in these models are insignificant individually, graphing the resulting probabilities illustrates statistically significant distinctions that support our theory.

5

Willing and Politically Able: Democratic Constraint and Coalition Joining

The prior two chapters investigated long-term global patterns, employing large, time-series, cross-sectional data sets. This allowed us to observe our key variables and theoretical predictions in action across many countries, conflicts, and years, which suggests that the findings are widely generalizable. It also allowed us to speak directly to the central literatures on the democratic peace (in terms of conflict initiation) and audience costs (in terms of conflict reciprocation).

That approach does, however, have limitations. To generalize across time, we necessarily sacrificed some degree of precision of measurement, particularly with respect to the relationship between our empirical indicators and the underlying concepts they are intended to measure. This could justifiably give some readers pause. How persuasive is a theory of micro-foundational factors if solely tested with such broad-stroke analyses as those presented in chapters 3 and 4? Can we be confident that we are measuring what we claim to be measuring?

In part to address such concerns, we take the opposite approach in chapter 7. There we undertake a deep dive into the decision-making processes of four countries—England, Germany, Spain, and Poland—with respect to the Iraq War. This approach allows us to carefully trace the roles played by our variables of interest in specific empirical cases, thereby greatly increasing our confidence in the relationships between our key causal variables. However, delving into specific cases to test theoretical predictions is also not without limitations. Most notably, it can be difficult to generalize findings beyond the specific cases under scrutiny, thereby possibly calling into question the applicability of any findings beyond the specific cases under investigation.

Chapter 5 adapts and expands upon portions of "The Iraq Coalition of the Willing and (Politically) Able: How Party Systems, the Press and Public Influence on Foreign Policy" by Matthew Baum in the *American Journal of Political Science* 57, no. 2 (2013): 442–58. Reprinted with permission.

In this chapter, we attempt to bridge the relative strengths of these approaches by pursuing a middle ground: a medium-N analysis of the wars in Iraq (2003) and Afghanistan (2001). We investigate the effects of party systems and media access on public attitudes and government decisions regarding coalition joining in the periods leading up to and immediately following the initiations of two distinct multinational military conflicts: Operation Iraqi Freedom in Iraq and Operation Enduring Freedom in Afghanistan. These are the periods when nations around the world made their initial decisions regarding whether or not to join the coalitions formed to overthrow the governments of the two target nations. By focusing on two individual conflicts we are able to hold constant each conflict's circumstances and location, the characteristics of the primary protagonists and of the international environment, as well as numerous other factors that might influence states' decisions regarding whether or not to become involved. Consequently, to the extent that similar relationships emerge in both cases, this will greatly increase our confidence in the generalizability of our findings.

We test our three coalition hypotheses against both conflicts. To refresh, the first two are our coalition support (H3) and joining (H4) hypotheses. They hold that in high-party states, public war support and the likelihood of joining a military coalition, respectively, will be inversely related to media access, while as the number of parties declines, these relationships will weaken and ultimately reverse. Finally, the parties and opinion-policy hypothesis (H5) predicts that in high-party states, governments' decisions regarding coalition joining will correspond more closely with public opinion as media access increases, while as the number of parties declines, the correspondence-enhancing effect of increased media access will weaken.

We begin the next section with the more comprehensive of our quantitative studies of coalition joining: the formation of the coalition of the willing (hereafter "the coalition") in the run-up to the 2003 Iraq War. We then replicate our key findings with our second case: the US- and NATO-led invasion of Afghanistan in 2001.

IRAQ (2003): OPERATION IRAQI FREEDOM

The George W. Bush administration employed a variety of economic and military carrots and sticks to persuade reluctant foreign leaders to join the Iraq coalition. For many world leaders whose populations overwhelmingly opposed the war, the decision to join the coalition was a fraught one. Elsewhere, public support was at best shallow, leaving little doubt that it could quickly erode if things went badly. Because of America's status as the world's most powerful nation, however, many states saw strategic advantages to joining the coalition. This conflict between *domestic political* and *international strategic* incentives makes Iraq an ideal case for investigating the conditions under which public opinion constrains foreign policy.

The Iraq War began on March 20, 2003. This was an unusually large-scale conflict involving a large number of states. It was also highly salient to citizens around the world, making it a politically risky endeavor for leaders contemplating involvement. In chapter 2 we discussed variation in the speed with which the information gap between leaders and the public closes (see figure 2.5 in particular). In the Iraq case, leaders were acutely aware that their window of opportunity was narrow.

Figure 5.1 shows the percentage of the public that opposed the Iraq War in each of the sixty-two countries for which we have opinion data. An average of 67 percent of those polled across these sixty-two nations expressed opposition to the war between mid-2002 and mid-2003. Opposition was lowest in the United States, averaging 29 percent, and highest in Brazil, at 96 percent. Ultimately, twenty-four of these sixty-two nations (39 percent) nonetheless sent troops to Iraq.[1] Among these coalition members, public opposition to the war averaged 62 percent.[2]

The Bush administration listed forty-nine nations as members of the coalition, five of which (United States, United Kingdom, Australia, Poland, and Denmark) contributed military forces to the original invasion. Another thirty-three subsequently provided troops. According to globalsecurity.org, more than three years after the start of hostilities, twenty-one nations continued to maintain a troop presence in Iraq, though the composition of states with troops varied over time.[3] Our full data set includes thirty-four nations that contributed troops to the coalition between 2003 and 2004. Table 5.1 lists these states, along with their contribution levels.[4]

We focus on the 2003–4 period because this is when most states made their primary decisions regarding whether or not to become involved. States subsequently joined or left the coalition for a variety of reasons, but the initial decision to participate or not represents the clearest point in time at which domestic political circumstances could have influenced these decisions. This was also the peak period of public awareness of the issue worldwide and hence the time

---

[1] For each country, these figures represent the average across all opinion observations in our data set. One consequence is that in several instances—most notably the United States and United Kingdom—postwar initiation rallies result in overall average opposition that is considerably lower than would have been the case had we excluded postwar initiation polls. Of course, these are the very cases where our theory would predict the most noteworthy opinion rallies. As we discuss in chapter 7, as well as briefly in the introduction, this helps account for British Prime Minister Tony Blair's willingness to buck public opinion, which strongly opposed intervention prior to the war's outbreak. He correctly surmised that opposition would drop once the bombs began to fall.

[2] This figure is averaged across twenty-two (out of twenty-four) coalition members for which we have opinion data.

[3] Data are based on troop contributions as of August 23, 2006, the latest date for which such data were available on globalsecurity.org.

[4] Note that we were able to obtain public opinion data only for twenty-four of the thirty-four states that contributed troops.

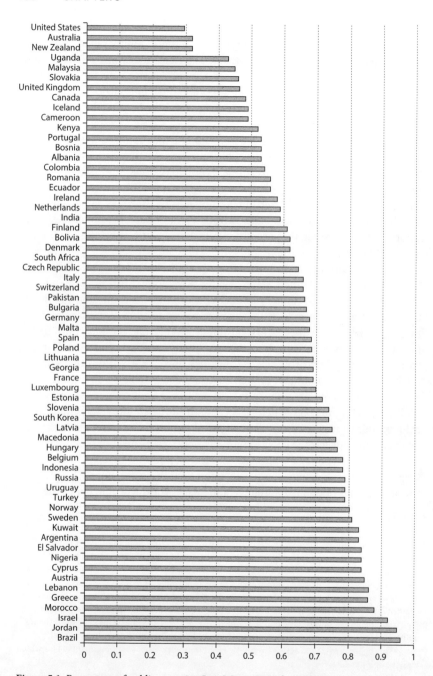

Figure 5.1. Percentage of public opposing Iraq War in 2003, by country

Table 5.1. Iraq Coalition Troop Commitment Levels (2003–4)

Country	Troops	Country	Troops
United States	145,000	Poland	200
United Kingdom	45,000	Norway	179
Italy	3,200	Mongolia	160
Australia	2,150	Azerbaijan	150
Ukraine	1,600	Portugal	128
Netherlands	1,345	Latvia	120
Spain	900	Lithuania	118
Romania	700	Slovakia	102
South Korea	700	Czech Republic	80
Japan	600	Philippines	80
Bulgaria	480	Albania	70
Thailand	440	Georgia	70
Denmark	420	New Zealand	61
Honduras	368	Estonia	55
El Salvador	361	Moldova	50
Dominican Republic	302	Macedonia	37
Hungary	300	Kazakhstan	25

period for which public opinion data are available for the maximum number of countries.

Data and Methods

For our empirical investigations, we compiled data on domestic electoral institutions and TV ownership for 180 countries, on public opinion regarding the Iraq War between mid-2002 and mid-2003 for the aforementioned 62 countries, and on troop commitments to the coalition for 191 countries, and a similar series of controls as employed in chapters 3 and 4.

DEPENDENT VARIABLES

We employ two dependent variables. The first is the average percentage of respondents *opposing* the Iraq War across all available survey questions regarding support for the war conducted within a given country between April 2002 and May 2003.[5] This variable, derived from thirteen multicountry surveys across sixty-two countries, ranges from 29.5 to 96 percent with a mean and standard deviation of 66.9 and 1.56 percent, respectively. Because the public war opposition variable is bounded between zero and one and potentially could be unduly influenced by extreme outliers, we employ the natural logarithm in our regressions.

Four of the thirteen surveys took place after the March 20, 2003 start date of the war, and therefore may have *followed* rather than preceded the decisions of several nations to deploy troops. This raises the possibility of reverse causality.

---

[5] See table 5.A.7 for all surveys, questions, and countries employed in this indicator.

We nonetheless believe the benefit of including these opinion observations outweigh the potential costs. The reason is that the exceptionally high salience of the prewar debate meant that public opinion had solidified in most nations well before the outbreak of war. In fact, there is only about a one-percentage-point difference in average levels of support expressed in surveys conducted prior to or following March 20, 2003. Consequently, it seems unlikely that many nations altered their decisions regarding participation in the coalition as a consequence of the effects on public attitudes of the conflict's first month. We nonetheless replicated all of our models excluding the post–March 2003 cases.[6] We also tested models excluding either the United States or United Kingdom. In each instance, the results essentially replicate those reported below.[7]

The second dependent variable is the maximum number of troops contributed to the coalition by each state during the first year of the war (March 2003–March 2004).[8] As noted earlier, thirty-four states contributed troops during this period. Of these, we have public opinion data for twenty-four. Excluding the 145,000 US troops, such contributions ranged from a low of 25 by Kazakhstan to a high of 45,000 by the United Kingdom. The average number of troops contributed by those states that contributed more than zero (again, excluding the United States) is 1,698, with a standard deviation of 7,787.

In order to further account for the varying capacities of states to contribute to the coalition, we divide this total by each state's total population (in thousands), yielding per capita troop commitment (henceforth "troops per capita"). Among states for which 2003 opinion data are available, this indicator varies from zero to .76 troops per thousand people, with a mean and standard deviation of .033 and .114, respectively (or, excluding the United States, .025 and .098, respectively). Finally, among contributing nations other than the United States that contributed, the mean and standard deviation for the per capita contribution level are .055 and .129, respectively.

INDEPENDENT VARIABLES

We include two key explanatory variables and as many as eight controls in our fully specified models. The first key independent variable (*TV access*) is identical to that employed in the prior two chapters: the number of televisions in a given country per one thousand inhabitants. We focus on TV for the reasons described in chapter 3, which we do not repeat here. However, it is worth noting that we tested all models with all measures of media access employed in

---

[6] Given the limited number of available observations, sacrificing all post-March data limits our ability to conduct a properly controlled analysis. Hence, we employ this post-invasion-only variation of the analysis solely as a robustness check.

[7] The results from these tests are shown at table 5.A.10 in the appendix.

[8] Troop commitment levels are from globalsecurity.org (http://www.globalsecurity.org /military/ops/iraq_orbat_coalition.htm, accessed May 23, 2014) and Perspectives on World History and Current Events (PWHCE, http://www.pwhce.org/willing.html, accessed May 23, 2014), as well as from a variety of supplemental sources.

prior chapters, with comparable results. We also tested models including controls for levels and annual changes in Internet access. For three reasons, we anticipated weaker results for the Internet variables. First, governments theoretically have less influence over Internet content relative to other media. Second, Internet users have greater capacity to self-select into websites that reinforce their preexisting beliefs. Finally, Internet penetration rates circa 2003 were quite modest in many nations. Likely owing to one or more of these factors, none of the findings for Internet penetration reached traditional levels of statistical significance, and, as a consequence, we exclude Internet access from our final models to preserve statistical leverage.[9]

Also as in the previous chapters, the second key independent variable measures the number of political parties within each state. We again operationalize this variable with Golder's measures of the effective number of *parliamentary* (ENPP) and *elective* (ENEP) parties.[10] These data are available for 51 of the 62 countries in our data set for which we also have public opinion data (104 and 100 countries overall for ENPP and ENEP, respectively). However, because we have far fewer cases in this cross-sectional analysis than we did in the time-series analyses in the previous two chapters (and fewer still for which we have ENPP or ENEP data), we also test our models against a third electoral system indicator with more complete data: a dummy, coded one for proportional representation (PR) electoral systems and zero for mixed, plurality, or majority-rule systems.[11]

As before, we consider ENPP, which captures the number of parties actually serving in the legislature, to be the best available measure of the domestic political environment pertinent to media actors seeking to frame their coverage to appeal to consumers. Hence, we employ ENPP in our primary model specifications. However, because this is an uncertain judgment, we replicate all models using both measures of the effective number of parties.

[9] That said, in appendix 2 to chapter 3 and in the concluding chapter we present some evidence that Internet users primarily consume domestically sourced news online, which makes typical users' Internet-based news consumption relatively similar to other types of media consumption. This, in turn, suggests that the same logic we apply to traditional media may also apply to the Internet, despite its potential as a global information source.

[10] Golder (2005). See chapter 3 for the formulas for deriving ENPP and ENEP. The ENPP data employed in this chapter vary from a low of 1.0 to a high of 9.05, with a mean and standard deviation of 3.29 and 1.56, respectively (3.97 and 1.61, respectively, among countries for which we have opinion data). ENEP varies from 1.59 to 10.29, with a mean and standard deviation of 4.05 and 1.78, respectively (4.80 and 1.86, respectively, among countries for which we also have public opinion data).

[11] The PR dummy has a mean and standard deviation of 0.39 and 0.49, respectively (or 0.63 and 0.49, respectively, for the sixty-two states with 2003 opinion data). These data are from the International Institute for Democracy and Electoral Assistance (IDEA, http://www.idea.int, accessed May 23, 2014). We employ data from January 2005 (the closest to 2003 available). To our knowledge (based on consultations with colleagues and more detailed checks of several uncertain cases), no state in our data changed their electoral system between 2003 and early 2005 sufficiently to change their coding from a zero to a one, or vice versa.

The PR dummy is the most indirect of the three measures. Nonetheless, since PR systems tend to produce larger numbers of parties than plurality or majoritarian systems and since the PR variable is available for a much larger set of countries—thereby substantially increasing the number of cases in our models—we employ it as a robustness check.[12]

For our data on democracy, we again employ the Polity IV democracy score.[13] To capture a state's capacity to contribute to the coalition, we estimate each state's overall economic power and current economic performance, as well as its level of development. The macroeconomic indicators include 2003 per capita GDP and, to capture growth rates, the percentage change in GDP from 2002 to 2003 (both in current US dollars). We also include inflation, measured as the annual percentage change in average consumer prices from 2002 to 2003. To measure a state's level of economic development, we employ infant mortality rates (circa 2004) and secondary school enrollment ratios (circa 2003).[14]

We also include dummies for NATO members and for membership in *any* formal alliance with the United States, respectively. These dummies account for the possibility that alliance relationships, or the similar electoral institutions of most NATO member states, might systematically influence states' propensities to contribute troops to the coalition.[15]

Finally, as we have argued, press freedom influences the credibility of information presented by the media, irrespective of the robustness of political opposition. Hence, it should mediate the effects of information on public opinion and leaders' decision making. To estimate press freedom, we employ the Reporters Sans Frontiers (RSF) World Press Freedom Ranking. This index is based on a survey of "journalists, researchers, jurists and human rights activ-

---

[12] Lijphart (1999). The actual number of cases varies from 50 to 129 depending on the mix of variables. The PR dummy correlates with ENPP and ENEP at .32 and .24, respectively. The higher correlation between PR and ENPP makes sense, given that the latter variable measures the number of parties in the legislature, rather than in the society. Nearly all democracies have more than two parties. The most direct effect of electoral rules is to mediate their capacity to enter the legislature, and hence their likelihood of gaining influence.

[13] Available at http://www.systemicpeace.org/polity/polity4.htm (accessed May 23, 2014). As in chapter 3, following convention, we subtract a state's score on the 10-point Polity autocracy scale from its score on the 10-point democracy scale (where 1 = min. and 10 = max., yielding a final scale running from −10 to 10). Unlike chapter 3, however, here we do not collapse the index into a binary democracy indicator.

[14] We did not include secondary enrollment as an additional development measure in chapters 3 and 4 because of very limited data early in the time series that we employed in those chapters (1965–2006).

[15] We tested additional controls, including states' total and urban populations, energy use, material capabilities, military expenditures, military personnel, and trade relations with and arms transfers from the United States. We also tested country- and region-specific dummies, as well as similarity in states' United Nations General Assembly voting records. Though several variables approached significance, none altered the key relationships. Hence, to preserve statistical leverage we exclude these model variations from our reported results.

ists" who "evaluat[ed] respect for press freedom in a particular country."[16] The index is on a 0 to 100 scale, where 0 represents the highest and 100 the lowest level of press freedom. In 2003 it included 166 countries, including nearly all countries in our 2003 cross section.[17] We employ this indicator instead of the composite Van Belle/Freedom House measure that we employ in our time-series analyses because it covers more of the countries included in this 2003 cross section. That said, once we account for wealth, media access, and the number of parties, the coefficient on this indicator becomes small and insignif-icant when employed solely as a control. Consequently, with the exception of a robustness test reported in the appendix, in order to preserve statistical lever-age we exclude it from models not directly testing the effects of press freedom on our key interaction.

Results

As we have done throughout the book, we again place all regression tables in the appendix to this chapter. Below we review our substantive findings. We in-vite interested readers to consult the appendix for details on regression analysis techniques and results.

Our coalition support hypothesis (H3) predicts that in high-party states, greater public access to the media will be associated with *increased* opposition to (that is, reduced support for) the war, while as the number of parties de-clines, the relationship will weaken and ultimately reverse, with greater media access associated with *reduced* public war opposition (that is, increased sup-port). In our initial statistical analyses we omit all control variables.[18] The re-sults, though not identical, are quite similar to those including all controls, sug-gesting that the relationships reported below are not artifacts of model specification. Consequently, we proceed more confidently to interpreting the fully specified model.

We test our predictions against all three previously described electoral sys-tem indicators.[19] As in previous chapters we employ statistical simulations to calculate the expected values and confidence intervals for the dependent vari-ables at different values of the key independent variables (depending on the model, these include the effective number of parties, media access, press free-dom, and public opinion), with all controls held constant at their mean values.[20] The top-left graphic in figure 5.2 illustrates the expected change in opposition

---

[16] http://en.rsf.org/press-freedom-index-2003,551.html.

[17] We use Freedom House press freedom data in prior chapters in part because they are avail-able for a much longer time frame. In 2003 the RSF and Freedom House press freedom indexes correlate at about .80.

[18] Table 5.A.3 in the appendix presents a series of OLS analyses testing H3 and H4. Models 1 to 6 omit all controls, while models 7 to 15 present the fully specified models

[19] Models 7 to 9 in table 5.A.3 thus employ ENPP, ENEP, and the PR dummy, respectively.

[20] King, Tomz, and Wittenberg (2000).

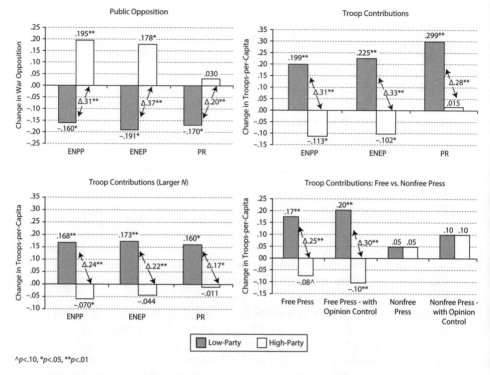

Figure 5.2. Expected change in public opposition and troop contributions to coalition of the willing as TV access increases by two standard deviations, low- versus high-party states and free versus nonfree press

to the Iraq War as the number of televisions per one thousand population increases from one standard deviation below to one standard deviation above the mean among countries with available public opinion data (from 157 to 727 TVs).[21] We separately present the results for low- and high-party states, defined as one standard deviation below or above the mean for the effective number of parties (2.36 vs. 5.58 for ENPP and 2.94 vs. 6.66 for ENEP), and zero or one for the PR dummy.[22]

The top-left graphic in figure 5.2 indicates that in low-ENPP states, a two-standard-deviation increase in the number of televisions per one thousand people (as noted, here and throughout this chapter from one below to one above the mean) is associated with a 16-percentage-point decline in public war opposition (from 71 to 55 percent, $p < .05$). The results are similar for the other two indicators. As TV access increases in low-ENEP nations, public opposition

[21] In the appendix, we graph the ENPP results for the full range of variation in TV access.

[22] This first set of results, for ENPP, ENEP, and the PR dummy, respectively, is based on models 7 to 9 in table 5.A.3.

to the war falls by nearly 19 percentage points (from 72 to 53 percent, $p < .05$). Finally, war opposition is nearly 17 points lower in non-PR states, relative to PR states (68 vs. 51 percent, $p < .10$). In short and as predicted by the coalition support hypothesis (H3), in countries with relatively few political parties, increased access to television is associated with a *decrease* in public opposition to (that is, increased support for) the war in Iraq.

The top-left graphic in figure 5.2 also indicates that in high-ENPP states, increased television access is associated with just over a 19-point *increase* in war opposition (from .65 to .84, $p < .01$). The corresponding increase in TV access in high-ENEP nations is associated with just over an 18-point increase in war opposition (from .65 to .83, $p < .05$). Finally, in PR states the corresponding effect is a statistically insignificant increase of less than 3 points (from .69 to .72), far smaller than that associated with non-PR states. We do not see a full reversal in this last case, presumably because the PR dummy is a noisier indicator than ENPP or ENEP. Hence, while we do see the expected reduction in the opposition-enhancing effects of increased TV access, the variable does not isolate low-party systems with sufficient precision in order to observe a full reversal, to opposition-*reducing* effects. Nonetheless, these results offer clear support for H3. In high-party states, the positive relationship between TV access and opposition to the war among low-party states weakens dramatically in one case (PR dummy) and reverses in two (ENPP and ENEP), with increased access to television associated with *increases* in opposition to the Iraq War.

We turn next to our troop contribution models, testing the coalition joining hypothesis (H4). The goal here is to determine the effects of leaders' expectations concerning the longer-term implications of public opinion, as distinct from contemporaneous support. Consequently, we include the log of contemporaneous public opposition as a control variable. H4 predicts that in high-party states, TV access will be inversely related to participation in the coalition, while as the number of parties declines this relationship will weaken and ultimately reverse.[23]

In the top-right graphic in figure 5.2, we illustrate the results of our tests of H4. The results indicate that in low-ENPP and low-ENEP states, an increase in TV access (again, from 157 to 727) is associated with increases of .199 ($p < .01$) and .225 ($p < .01$) troops per capita, respectively. Finally, in non-PR states, the corresponding effect is an increase of .299 troops per capita ($p < .01$). In other words, as anticipated by H4, in countries with relatively few political parties, increased access to television is associated with *increased* troop contributions to the coalition.

In high-ENPP and high-ENEP states, the same increase in TV access is associated with *decreases* of .113 ($p < .05$) and .102 ($p < .05$) troops per capita, respectively, contributed to the coalition. In PR states, the corresponding effect

[23] Models 10 to 12 in table 5.A.3 test this hypothesis.

is a statistically insignificant increase of .015 troops per capita. The absence of any effect in PR states stands in sharp contrast to the large and significant increase associated with low-party states. Once again, the bluntness of the PR dummy as a proxy for the party system likely explains the absence of a full reversal. Nonetheless, on balance these results clearly support H4 across all three measures of party systems. In high-party states, the relationship between TV access and troop commitments to the coalition is essentially nil in one case (again, the PR dummy) and reverses in two (ENPP and ENEP), with increased access to television associated with *declines* in the expected contributions to the coalition.

One of the primary limitations in the analyses thus far is the limited number of available observations—ranging from 50 to 59 in our models. Hence, as a robustness test, we replicate the above analyses excluding war opposition, which, as noted, is available for only 62 countries.[24] Doing so increases the number of observations to 80 in our ENPP and ENEP models and 129 in our PR model. In the bottom-left graphic in figure 5.2, we again graphically illustrate the results.

The results confirm our expectations. Comparing the bottom-left and top-right graphics in figure 5.2, we see quite similar patterns. The only noteworthy distinction is that, presumably due to the greater number of noncoalition participants included in the models, many of the substantive differences are slightly smaller than those shown in the top-right graphic in figure 5.2. This increases our confidence in the reliability of the results reported above.

Before turning to our final hypothesis, we assess whether, as our theory anticipates and as was the case with initiation and reciprocation, press freedom mediates the constraining effects of robust opposition and media access on leaders' coalition joining decisions. As in prior chapters, we do so by interacting press freedom with TV access and the effective number of parties. For this analysis, we employ the aforementioned RSF Press Freedom Index. A score of 20 or below on the index indicates a free press, while a score above 20 indicates that a state has a "problematic free press situation."[25] In keeping with our treatment of the Van Belle and Freedom House data in the prior chapters we collapse the index to a dummy variable, coded one for free press states (scoring 0–20 on the RSF Index) and zero for non–free press states (scoring 21–100 on the Index).[26] For purposes of brevity, we present only the results for our primary party indicator, ENPP. The results, however, are similar across all three party system indicators.

---

[24] Models 13 to 15 in table 5.A.3 replicate models 10 to 12.

[25] Ekman (2009: 13).

[26] The results are robust to variations in the threshold for dividing free press from non–free press countries. For instance, rerunning our models with a stricter threshold of 15 as the cut point (that is, index scores of 1–15 instead of 1–20 as representing a free press) has no material effect on the reported results.

The bottom-right graphic in figure 5.2 illustrates the results from this investigation.[27] As noted, we derive these expected values from a three-way interaction among ENPP, TV access, and press freedom. The graphic presents the results from two models, one including and the other excluding war opposition as a control variable. As before, we ran the latter model to increase the number of observations (which rises from forty-nine to seventy-six absent war opposition), and hence our statistical leverage.

The results indicate that, as anticipated, the conditional effects of opposition and access importantly depend on a free and hence credible press. When the media are free, the interaction is strong and consistent with our theory. However, when they are not, the conditional relationship disappears. Beginning with low-party, free press states, an increase in TV access (again, from 157 to 727) is associated with increases of .174 ($p < .01$) and .203 ($p < .01$) troops per capita, respectively, for the models with and without the war opposition control. In sharp contrast, among high-party, free press states, the effects once again reverse. Here, the same increase in TV access is associated with *decreases* of .075 ($p < .06$) and .104 ($p < .01$) troops per capita contributed to the coalition, respectively. In each case, the differences in the effects of increased TV access given a high- versus low-party system are themselves statistically significant ($p < .01$). In sharp contrast, and as noted above, in non–free press states, we find no significant direct or conditional effects of opposition and access. This makes sense, as when the press are not free from government influence, they are in most circumstances less credible to citizens than their free counterparts. Hence, nonfree presses are less well situated to influence leaders' political risk assessments.

Our final coalition hypothesis (H5, parties and opinion-policy correspondence hypothesis) predicts that in high-party states, governments' decisions regarding coalition joining will correspond more closely with public opinion as media access increases, while in low-party states, variations in media access will have a weaker effect on the correspondence between public opinion and coalition joining decisions.[28] Figure 5.3 plots the results from our tests of H5 for our primary party measure, ENPP, over a two-standard-deviation increase in television access (again, centered on the mean).[29]

---

[27] The results shown in the graphic are based on models 10 (excludes war opposition) and 11 (includes war opposition) in table 5.A.4.

[28] Models 1 to 3 of table 5.A.4 (in the appendix) test this prediction by interacting the number of parties with TV access and logged public opposition to the war, replicating the model for all three party system indicators. (Note that model 3 in table 5.A.4 excludes the largest residual outlier, Canada, the inclusion of which modestly weakens the reported results.) In table 5.A.5 in the appendix, we transform the coefficients into expected numbers of troops contributed to the coalition as TV access and opposition to the war vary for all three measures of partisan opposition.

[29] The corresponding relationships for the ENEP and PR models are quite similar to those represented in figure 5.3, and so we do not review them in the main text, but instead refer interested readers to table 5.A.5.

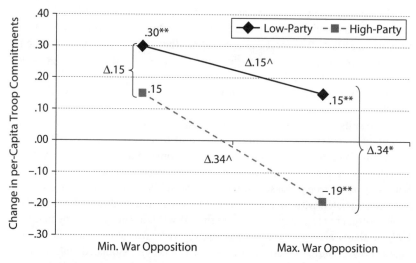

Figure 5.3. Effect of a two-standard-deviation increase in TV access on Iraq troop commitments as war opposition varies, low- versus high-party states

^p<.10, *p<.05, **p<.01

With minimum war opposition, as TV access increases in low-party states, the number of troops contributed to the coalition increases by almost .30 per one thousand population ($p < .01$). The corresponding increase given maximum war opposition is just over .15 troops per capita ($p < .01$). Hence, the predicted difference in the increases in contributions given reduced war opposition (that is, increased war support) for low- versus high-TV access states is nearly .15 troops per capita ($p < .10$). This suggests that when the number of parties is low—which we argue is associated with more compliant media coverage than in multiparty systems—leaders will view enhanced public access to the media as an opportunity to gain greater public support over the longer term. While opposition to the war has some constraining effect, it is relatively muted. If a leader discounts contemporaneous public opinion, then even intense public opposition may not fully deter her from her preferred policies.

In high-party states, increased TV access, given minimum war opposition, is associated with a statistically insignificant .15 increase in troops per capita. Conversely, given maximum war opposition, the corresponding effect is a .19 *decrease* in troops per capita ($p < .01$). This .34 difference between the effects of TV access given minimum versus maximum war opposition is significant at $p < .10$. Increased media access can thus cut either way. This suggests that because media coverage in high-party states is likely to be more policy-centric and more prone to challenge the government, contemporaneous public opposition or support likely represents a relatively more reliable indicator of the longer-term political implications of a policy. Consequently, leaders are *more* constrained by public opposition. These results offer clear support for H5.

Finally, the difference between the differential effects of enhanced TV access given minimum versus maximum war opposition is over twice as large in high-relative to low-party states (roughly .34 vs. .15). This approximately .2 troops per capita gap in the differences ($p < .05$) is equivalent to nearly 1.4 standard deviations.

According to the Downsian Premise, the number of parties should influence the nature of political news coverage. We argue that the resulting tenor of news coverage influences public opinion and foreign policy decision making, albeit through partially distinct paths and to varying degrees depending on the party system. This implies that the party system helps predict the likely nature of news coverage, which in turn influences public opinion and decision making.

In part to determine whether or not this is the case for the Iraq conflict, we analyzed the content of all newspaper articles available through the LexisNexis and ISI Emerging Markets databases for democratic countries that included the word "Iraq" between December 20, 2002, and April 28, 2003.[30] We describe the data in detail in chapter 6, where we undertake a series of empirical tests of the Downsian Premise. To briefly summarize here, the data cover forty-one democracies and include 424 newspapers (or about 10 papers per country).[31] We coded all articles on a variety of dimensions (again, see chapter 6). For instance, previewing chapter 6, one such dimension is valence. We coded each article as positive, negative, or neutral with respect to the government's policy toward Iraq. Employing the average valence for each country, we find that ENPP and average news valence correlate at –.26 overall and –.43 with countries above the mean level of TV access among democracies. The corresponding correlations with ENEP are –.43 and –.59, respectively. Consistent with the Downsian Premise, these correlations indicate that as the number of parties rises, news coverage becomes less supportive of the government's position on Iraq.

Robustness Tests

EFFECTS OF NEWS VALENCE

Our theory treats news content as following in significant measure from the party system. In the analyses thus far, we have in effect employed the party

---

[30] For purposes of this analysis, "democratic countries" are those that score 6 or higher on the Polity IV DEMOC-AUTOC scale.

[31] Our full analysis included 2,310 newspapers across sixty-three countries. These smaller figures represent newspapers in democracies that covered the Iraq story during the time period we investigated. Comparable multicountry TV transcripts do not exist, forcing us to explore newspapers rather than television as we have done elsewhere in this analysis. Since the criterion for inclusion in these databases is unknown to us, this could potentially be an unrepresentative sample of newspapers, though there is no *ex ante* reason to anticipate that this should work in favor of our predictions.

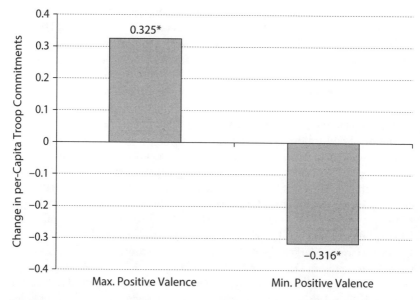

*p<.05

Figure 5.4. Effects of a two-standard-deviation increase in TV access, given minimum versus maximum positive news coverage of government's Iraq policy

system as the underlying causal factor driving the proximate variable of interest, news content. Arguably a more direct predictor of the differential effects of media access on leaders' decision making would be the actual content of news. Valence of coverage, in turn, is perhaps the clearest representation of news content that is consequential to decision making. Unfortunately, we do not have news valence data for enough countries to replicate our full model specifications. However, we can interact news valence with TV access in place of the number of parties in models with a reduced set of controls. When we do so, the effects on troop commitments largely replicate the previous results, thereby enhancing our confidence in their validity.[32] In other words, this replication increases our confidence that we have correctly specified the relationship among the party system, news content, and leaders' coalition-joining decisions. In figure 5.4, we illustrate the results.

Controlling for development,[33] and given *minimum* progovernment news valence in Iraq-related coverage, an increase in TV access from one standard deviation below to one standard deviation above the mean is associated with a drop of .316 troops per capita ($p < .05$). Conversely, the corresponding increase

[32] See models 6 and 7 of table 5.A.4.

[33] In this model we control for secondary enrollment because it allows for a slightly higher N, but the results are equivalent for infant mortality.

in TV access given *maximum* progovernment news valence in Iraq coverage is a .325 *increase* in troops per capita ($p < .01$).[34]

Though derived from a model with only thirty-four observations and therefore far from definitive on their own, these results are consistent with the coalition joining hypothesis (H4) and therefore bolster our confidence in the previously reported results employing party system indicators as predictors of media content. Controlling for public war opposition further reduces the N to twenty-six, but despite the substantial decline in statistical leverage, does not materially change the results.[35] The takeaway point from these and other replications presented in the appendix is that our results are durable and emerge across a wide range of tests, including multiple operationalizations of the key independent and dependent variables.

RECURSIVE ANALYSIS

Thus far, we have implicitly assumed that the effects of media access and party systems on public attitudes toward the war in Iraq and states' decisions to send troops to join the coalition were independent from one another. However, our theory and evidence suggest that public attitudes influence troop contribution decisions while media access and party systems influence *both* public attitudes and troop contributions. It is thus possible that media access and party systems also influence troop contribution decisions indirectly *through* their direct influence on public attitudes. This suggests a recursive relationship, whereby media access and party systems directly influence both public opinion and troop contributions, and public opinion directly influences contributions, but there is no hypothesized feedback loop of troop contributions influencing public opinion.[36]

To assess this possibility, we employ recursive regression to test whether this indirect path is statistically and substantively significant, using the delta method to derive confidence intervals surrounding the predicted indirect effects on troop contributions, via public opinion, of media access and party systems.[37] Given our limited statistical leverage, we employ this approach solely as a robustness test that is intended to supplement the main statistical findings presented above with a more precise assessment of our theoretical mechanism.

In order to properly identify an instrument for public war opposition, we added several variables to the recursive system, including the total volume of

---

[34] See model 6 in table 5.A.4.

[35] See model 7 in table 5.A.4. Table 5.A.9 in the appendix presents a more complete set of analyses, including models employing war opposition as the dependent variable.

[36] As noted, public attitudes solidified in most countries prior to the outbreak of war. Moreover, most surveys employed herein took place either prior to or roughly in parallel with troop contribution decisions. This further reduces the likelihood that the latter caused the former.

[37] See Baum and Lake (2003) for an explication of recursive regression analysis and the delta method.

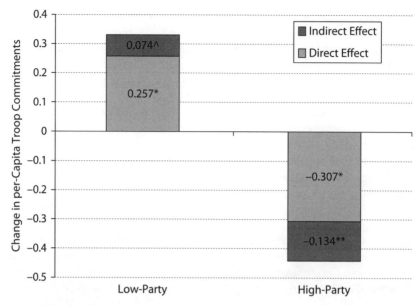

^p<.10, *p<.05, **p<.01

Figure 5.5. Direct and indirect effects on troop commitments of increased TV access, given low- versus high-party states

trade between each country and the United States, the total amount of energy consumed by each country, and a dummy for majority Muslim countries. Each *directly* influences attitudes to a much greater extent than troop commitments (net of the other factors included in the models).[38] In figure 5.5 we graphically illustrate the results from our recursive model.

The results support the anticipated indirect path of influence for media access and party systems. Given the minimum number of parties (measured via ENPP), a two-standard-deviation increase in TV access directly yields an increase in per capita troop commitments of .257 ($p < .05$). However, there also emerges a substantial indirect effect, through public war opposition. The corresponding indirect effect is an increase of .074 troops per capita ($p < .10$), representing over 22 percent of the total combined effect of increased TV access on troop commitments.

Given the maximum number of parties observed in the data, the relationships reverse, as in the previous analyses. In this case, the direct effect of a maximum increase in TV access is a *decrease* in troop contributions of about .307 troops per capita ($p < .05$). The corresponding indirect effect is a decrease

---

[38] Models 4 and 5 in table 5.A.4 present the results of an instrumental variable regression, which forms the basis for the recursive regression approach.

of .134 troops per capita ($p < .01$), accounting for 30 percent of the total combined effect of TV access on troop contributions. As noted, due to the small Ns in the recursive regression models, these results should be interpreted with caution. Nonetheless, they do appear consistent with our core findings, offering additional support for H4.

Taken together, our findings strongly suggest that media access, conditional on the extent of partisan opposition, plays a central role in generating democratic constraints on leaders. The primary alternative explanation—that greater representativeness of consensual relative to majoritarian democracies accounts for any differences across party systems in the relationship between public opinion and troop contributions—cannot account for the observed effects of TV access, holding the number of parties constant. Nor can it account for either the reversal in the direction of those effects in low- versus high-party states or the differential effects of news valence on troop commitments as media access varies. We next replicate our key findings against a second case: Afghanistan.

AFGHANISTAN (2001): OPERATION ENDURING FREEDOM

Data and Methodology

In this section we undertake a second set of tests of our core hypotheses (H3 through H5) against a data set based on the Afghanistan conflict. The US- and NATO-led war in Afghanistan—originally called Operation Infinite Justice and later Operation Enduring Freedom—began on October 7, 2001.[39] Far fewer troops fought in Afghanistan than in Iraq, though the Afghanistan conflict continued far longer than the Iraq War—thirteen years as of this writing. As in Iraq, the United States provided the bulk of the military force, reaching a maximum of 31,000 troops in the first three years of the conflict. This accounted for just over half of the total force. The United Kingdom contributed the next highest number, at 7,800 troops. In total, during the first three years of the conflict, thirty-seven countries—twenty-five of which were NATO members—contributed an average of 313 troops (151 excluding the United States) to the coalition. This is equivalent to .045 troops per one thousand people (with a standard deviation of .039 troops per one thousand people). Excluding the United States, the average per capita troop contribution falls to just below .01 troops per one thousand people (with a standard deviation of .023 troops per one thousand people).[40] Table 5.2 lists countries contributing troops between 2002 and 2005, as well as the numbers of troops contributed by each country.

---

[39] The Bush administration changed the name because it feared offending Muslims. As they apparently learned after the fact, the term "infinite justice" is commonly employed by several religions, including Islam, as a unique description of God.

[40] Troop level data are from the same sources as the Iraq War troop data.

Table 5.2. Afghanistan Coalition Troop Commitment Levels (2002–5)

Country	Troops	Country	Troops
United States	31,000	Greece	171
United Kingdom	7,800	Portugal	160
Germany	3,210	Albania	140
Italy	2,880	South Korea	140
Canada	2,500	Czech Republic	135
Netherlands	1,650	Estonia	130
France	1,515	Macedonia	130
Poland	1,100	New Zealand	115
Turkey	825	Finland	105
Denmark	780	Latvia	100
Spain	740	Slovakia	70
Belgium	616	Slovenia	70
Romania	535	Azerbaijan	50
Norway	495	Iceland	20
Bulgaria	420	Ireland	10
Sweden	345	Luxembourg	10
Lithuania	260	Switzerland	4
Hungary	230	Austria	3
Croatia	190		

Our statistical models are nearly identical to those employed in our analysis of the Iraq War case. We therefore do not redefine previously employed variables, except to note that all variables in this analysis use 2001, or the change from 2000 to 2001, as the target year(s) for measurement (whereas the Iraq analysis employed 2003 or the change from 2002 to 2003). There are slightly more missing data on key variables in this case, relative to the Iraq data. Our fully specified models thus include only forty-seven or forty-eight observations for the opinion and troop commitment models, respectively. Due to missing data, we exclude the secondary enrollment ratio as an indicator of development, as including it reduces the N to a maximum of forty observations without materially affecting the key relationships (as well as being itself statistically insignificant).

There are several differences between the Iraq and Afghanistan models. To begin with, while press freedom remains statistically insignificant in the fully specified models, it performed better in some model specifications than in the Iraq models. Moreover, unlike the Iraq case, its presence in the Afghanistan models also somewhat improves their overall fit. Hence, because it is a theoretically compelling control, we do not drop it from the reported results in this case. We also add three additional controls. First, recall that we tested an Iraq model specification employing the similarity of voting records between the United States and the other country in question.[41] Though the variable was statistically significant, in the expected direction, it had no material effect on the key relationships. To preserve statistical leverage, we excluded it from the final models.

[41] See note 15.

In this case, however, the variable both is significant in its own right and affects the key relationships. We therefore include it in our reported results.

Two additional new variables count by country the number of *publicly* owned newspapers and *privately* owned television stations out of the top five papers and TV stations in each country, respectively. (They are literally the inverse of the number of private newspapers or public television stations, and hence the variables are interchangeable in this respect.) This captures the proportion of the top media outlets in each country that are publicly versus privately owned. We include these variables to help better account for the nature of the media environment in each country. As we discuss in the chapter 8 and as additional research has shown,[42] the ownership structure of the media influences news content in important ways, potentially either mitigating or exacerbating the relationships predicted by our theory. Neither variable influenced the key relationships in the Iraq models, and so we excluded them in that case. However, in the Afghanistan models, these variables are statistically significant and/or substantially improve the overall fit of the models.

In order to ensure that excluding these four variables does not meaningfully alter the Iraq results, we replicate our key troop commitment model from the Iraq analysis, with all four additional variables included.[43] Though including these additional controls considerably reduces the N and with it our statistical leverage (from fifty to thirty-eight observations in the fully specified model), all of the key relationships remain in the predicted directions, comparable in magnitude, and statistically significant—in fact, the key relationship are even stronger than those reported in figure 5.2.

The final difference between the Iraq and Afghanistan analyses concerns the troop commitment models. When we include public opposition to the war in Afghanistan as a control, the N drops considerably further than it did in the Iraq models (due to missing data we preserve at best thirty-five observations, compared to fifty in the Iraq models). For our three-way interaction models we have no choice but to include the opinion indicator, despite the drop in statistical leverage. To retain sufficient statistical leverage with war opposition included as a control, we drop the four new control variables (that is, those not employed in the Iraq models, including newspaper and television public vs. private ownership, press freedom, and UN General Assembly voting similarity with the United States), as including each results in additional dropped observations, thereby rendering the model intractable. To retain sufficient statistical leverage without dropping other controls, we exclude war opposition from models not directly interpreting public war opposition in conjunction with the numbers of parties and television access.

For this analysis, we have public opinion data from sixty-three countries, derived from six cross-national and national surveys conducted between Sep-

---

[42] Baum and Zhukov (2011, 2013a, 2013b).
[43] See model 8 in table 5.A.4 in the appendix.

tember and December 2001 (see table 5.A.8 for details on the opinion surveys). Across these sixty-three countries, an average of about 56 percent of respondents opposed the conflict (with a range of 0 to 90 percent opposition and a standard deviation of about 21 percentage points). This suggests that a majority of respondents worldwide opposed the Afghanistan invasion, though opposition was about 11 percentage points lower than for the Iraq War. Figure 5.6 summarizes the level of public opposition to Afghanistan across the sixty-three countries in our data set.

Our opinion data in nearly all cases precede, or at most parallel, nations' troop commitment decisions. We employ a larger time window for capturing maximum troop commitments in this case (three years) than we did for Iraq (one year). We did so to maximize the number of cases included in our analysis, albeit at the obvious cost of some precision in the direct relationship between public opinion on the war and leaders' decisions regarding troop commitments. However, increasing the potential time lag between opinion measures and troop commitments ought almost certainly to work against our predictions, thereby making our tests relatively conservative. Moreover, reducing the time window of the troop commitment indicator by a year, though it reduces our statistical leverage, does not materially alter the key relationship among parties, media access, and troop commitment decisions. The reason, presumably, is that while some states did not send troops into Afghanistan for several years into the conflict, in most cases there was a substantial time lag between the policy debates and ultimate decisions to support the coalition and the actual deployment of troops. Nonetheless, the longer time lag makes this a less precise test than our Iraq case analysis and is partly why we view the Afghanistan case primarily as a robustness check. (See table 5.A.2 for summary statistics on the variables in our regression analyses.)

Results

In order to keep this presentation manageable in length, rather than run through the full set of party-system indicators and model specifications, for our Afghanistan analyses we focus solely on our most preferred party system indicator (ENPP) and cut straight to interpreting the full model specifications.[44]

The coalition support hypothesis (H3) predicts that in high-party states, greater public access to the media will be associated with *increased* opposition to the war, while as the number of parties drops the relationship will weaken and ultimately reverse.[45] As before, we calculate expected public war opposition as media access and the number of parties vary, with all controls held constant at their mean values. Figure 5.7 illustrates the expected change in opposi-

[44] Table 5.A.6 (in the appendix) presents a series of OLS analyses testing our hypotheses.
[45] Model 1 in table 5.A.6 tests these predictions.

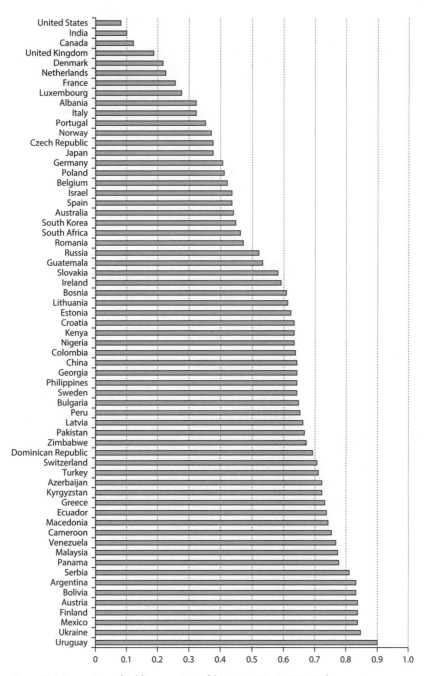

Figure 5.6. Percentage of public opposing Afghanistan War in 2001–2, by country

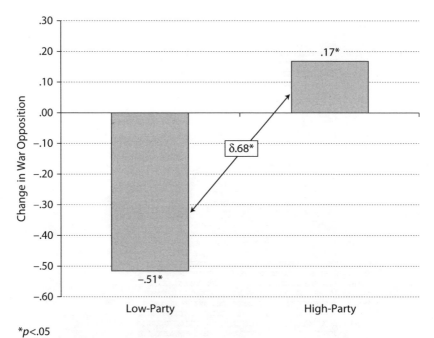

*p<.05

Figure 5.7. Effects of a two-standard-deviation increase in TV access on opposition to Afghanistan conflict, low- versus high-party states

tion to the Afghanistan War, as TV access increases from one standard deviation below to one standard deviation above the mean among countries with available public opinion data (from 135 to 719 TVs). We separately present the results for low- and high-party states, as before defined as one standard deviation below or above the mean, respectively, in the Afghanistan data set (from 1.70 to 4.86 for ENPP).

In low-party states, increased TV access is associated with a 51-percentage-point *decline* in public war opposition (from 98 to 47 percent, $p < .05$). Conversely, in high-party states, increased TV access is associated with a 17-point *increase* in war opposition (from .39 to .56, $p < .05$). In short and consistent with H3, in countries with relatively few parties, increased TV access is associated with reduced public opposition to the war in Afghanistan, while in countries with relatively large numbers of political parties, the relationship reverses, with increased access to television associated with *increases* in expected opposition to the Afghanistan War. It is also worth noting that the .68-percentage-point difference between the effects of increased TV access in low- versus high-party states is itself significant at the .05 level.

We turn next to our troop contribution analysis.[46] The coalition joining hypothesis (H4) predicts that among high-party states, there will be an inverse

---

[46] This analysis is shown at model 2 in table 5.A.6.

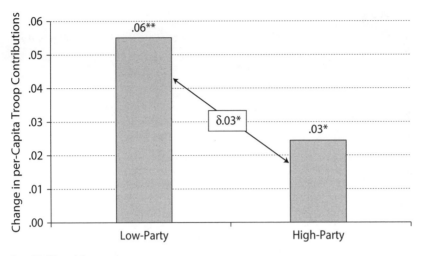

*p<.05, **p<.01

Figure 5.8. Effects of a two-standard-deviation increase in TV access on per capita troop contributions to Afghanistan conflict, low- versus high-party states

relationship between TV access and participation in the coalition, while this relationship will weaken and eventually reverse as the number of parties declines. Figure 5.8 illustrates the results of our tests of these propositions.

The results indicate that in low-party states, increased television access is associated with an increase of .06 ($p < .01$) troops per capita. Conversely, in high-party states, increased TV access is associated with half as large an increase—.03 troops per capita ($p < .05$). In other words, as anticipated by H4, in countries with relatively few political parties, increased access to television is associated with substantial increases in troop contributions, while in countries with relatively large numbers of parties, the relationship between TV access and troop commitments to the coalition, though remaining positive, is only half as large. As before, the .03-percentage-point difference between the effects of TV access in low- versus high-party states is itself significant at the .05 level.

Unlike the Iraq analysis, in this instance we see a small (relative to low-party states), positive effect of increased TV access on troop contributions in high-party states. Though consistent with our expectations, this difference warrants some further consideration. One likely explanation is that, as noted, public opinion in most countries was less hostile to the Afghanistan intervention than to Iraq. So, while we do observe a substantial and statistically significant differential between high- and low-party states, we do not see the full reversal that we saw in the Iraq case.

Finally, our parties and opinion-policy correspondence hypothesis (H5) predicts that in high-party states, increased media access will tighten the link be-

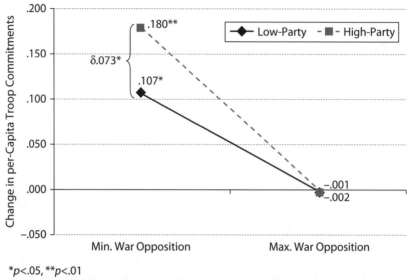

*p<.05, **p<.01

Figure 5.9. Effects of a two-standard-deviation increase in TV access on Afghanistan troop commitments as war opposition varies, low- versus high-party states

tween public opinion and governments' decisions regarding whether or not to join the coalition, whereas in low-party states, this linkage-enhancing effect will be weaker. As with the Iraq case, we test this prediction by interacting the number of parties with TV access and logged public opposition to the war.[47] In figure 5.9, we graphically illustrate the expected number of troops contributed to the coalition as TV access, the number of parties, and opposition to the war vary.

As predicted by H5, figure 5.9 shows that in high-party states public opposition to the war appears to inhibit leaders from joining the coalition to a greater extent when TV access is high than when it is low. Also as anticipated, this effect is weaker in low-party states. With minimum war opposition, as TV access increases in low-party states, the expected number of troops contributed to the coalition increases by about .11 troops per capita ($p < .05$). The corresponding effect given maximum war opposition is insignificant and near zero (−.002, ns). Hence, the predicted difference in the increases in troop contributions given variations in war opposition for states with low- versus high-TV access is .107 troops per capita ($p < .05$).

Conversely, increased TV access in high-party states, given minimum war opposition, is associated with a .18 increase in troops per capita ($p < .01$), whereas, given maximum war opposition, the corresponding effect is again

[47] Model 3 in table 5.A.6 tests H5. Note that this analysis excludes the largest residual outlier, Russia, the inclusion of which modestly weakens the reported results. In order to preserve sufficient statistical leverage, it also excludes the several new variables introduced for our tests of H3 and H4.

near zero ($-.001$, ns). This .18 difference is significant at $p < .01$. Finally, the .07 difference in troops per capita between the effects of increased TV access given low- versus high-party systems is itself statistically significant ($p < .05$). This again indicates greater responsiveness to public opinion in high-party states (and support for H5).

One question that these results raise is why, given minimum public opposition, high-party countries contributed more troops to Afghanistan than their low-party counterparts, while the opposite pattern emerged for Iraq. There are two possible answers. First, as noted earlier, Iraq was less popular globally (67 vs. 56 percent opposition, on average). Second, NATO more heavily dominated the conflict in Afghanistan (67 percent of countries sending troops to Afghanistan were NATO members, compared to vs. 46 percent Iraq). The reason for this is presumably that NATO invoked its charter after 9/11, formally obligating member states to participate in the NATO-led mission in Afghanistan. NATO states, in turn, have on average about 25 percent higher ENPP scores— that is, a higher effective number of parties—than non-NATO states. So the relatively greater NATO orientation of the Afghanistan intervention force could explain a higher propensity to contribute troops in Afghanistan, relative to Iraq, absent significant public opposition.

Regardless, these patterns suggest that when the number of parties is low, leaders are likely to view enhanced public access to the media as an opportunity to gain greater public support over the longer term. While opposition to the war has some constraining effect, such an effect is limited. If a leader discounts contemporaneous public opinion, then even intense public opposition may prove insufficient to fully deter her from her preferred foreign policy course.

Finally, the difference between the differential effects of enhanced TV access given minimum versus maximum war opposition is over twice as large in high- relative to low-party states (.08 vs. .001). This "difference between the differentials" of .08 troops per capita between low- and high-ENPP states is itself statistically significant ($p < .05$).

CONCLUSION

Evidence from the Iraq and Afghanistan cases suggest that, as we found in our studies of conflict initiation and reciprocation in the prior two chapters, the media influence states' conflict behavior in differing ways and to varying degrees, depending in part on the institutional environment in which they operate. In multiparty states, increased public access to television reduced public support for, and the propensity to commit troops to, the respective conflicts. In contrast, greater media access in two-party states is associated with *lower* opposition and *higher* troop commitments, but there is a weaker link between the two. This again is consistent with the Downsian Premise, which holds that multiparty systems promote policy-centric media coverage of politics, which in turn empowers citizens to more effectively monitor their leaders' activities. Because citizens in multiparty democracies are more likely to encounter information conflicting with their leaders' preferred framing of foreign conflicts, they are more likely to punish leaders who engage in risky foreign adventures and fail. Consequently, media coverage in most instances weighs more heavily on leaders' political calculations in multi-party than in two-party states. Variations in press freedom alone are insufficient to account for these patterns.

In the next chapter, we turn from our investigations of conflict decision making by democratic governments to in-depth testing of the Downsian Premise, which underlies our theoretical argument.

APPENDIX: STATISTICAL TABLES AND ROBUSTNESS TESTS

Summary Statistics

Table 5.A.1 and 5.A.2 present summary statistics on the variables employed in the Iraq and Afghanistan models.

Table 5.A.1. Iraq Summary Statistics

	M	SD	Min	Max	N
Overall					
Troops per 1,000 pop.	0.025	0.07	0.00	0.76	191
Free press scale	0.51	0.50	0.00	1.00	160
PR electoral system	0.39	0.49	0.00	1.00	183
ENPP	3.29	1.56	1.00	9.05	104
ENPP	4.05	1.78	1.59	10.29	100
Democracy level	3.46	6.71	−10	+10	151
TVs per 1,000 pop	274	251	5	1552	180
GDP per capita	7382	11623	83	64348	177
Annual % change in per capita GDP	0.14	0.14	−0.66	0.56	177
Infant mortality rate (2004)	42.19	40.91	2	165	185
Secondary enrollment ration (2003)	74.88	33.82	6	179	159
Inflation (2003)	8.50	28.71	−3.50	365	177
NATO member	0.13	0.34	0.00	1.00	191
US ally	0.28	0.45	0.00	1.00	191
Observations with opinion data					
% opposing war	0.67	0.16	0.30	0.96	62
Troops per 1,000 pop.	0.03	0.11	0.00	0.76	62
Free press scale	0.77	0.43	0.00	1.00	60
PR electoral system	0.63	0.49	0.00	1.00	62
ENPP	3.97	1.61	1.99	9.05	51
ENPP	4.80	1.86	2.04	10.29	51
Democracy level	7.44	4.45	−7	+10	59
TVs per 1,000 pop	442	285	18	1552	62
GDP per capita	14813	15405	232	64348	62
Annual % change in per capita GDP	0.19	0.10	−0.08	0.48	62
Infant mortality rate (2004)	19.06	24.01	2	101	62
Secondary enrollment ratio (2003)	93.08	30.48	20	179	61
Inflation (2003)	4.37	5.04	−1.10	25.30	62
NATO member	0.40	0.49	0.00	1.00	62
US ally	0.42	0.50	0.00	1.00	62

Table 5.A.2. Afghanistan Summary Statistics

	M	SD	Min	Max	N
Overall					
Troops per 1,000 pop.	0.01	0.02	0.00	0.15	191
Free press scale	72.54	23.07	2.50	99.50	133
PR electoral system	0.51	0.50	0.00	1.00	183
ENPP	3.28	1.58	1.00	9.05	101
ENEP	4.03	1.80	1.59	10.29	99
Democracy level	3.22	6.61	−10.00	10.00	151
TVs per 1,000 pop	261	230	1.90	970	180
GDP per capita	6280	10215	95	74996	190
Annual % change in GDP per capita	0.005	0.10	−0.28	0.39	190
Infant mortality rate (2004)	41.75	37.69	3.00	165.00	189
Inflation (2003)	10.33	31.60	−8.80	357.90	171
NATO member	0.13	0.34	0.00	1.00	191
US ally	0.28	0.45	0.00		191
# of top 5 TV stations that are privately owned	0.39	0.33	0.00	1.00	95
# of top 5 newspapers that are publicly owned	0.29	0.40	0.00	1.00	95
UN General Assembly voting similarity to US	−0.24	0.34	−0.60	0.96	183
Observations with opinion data					
% opposing war	0.56	0.21	0.08	0.09	63
Troops per 1,000 pop.	0.02	0.04	0.00	0.15	63
Free press scale	82.41	17.94	3.00	99.50	52
PR electoral system	0.77	0.42	0.00	1.00	
ENPP	3.80	1.64	1.99	9.05	50
ENEP	4.68	1.84	2.16	10.29	50
Democracy level	6.97	4.65	−7.00	10.00	60
TVs per 1,000 pop	415	244	36	970	62
GDP per capita	10254	11764	306	43608	63
Annual % change in GDP per capita	0.03	0.10	−0.28	0.35	63
Infant mortality rate (2004)	22.54	24.71	3.00	107.00	63
Inflation (2003)	9.04	16.89	−1.10	91.10	60
NATO member	0.35	0.48	0.00	1.00	63
US ally	0.48	0.50	0.00	1.00	63
# of top 5 TV stations that are privately owned	0.55	0.27	0.00	1.00	49
# of top 5 newspapers that are publicly owned	0.10	0.24	0.00	1.00	49
UN General Assembly voting similarity to US	−0.18	0.25	−0.56	0.73	62

Regression Tables Employed in Text of Chapter 5

Table 5.A.3. OLS Analyses of Effects of Variations in TV Access and Number of Parties on Public Opposition to Iraq War and Troop Commitments

	Troops Deployed (Base Models)			War Opposition (Base Models)		
	ENPP	ENPP	PR	ENPP	ENPP	PR
	1	2	3	4	5	6
% oppose war	−0.068	−0.084	−0.068	—	—	—
	(0.063)	(0.057)	(0.041)			
Parties/PR	0.067^	0.054^	0.098*	−0.076^	−0.071^	−0.047
	(0.035)	(0.030)	(0.041)	(0.041)	(0.039)	(0.114)
Access (× 100)	0.084*	0.080^	0.043*	−0.124**	−0.132**	−0.044^
	(0.041)	(0.041)	(0.017)	(0.039)	(0.040)	(0.022)
Parties × access (× 100)	−0.017^	−0.014^	−0.041*	0.028**	0.025**	0.046^
	(0.009)	(0.007)	(0.017)	(0.009)	(0.008)	(0.024)
GDP per capita (× 1,000)	—	—	—	—	—	—
Annual change in GDP per capita (2002 to 2003)	—	—	—	—	—	—
Infant mortality (× 100)	—	—	—	—	—	—
Secondary enrollment (× 100)	—	—	—	—	—	—
Inflation	—	—	—	—	—	—
Democracy	—	—	—	—	—	—
NATO	—	—	—	—	—	—
US ally	—	—	—	—	—	—
Constant	−0.331*	−0.325^	−0.121**	−0.050	−0.017	−0.355***
	(0.155)	(0.163)	(0.043)	(0.178)	(0.185)	(0.096)
Observations	51	51	62	51	51	62
R^2–	.504	.456	.575	.277	.269	.134

Robust standard errors in parentheses. ^p < .10. *p < .05. **p < .01. ***p < .001.

	War Opposition			Troops Deployed (Full Models)			Troops Deployed (Excludes War Opposition)		
	ENPP	ENPP	PR	ENPP	ENPP	PR	ENPP	ENPP	PR
	7	8	9	10	11	12	13	14	15
	—	—	—	-0.011	-0.025	-0.038	—	—	—
				(0.053)	(0.054)	(0.032)			
	-0.068	-0.070	-0.063	0.051**	0.051*	0.166**	0.037*	0.026^	0.050*
	(0.047)	(0.044)	(0.152)	(0.017)	(0.019)	(0.054)	(0.016)	(0.013)	(0.023)
	-0.110*	-0.132*	-0.050^	0.075***	0.084**	0.053**	0.062**	0.061*	0.028*
	(0.045)	(0.051)	(0.028)	(0.021)	(0.026)	(0.015)	(0.023)	(0.024)	(0.012)
	0.028*	0.026*	0.057*	-0.017**	-0.015**	-0.050**	-0.013*	-0.010*	-0.030*
	(0.010)	(0.010)	(0.027)	(0.005)	(0.005)	(0.015)	(0.005)	(0.004)	(0.013)
	-0.002	0.001	-0.002	0.000	-0.001	-0.000	-0.000	-0.001	0.000
	(0.002)	(0.002)	(0.003)	(0.001)	(0.001)	(0.001)	(0.001)	(0.001)	(0.001)
	0.050	-0.102	0.025	-0.428*	-0.349*	-0.265**	-0.269*	-0.244*	-0.105*
	(0.462)	(0.443)	(0.394)	(0.160)	(0.146)	(0.092)	(0.110)	(0.105)	(0.052)
	-0.076	-0.094	-0.304	0.178^	0.193^	0.221*	0.161^	0.178^	0.083
	(0.200)	(0.183)	(0.233)	(0.090)	(0.099)	(0.097)	(0.083)	(0.097)	(0.053)
	-0.233	-0.236	0.112	0.318**	0.318*	0.088	0.169^	0.164	0.035
	(0.239)	(0.225)	(0.200)	(0.106)	(0.130)	(0.085)	(0.093)	(0.108)	(0.053)
	0.753^	0.814^	0.743	-0.389*	-0.381^	-0.177	-0.065	-0.063	-0.015
	(0.414)	(0.462)	(0.562)	(0.185)	(0.201)	(0.150)	(0.092)	(0.079)	(0.010)
	0.024	0.023	-0.014	-0.039**	-0.039*	-0.002	-0.003	0.000	0.002^
	(0.033)	(0.031)	(0.009)	(0.014)	(0.016)	(0.003)	(0.003)	(0.003)	(0.001)
	-0.058	-0.058	-0.083	0.087**	0.083**	0.064*	0.062*	0.066*	0.073*
	(0.102)	(0.101)	(0.105)	(0.027)	(0.029)	(0.026)	(0.024)	(0.026)	(0.029)
	0.077	0.060	0.055	-0.073*	-0.062*	-0.050*	-0.042^	-0.040^	-0.027
	(0.093)	(0.092)	(0.083)	(0.030)	(0.029)	(0.022)	(0.023)	(0.022)	(0.017)
	-0.160	-0.055	-0.286	-0.105	-0.171	-0.213*	-0.256^	-0.272^	-0.092
	(0.370)	(0.371)	(0.221)	(0.120)	(0.134)	(0.098)	(0.132)	(0.147)	(0.067)
	50	50	59	50	50	59	80	80	125
	.349	.347	.250	.747	.714	.716	.573	.530	.492

Table 5.A.4. Effects of Variations in TV Access, Number of Parties, and News Valence on Public Opposition to Iraq War and Troop Commitments

	ENPP	ENEP	PR	IV Regression (War Opposition)	IV Regression (Troops)
	1	2	3	4	5
% oppose war (log)	0.008	−0.040	−0.054	—	−0.197^
	(0.172)	(0.180)	(0.075)		(0.113)
PR/parties	0.061**	0.060**	0.217***	−0.0691	0.0414*
	(0.017)	(0.018)	(0.054)	(0.0473)	(0.0203)
Access (× 100)	0.069**	0.072**	0.057***	−0.0009*	0.0574*
	(0.023)	(0.026)	(0.014)	(0.0004)	(0.0252)
Parties × access (× 100)	−0.019**	−0.016**	−0.063***	0.0002*	−0.0124*
	(0.006)	(0.006)	(0.016)	(0.0001)	(0.0057)
Parties × % oppose war (log)	0.039	0.051	0.150	—	—
	(0.038)	(0.032)	(0.098)		
Parties × access × % oppose war (log)	−0.009^	−0.009^	−0.023	—	—
	(0.005)	(0.005)	(0.015)		
Free press	—	—	—	—	—
Free press × ENPP	—	—	—	—	—
Free press × access	—	—	—	—	—
Free press × access × parties	—	—	—	—	—
GDP per capita (× 1,000)	0.000	−0.001	0.000	—	—
	(0.001)	(0.001)	(0.001)		
Annual change in GDP per capita (2002 to 2003)	−0.394*	−0.313^	−0.247*	−0.4519	−0.368*
	(0.168)	(0.157)	(0.102)	(0.4513)	(0.184)
Infant mortality (× 100)	0.182^	0.192*	0.212*	−0.0013	0.00146^
	(0.093)	(0.094)	(0.087)	(0.0018)	(0.000817)
Secondary enrollment (× 100)	0.285*	0.265^	0.054	−0.0026	0.00265*
	(0.123)	(0.135)	(0.068)	(0.0020)	(0.00107)
Inflation (× 100)	−0.441*	−0.448*	−0.184	0.0044	—
	(0.190)	(0.210)	(0.149)	(0.0059)	
Democracy	−0.036*	−0.034*	−0.002	0.0273	−0.0302*
	(0.015)	(0.016)	(0.003)	(0.0318)	(0.0119)
NATO	0.087**	0.084**	0.079**	0.0022	0.0692*
	(0.028)	(0.031)	(0.027)	(0.1005)	(0.0324)
US ally	−0.062^	−0.050	−0.039^	0.0049	−0.0429
	(0.031)	(0.030)	(0.021)	(0.0862)	(0.0282)
# of top 5 TV stations that are privately owned	—	—	—	—	—
# of top 5 newspapers that are publicly owned	—	—	—	—	—
UN General Assembly voting similarity to US	—	—	—	—	—
Press freedom	—	—	—	—	—

News Valence I (Troops)	News Valence II (Troops)	ENPP (Extra Controls)	ENPP Cabinet & Elections Controls	ENPP (Press Freedom)	ENPP Press Freedom & War Opposition
6	7	8	9	10	11
—	-0.204*** (0.049)	0.083 (0.068)	0.025 (0.064)	—	-0.0213 (0.0535)
—	—	0.073** (0.024)	0.093* (0.044)	0.0092 (0.0079)	0.0176 (0.0154)
-0.002* (0.001)	-0.0019^ (0.0010)	0.0009** (0.0003)	0.001** (0.0003)	0.0001 (0.0001)	0.0002 (0.0003)
—	—	-0.0002** (0.0001)	-0.0002** (0.0001)	—	—
—	—	—	—		
—	—	—	—	—	—
—	—	—	—	-0.0992 (0.0826)	-0.0963 (0.1534)
—	—	—	—	0.0293 (0.0193)	0.0340 (0.0243)
—	—	—	—	0.0005* (0.0002)	0.0006^ (0.0003)
—	—	—	—	-0.00014* (0.00056)	-0.0002* (0.0001)
-0.004* (0.002)	-0.005 (0.003)	-0.001 (0.002)	0.001 (0.001)	0.0006 (0.0001)	0. 0002 (0.0001)
—	—	-0.112 (0.165)	-0.141 (0.417)	-0.2731* (0.1182)	-0.4536* (0.1738)
—	—	0.002* (0.001)	0.009 (0.007)	0.0015^ (0.0009)	0.0020 (0.0015)
0.000 (0.001)	0.0006 (0.0015)	0.004** (0.001)	0.004* (0.001)	0.0017 (0.0011)	0.0031* (0.0012)
—	—	-0.003 (0.002)	-0.010 (0.006)	-0.0010 (0.0012)	-0.0055^ (0.0032)
—	—	-0.034** (0.012)	-0.015 (0.016)	-0.0025 (0.0034)	-0.0347* (0.0134)
—	—	0.067^ (0.035)	0.107* (0.048)	0.0573* (0.0248)	0.0781** (0.0286)
—	—	-0.031 (0.039)	-0.077^ (0.044)	-0.0420^ (0.0250)	-0.0726* (0.0322)
—	—	-0.194* (0.088)	—	—	—
—	—	-0.876* (0.399)	—	—	—
—	—	0.054 (0.049)	—	—	—
—	—	-0.075 (0.057)	—	—	—

Table 5.A.4. (*continued*)

	ENPP	ENEP	PR	IV Regression (War Opposition)	IV Regression (Troops)
	1	2	3	4	5
Majority Muslim	—	—	—	0.1674	—
				(0.1174)	
Trade with US (× 1,000)	—	—	—	−1.0e−06*	−2.70e−07^
				−0.0−06	(1.49e−07)
Energy consumption (× 1,000)	—	—	—	0.0000003^	—
				(0.0000002)	
News valence	—	—	—	—	—
Access × news valence	—	—	—	—	—
Number of parties in cabinet	—	—	—	—	—
Number of days between elections	—	—	—	—	—
Constant	−0.088	−0.134	−0.206*	−0.0797	−0.198
	(0.124)	(0.123)	(0.090)	(0.3834)	(0.127)
Observations	50	50	58	49	49
R^2	.76	.74	.80	.23	.55

Robust standard errors in parentheses. ^$p < .10$. *$p < .05$. **$p < .01$. ***$p < .001$.

News Valence I (Troops)	News Valence II (Troops)	ENPP (Extra Controls)	ENPP Cabinet & Elections Controls	ENPP (Press Freedom)	ENPP Press Freedom & War Opposition
6	7	8	9	10	11
—	—	—	—	—	—
—	—	—	—	—	—
—	—	—	—	—	—
−9.937*	−1.091^	—	—	—	—
(4.855)	(5.546)				
0.037*	0.036**	—	—	—	—
(0.015)	(0.017)				
—	—	—	0.011	—	—
			(0.008)		
—	—	—	0.00001	—	—
			(0.00004)		
0.573	0.500	−0.150	−0.772*	−0.1646	−0.0294
(0.346)	(0.407)	(0.133)	(0.357)	(0.1063)	(0.1643)
34	26	38	32	76	49
.60	.64	.82	.85	.57	.75

Table 5.A.5. Effects of Variations in War Opposition, TV Access, and Number of Parties on Number of Troops Contributed to Iraq Coalition of the Willing

	Minimum War Opposition	Maximum War Opposition	Difference (Low vs. High TV Access)	Difference (in Diff. between Low vs. High TV Effects, Low vs. High Parties)
ENPP low				
Low TV access	−0.091	−0.007	−0.084	
High TV access	0.205	0.145	0.060	
Difference	*0.296***	*0.152**	*0.144**	
ENPP high				*.204* (.348—.144)*
Low TV access	−0.083	0.095	0.178	
High TV access	0.065	−0.095	−0.160	
Difference	*0.148*	*−0.190***	*0.348**	
ENEP low				
Low TV access	−0.096	−0.014	−0.082	
High TV access	0.234	0.132	0.102	
Difference	*0.330***	*0.147**	*0.184**	
ENEP high				*.232* (.416—.184)*
Low TV access	−0.134	0.109	−0.243	
High TV access	0.088	−0.085	0.173	
Difference	*0.222*	*−0.194***	*0.416**	
NOT PR				
Low TV access	−0.016	−0.081	0.065	
High TV access	0.276	0.211	0.065	
Difference	*0.292***	*0.292***	*0.000*	
PR				*.106 (.106—.000)*
Low TV access	−0.009	0.033	−0.042	
High TV access	0.082	0.018	0.064	
Difference	*0.091*	*−0.015*	*0.106**	

*$p < .05$. **$p < .01$.

Table 5.A.6. OLS Analysis of Effects of Variations in TV Access and Number of Parties on Public Opposition to Afghanistan War and Troop Commitments to Afghanistan Coalition

Independent Variables	War Opposition 1	Troop Contributions 2	Troop Contributions 3
Effective number of parliamentary parties (ENPP)	−0.287^	0.0130*	−0.00846^
	(0.150)	(0.00524)	(0.00466)
Access	−0.00270*	0.000158**	−1.42e−05
	(0.00116)	(4.76e−05)	(3.53e−05)
War opposition (logged)	—	—	0.0578
			(0.0426)
ENPP × access	0.000697*	−2.08e−05^	—
	(0.000276)	(1.07e−05)	
% oppose war (log) × access	—	—	−6.32e−05
			(5.24e−05)
% oppose war (log) × ENPP	—	—	−0.00615
			(0.00740)
% oppose war (log) × access × ENPP	—	—	−1.99e−05*
			(9.60e−06)
GDP per capita (2001) (× 1,000)	−0.024**	0.001	−0.001
	(0.009)	(0.001)	(0.001)
Annual change in GDP per capita (2000 to 2001)	−1.002^	−0.0317	0.0406
	(0.590)	(0.0343)	(0.0361)
Infant mortality (2000)	−0.0116^	0.000260^	−1.20e−05
	(0.00618)	(0.000140)	(0.000264)
NATO member	−0.475***	0.0535***	0.0193^
	(0.130)	(0.0101)	(0.0106)
Democracy score	0.0116	−0.00567*	0.000322
	(0.0258)	(0.00248)	(0.00278)
Inflation (2000)	0.0108	−0.000589	−0.000434
	(0.00668)	(0.000407)	(0.000408)
US ally	−0.00670	0.00471	−0.0187*
	(0.146)	(0.00667)	(0.00826)
# of top 5 TV stations that are private	—	−0.0400*	—
		(0.0177)	
# of top 5 newspapers that are public	—	0.0319	—
		(0.0246)	
Similarity to US in UN General Assembly votes	—	−0.0299^	—
		(0.0149)	
Press freedom	—	0.000285	—
		(0.000439)	
Constant	0.895	−0.0548	0.0552
	(0.653)	(0.0463)	(0.0370)
Observations	48	46	47
R^2-	.553	.785	.794

Robust standard errors in parentheses. ^p < .10. *p < .05. **p < .01. ***p < .001.

Survey Data

Table 5.A.7. Iraq War Survey Questions and Participating Countries

Date	Sponsor	Question	Countries Included
April 2002	Pew	"Would you favor or oppose the US and its allies taking military action in Iraq to end Saddam Hussein's rule as part of the war on terrorism?" (Figures represent percentage responding "oppose.")	France, Germany, Italy, United Kingdom, USA
August to September 2002	Gallup	"Would you favor or oppose sending American ground troops (the United States sending ground troops) to the Persian Gulf in an attempt to remove Saddam Hussein from power in Iraq?" (Figures represent percentage responding "oppose.")	Canada, Great Britain, Italy, Spain, USA
September 2002	Dagsavisen	"The USA is threatening to launch a military attack on Iraq. Do you consider it appropriate of the USA to attack [WITHOUT/WITH] the approval of the UN?" (Figures represent average across the two versions of the UN approval question wording responding "under no circum-stances.")	Norway
January 2003	Gallup	"Are you in favor of military action against Iraq: under no circumstances; only if sanctioned by the United Nations; unilaterally by America and its allies?" (Figures represent percentage responding "under no circumstances.")	Albania, Argentina, Australia, Bolivia, Bosnia, Bulgaria, Cameroon, Canada, Colombia, Denmark, Ecuador, Estonia, Finland, France, Georgia, Germany, Iceland, India, Ireland, Kenya, Luxembourg, Macedonia, Malaysia, Netherlands, New Zealand, Pakistan, Portugal, Romania, Russia, South Africa, Spain, Switzerland, Uganda, United Kingdom, Uruguay, USA
January 2003	CVVM	"Would you support a war against Iraq?" (Figures represent percentage responding "no.")	Czech Republic
January 2003	Gallup	"Would you personally agree with or oppose a US military attack on Iraq without UN approval?" (Figures represent percentage responding "oppose.")	Hungary
January 2003	EOS-Gallup	"For each of the following proposi-tions tell me if you agree or not. The United States should intervene militarily in Iraq even if the United Nations does not give its formal agreement." (Figures represent percentage responding "rather" or "absolutely" unjustified.)	Austria, Belgium, Bulgaria, Cyprus, Czech Republic, Denmark, Estonia, Finland, France, Germany, Greece, Hungary, Ireland, Italy, Latvia, Lithuania, Luxembourg, Malta, Netherlands, Norway, Poland, Romania, Slovakia, Slovenia, Spain, Sweden, Switzerland, Turkey, United Kingdom

Table 5.A.7. (*continued*)

Date	Sponsor	Question	Countries Included
March 2003	Pew	"Thinking about possible war with Iraq, would you favor or oppose [survey country] joining the U.S. and other allies in military action in Iraq to end Saddam Hussein's rule?" (USA asked "Would you favor or oppose taking military action in Iraq to end Saddam Hussein's rule?") (Figures represent percentage responding "oppose.")	Italy, Poland, Spain, United Kingdom, USA
March to April 2003	Centro de Opinion Publica	"Do you agree with the war against Iraq?" (Figures represent percentage responding "no.")	El Salvador
May 2003	IPSOS	"Do you think the US did the right thing or the wrong thing when it took military action against the Saddam Hussein regime in Iraq?" (Figures represent percentage responding "wrong thing.")	Canada, France, Germany, Italy, Russia, Spain, United Kingdom, USA
May 2003	Pew	"On the subject of Iraq, did [survey country] make the right decision or the wrong decision to use military force against Iraq?" (Figures represent percentage responding "wrong" decision.)	Australia, Spain, United Kingdom, USA
May 2003	Pew	"On the subject of Iraq, did [survey country] make the right decision or the wrong decision to not use military force against Iraq?" (Figures represent percentage responding "right" decision.)	Brazil, Canada, France, Germany, Indonesia, Israel, Italy, Jordan, Lebanon, Morocco, Nigeria, Pakistan, Russia, South Korea
May 2003	Pew	"On the subject of Iraq, did [survey country] make the right decision or the wrong decision to allow the US and its allies to use bases for military action in Iraq?" (Figures represent percentage "wrong" decision.)	Kuwait, Turkey

Table 5.A.8. Afghanistan War Survey Questions and Participating Countries

Date	Sponsor	Question	Countries Included
Late September 2001	Gallup International	"Some countries and all NATO members states have agreed to participate in any military action against the terrorists responsible for the attacks or against those countries harboring the terrorists. Do you agree or disagree that [your country] should take part in military actions against terrorists with the United States?" (Figures represent % "disagree")	Argentina, Austria, Bosnia, Bulgaria, Colombia, Croatia, Czech Republic, Denmark, Ecuador, Estonia, Finland, France, Germany, Greece, India, Israel, Italy, Latvia, Lithuania, Luxembourg, Mexico, Netherlands, Norway, Pakistan, Panama, Peru, Portugal, Romania, South Korea, Spain, Switzerland, UK, Ukraine, USA, Venezuela, Zimbabwe
October 19–21, 2001	Gallup USA	"Do you approve or disapprove of U.S. military action in Afghanistan?" (% "disapprove")	USA
November 14–30, 2001	Harris Poll	"How strongly do you approve or disapprove of the United States government's decision to begin the military operations in response to the terrorists' attacks? Would you say you strongly approve, somewhat approve, somewhat disapprove or strongly disapprove?" (% "strongly" or "somewhat" disapprove)	China, Japan, South Korea, USA
November 7, 2001–December 29, 2001	Gallup International	"Some countries and all NATO members states have agreed to participate in the military action against Afghanistan. Do you agree or disagree that [your country] should take part with the United States in military action against Afghanistan?" (% "disagree")	Albania, Argentina, Austria, Azerbaijan, Belgium, Bolivia, Bosnia & Herzegovina, Bulgaria, Cameroon, Colombia, Costa Rica, Croatia, Czech Republic, Denmark, Dominican Republic, Ecuador, Estonia, Finland, France, FYR Macedonia, Georgia, Germany, Greece, Guatemala, Hong Kong, Iceland, India, Ireland, Israel, Italy, Japan, Kenya, Kosovo, Kyrgyzstan, Latvia, Lithuania, Luxembourg, Malaysia, Mexico, Netherlands, Nigeria, Northern Ireland, Norway, Pakistan, Panama, Peru, Philippines, Poland, Portugal, Romania, Russia, Slovak Republic, South Korea, Spain, Sweden, Switzerland, Turkey, UK, Ukraine, Uruguay, USA, Venezuela, Yugoslavia

Table 5.A.8. (*Continued*)

Date	Sponsor	Question	Countries Included
October 13–14, 2001	Public Opinion Foundation	"Do you approve or disapprove of Putin's support for U.S. operations in Afghanistan?" (% "disapprove")	Russia
August 14, 2002	UMR Research	"Do you approve or disapprove of Australia's armed forces being involved in military operations in [Afghanistan]?" (% "disapprove")	Australia
October 16–21, 2001	Leger Marketing	"Question: When the strikes against Afghanistan began, Canada decided to offer military support to the United States. Do you support this military assistance FULLY, IN PART, or NOT AT ALL?" (% "not at all")	Canada

Additional Iraq Robustness Tests

We undertake three additional sets of robustness tests and then present an alternative graphic illustration of some of the core results. The first employs news valence (where larger values represent greater positive valence in Iraq coverage) in place of party systems. The second selectively excludes potential disproportionately influential observations as well as public opinion observations taken after the start of the Iraq conflict on March 20, 2003. The third empirically tests for the potential effects of "clarity of responsibility" on democratic constraint, as discussed in chapter 2. Table 5.A.9 presents the first set of tests and table 5.A.10 presents the second. Finally, model 9 in table 5.A.4 presents the third robustness test. We begin by discussing the first set of tests.

The first six models in table 5.A.9 interact TV access and news valence while varying the control variables included in the model, while models 7 and 8 replicate models 1 and 2, with public war opposition as the dependent variable.

The most basic empirical model we could run to test our troop commitment predictions would include an interaction between TV access and TV content. Unfortunately, when we run this model controlling only for public war opposition, we end up with an N of twenty-six states. This is far too low to allow a fully controlled model. Excluding the opinion indicator raises the N to thirty-five, which is still too low for our complete model specifications (some of which include three-way interactions). Consequently, we limit this analysis to testing hypotheses that could be assessed with two-way interactions, while also testing each control variable separately. We found that only three controls appeared to materially influence the key relationships: secondary enrollment ratios, infant

Table 5.A.9. OLS Analyses of Effects of News Valence, TV Access, and Effective Number of Parliamentary Parties on Iraq War Opposition and Troop Commitments

	Troops	Troops	Troops	Troops	Troops	Troops	War Opposition	War Opposition
	1	2	3	4	5	6	7	8
News valence	-9.101^ (4.754)	-9.937^ (4.855)	-16.60** (5.492)	-10.53 (6.309)	-10.09^ (5.546)	-23.48* (9.448)	-1.381 (8.073)	4.044 (9.386)
Access	-0.00170^ (0.0009)	-0.00198* (0.00089)	-0.00252** (0.00089)	-0.00160 (0.0011)	-0.00194^ (0.00099)	-0.00296* (0.0012)	0.00159 (0.0010)	0.00249* (0.0011)
Access × news valence	0.0302* (0.0141)	0.0368* (0.0145)	0.0462** (0.0138)	0.0287 (0.0180)	0.0358* (0.0174)	0.0529* (0.0198)	-0.0299^ (0.0158)	-0.0475* (0.0193)
GDP per capita (× 1,000)	—	-0.004 (0.003)	-0.003 (0.002)	—	-0.005 (0.003)	-0.002 (0.003)	—	0.004 (0.005)
Secondary enrollment	—	-6.72e-05 (0.00132)	—	—	0.000633 (0.00149)	—	—	0.00209 (0.00276)
Infant mortality	—	—	0.00393* (0.00143)	—	—	0.00549^ (0.00264)	—	—
% oppose war (log)	—	—	—	-0.0990 (0.142)	-0.0602 (0.172)	-0.0373 (0.141)	—	—
Constant	0.527^ (0.292)	0.573 (0.346)	0.894** (0.320)	0.567 (0.402)	0.500 (0.407)	1.280* (0.561)	-0.213 (0.556)	-0.712 (0.765)
Observations	35	34	34	26	26	26	26	26
R^2	.538	.601	.678	.571	.640	.697	.448	.504

Robust standard errors in parentheses. ^$p < .10$. *$p < .05$. **$p < .01$. ***$p < .001$.

mortality, and per capita GDP. Hence, we employ only these controls and include public war opposition in some models. Interestingly, in the primary models employed in the chapter, infant mortality had no material effects and so was excluded. With news valence included in the models, however, infant mortality outperforms secondary enrollment ratios in the troop commitments models. We therefore report the controlled troop commitment models two ways: once with secondary enrollment and a second time with infant mortality. The results are somewhat stronger in the latter models. Since infant mortality did no better than secondary enrollment in the opinion models, we do not include it therein.

Models 1 and 2 interact TV access and news valence, employing the news valence indicator as the measure of news content. This variable is the most direct measure available of the content of news coverage. Theoretically, because news valence is measured with respect to government policy, it could cut both ways, with greater policy valence indicating greater support for a government's policy of *not* committing troops. However, the Iraq case is unlikely to work in this manner in practice for two reasons. The first is a floor effect: a state cannot commit less than zero troops in response to greater media support for not committing troops. Conversely, it is possible to raise troop commitment levels essentially infinitely in response to supportive news coverage of a government's decision to participate in the coalition. The second reason is an artifact of the data. As it happens, 57 percent of the countries for which we have news valence and party data (twenty of thirty-five) contributed troops, so the data are weighted disproportionately toward states for which "positive valence" indicates support for a government decision to participate in the coalition.

Model 1 excludes all controls, model 2 controls for secondary enrollment and GDP growth, model 3 substitutes infant mortality for secondary enrollment, model 4 controls for public war opposition, model 5 includes all three controls, and model 6 also includes three controls, with infant mortality replacing secondary enrollment. We discuss models 2 and 5 in the main text (see table 5.A.4) and include them here solely to facilitate comparison. We present models 1, 3, 4, and 6 as additional robustness tests to see if the results persist with no controls or with all key controls included. In five of the six models, the key coefficients are statistically significant and in the predicted directions. In the sixth case (model 4), the coefficients are not significant, though they do remain in the predicted directions. However, once controls are introduced, in model 5 (per capita GDP and secondary enrollment) and model 6 (per capita GDP and infant mortality), the key coefficients become significant. Since these models essentially replicate those reported in the main text, we do not discuss their substantive interpretations in detail here.

Models 7 and 8 employ public war opposition as the dependent variable, with model 7 excluding all controls and model 8 including controls for secondary enrollment ratios and GDP growth. The N slips to twenty-six in both models, which further reduces our statistical leverage. Despite this limitation, how-

Table 5.A.10. OLS Robustness Tests of Iraq Troop Commitment Models Excluding Postwar Initiation Opinion Cases, US and UK Cases

	ENPP			
	Full Model	Exclude Postwar Initiation Cases	Exclude US	Exclude UK
	1	2	3	4
% oppose war (log)	−0.0113	−0.0199	0.0305	−0.0751^
	(0.0532)	(0.0605)	(0.0447)	(0.0394)
Access (× 1,000)	0.0753***	0.0746**	0.0696*	0.0317^
	(0.0207)	(0.0212)	(0.0258)	(0.0187)
Parties	0.0515**	0.0510*	0.0488*	0.0185
	(0.0173)	(0.0197)	(0.0204)	(0.0139)
Access × parties (× 1,000)	−0.0171**	−0.0169**	−0.0157*	−0.00693
	(0.0048)	(0.00495)	(0.00603)	(0.00437)
GDP per capita (× 10,000)	0.00397	0.0045	−0.00180	0.00604
	(0.00774)	(0.00822)	(0.00748)	(0.00711)
Annual change in GDP per capita (2002 to 2003)	−0.428*	−0.400*	−0.281^	−0.325^
	(0.160)	(0.164)	(0.157)	(0.191)
Infant mortality (× 100)	0.178^	0.192*	0.173^	0.0659
	(0.0903)	(0.0918)	(0.0859)	(0.0595)
Secondary enrollment ratio (× 100)	0.318**	0.334**	0.337**	0.101^
	(0.106)	(0.110)	(0.119)	(0.0551)
Inflation (× 100)	−0.389*	−0.302	−0.432*	−0.161
	(0.185)	(0.180)	(0.186)	(0.108)
DEMOC-AUTOC	−0.0393**	−0.0373*	−0.0384*	−0.0174^
	(0.0141)	(0.0139)	(0.0152)	(0.00934)
NATO member	0.0866**	0.0886**	0.0655*	0.0619^
	(0.0275)	(0.0285)	(0.0285)	(0.0308)
US ally	−0.0734*	−0.0749*	−0.0460	−0.0557
	(0.0301)	(0.0330)	(0.0295)	(0.0345)
Constant	−0.105	−0.156	−0.127	0.0118
	(0.120)	(0.127)	(0.112)	(0.0770)
Observations	50	45	49	49
R^2–	.747	.757	.709	.554

Robust standard errors in parentheses. ^p < .10. *p < .05. **p < .01. ***p < .001.

ever, the results remain significant in key respects and in the predicted directions. Transforming the coefficients from model 8 into expected percentages opposing the war (based on simulations), the results indicate that given low TV access (a standard deviation below the mean), variations in news tone have no statistically significant effect. However, with high levels of TV access (a standard deviation above the mean), more positive coverage leads to significantly reduced war opposition (a decline of .41, p < .01). Moreover, when news coverage is positive, increased TV access is associated with a .53 drop in war opposition (p < .01). In contrast, when news coverage is least positive, increased TV access is associated with a .12 increase in war opposition, though this latter effect is not statistically significant. The .52 difference between the

	ENEP				PR/MAJ		
Full Model	Exclude Postwar Initiation Cases	Exclude US	Exclude UK	Full Model	Exclude Postwar Initiation Cases	Exclude US	Exclude UK
5	6	7	8	9	10	11	12
−0.0248	−0.0294	0.00941	−0.0759^	−0.0381	−0.0396	−0.0240	−0.0555*
(0.0542)	(0.0617)	(0.0442)	(0.0401)	(0.0315)	(0.0420)	(0.0287)	(0.0232)
0.0845**	0.0877**	0.0746*	0.0394^	0.0530**	0.0517**	0.0472*	0.0308*
(0.0263)	(0.0278)	(0.0338)	(0.0207)	(0.0152)	(0.0156)	(0.0224)	(0.0142)
0.0507*	0.0559*	0.0447^	0.0225	0.166**	0.158*	0.143^	0.100^
(0.0188)	(0.0222)	(0.0226)	(0.0142)	(0.0539)	(0.0593)	(0.0758)	(0.0503)
−0.0154**	−0.0161**	−0.0135*	−0.00709^	−0.0504**	−0.0495**	−0.0439^	−0.0298*
(0.00501)	(0.00538)	(0.00638)	(0.00396)	(0.0147)	(0.0152)	(0.0224)	(0.0148)
−0.00625	−0.00557	−0.0103	0.0015	−0.00112	0.00077	−0.00477	.00381
(0.00871)	(0.00912)	(0.00843)	(0.00572)	(0.00664)	(0.00654)	(0.00685)	(.00608)
−0.349*	−0.315*	−0.233	−0.269	−0.265**	−0.282*	−0.206	−0.193^
(0.146)	(0.152)	(0.156)	(0.161)	(0.0924)	(0.108)	(0.128)	(0.107)
0.193^	0.216*	0.188^	0.0648	0.221*	0.222*	0.222*	0.0728^
(0.0986)	(0.104)	(0.0995)	(0.0584)	(0.0968)	(0.0948)	(0.106)	(0.0412)
0.318*	0.340*	0.336*	0.0884^	0.0880	0.118	0.117	−0.0206
(0.130)	(0.134)	(0.142)	(0.0487)	(0.0853)	(0.107)	(0.0819)	(0.0360)
−0.381^	−0.254	−0.416*	−0.154	−0.177	−0.103	−0.204	−0.0635
(0.201)	(0.175)	(0.203)	(0.105)	(0.150)	(0.160)	(0.132)	(0.105)
−0.0385*	−0.0363*	−0.0374*	−0.0167^	−0.00249	−0.00317	−0.00284	−0.000105
(0.0161)	(0.0158)	(0.0174)	(0.00878)	(0.00324)	(0.00388)	(0.00307)	(0.00154)
0.0833**	0.0836*	0.0643^	0.0595*	0.0645*	0.0673*	0.0537	0.0486*
(0.0294)	(0.0307)	(0.0323)	(0.0292)	(0.0259)	(0.0282)	(0.0326)	(0.0239)
−0.0624*	−0.0629^	−0.0389	−0.0495	−0.0499*	−0.0582*	−0.0352	−0.0423
(0.0295)	(0.0325)	(0.0308)	(0.0310)	(0.0225)	(0.0284)	(0.0262)	(0.0252)
−0.171	−0.258^	−0.174	−0.0269	−0.213*	−0.230*	−0.222*	−0.0647^
(0.134)	(0.148)	(0.133)	(0.0830)	(0.0981)	(0.100)	(0.101)	(0.0334)
50	45	49	49	59	51	58	58
.714	.729	.652	.569	.716	.737	.630	.596

effects on war opposition given the least versus most positive coverage is itself significant at $p < .05$.

Turning next to table 5.A.10, we rerun all two-way interaction models presented in the Iraq analysis in the main text, separately excluding, first, all post–March 2003 observations, second, the US case, and, third, the UK case. We repeat this with sets of models employing all three dependent variables.

In each case, while the results predictably vary somewhat depending on which observations we exclude, they fundamentally replicate those reported in the main text; the directions of the effects remain the same and the substantive effects remain statistically significant and in most instances comparable in magnitude. Nearly all of the coefficients remain significant as well, though in one out of the twenty-four key variables across the various models[48]—the ENPP variable in the UK exclusion model—the interaction term is not quite statistically significant ($p < .12$). Even in that instance, however, the substantive interaction indicates that the effects of TV access given a high number of parties or a PR system are statistically significantly distinct from those given a low number of parties or a majoritarian system, and in the predicted direction.

The key coefficients do become somewhat smaller in magnitude in many of the UK exclusion models (though they nearly always—with a single exception—remain statistically significant and always in the predicted directions). This difference must, however, be interpreted with at least some caution. Single case exclusions are more likely to exert fairly substantial effects given small-N models, by virtue of the limited number of cases. To illustrate this point, if we also exclude Canada, Italy, or South Africa—the other three largest residual outliers in the regression models shown in table 5.A.10—the coefficients on TV access and the interaction term in the ENPP models excluding the United Kingdom become substantially larger in magnitude and significant at $p < .05$. The United Kingdom only weakens the results if all three of these other countries are included in the model. If any one of them is excluded, then dropping the UK case does not weaken the results. One might be able to tell a substantive story in each case to account for this, but it is also the case that sensitivity to individual case exclusions is heightened with regressions involving a relatively small number of observations (and hence limited statistical leverage). We are therefore hesitant to over-interpret the implications of any individual exclusion. Nonetheless, most such exclusions strengthen, rather than weaken, the results, and even the sole exclusion (out of twenty-four key coefficients) that somewhat weakens the significance of the results does not fundamentally alter them.

We conducted one final robustness test, aimed at addressing the concern raised in chapter 2 that clarity of responsibility—that is, the ability of citizens to determine who to hold to account for policy failures—may be more important than the number of parties in influencing democratic constraint or, alternatively, may condition the effects of parties on constraint. According to this view, having an especially fragmented party system, or a highly stable or oversized governing coalition, may obscure rather than clarify responsibility, or alternatively may reduce the incentives of opposition parties to criticize the government. Unfortunately, scholars have not yet measured these factors on a global scale. However, such data are available for thirty-four OECD countries via the ParlGov data set.[49] We employed ParlGov to measure the number of parties serving in the governing cabinet when the Iraq War began in March 2003 and the number of days between the elections immediately preceding and

---

[48] The 24 key causal variables include 12 × party system + 12 × (party system × TV access).

[49] Döring and Manow (2012).

immediately following the start of the war.[50] This allows us to determine whether cabinet size (measured as the number of parties serving in the cabinet) or differences in the stability or volatility of governments (measured as the number of days between elections) influence coalition-joining behavior either directly or indirectly, by mitigating or mediating the influence of the effective number of parties. If so, these variables should improve the fit of our model, and most likely also alter the relationship between our party system indicator and the dependent variable (troop commitments).

In fact, the results from our core troop contribution model, with these two variables added as controls, do not support this hypothesized alternative source of democratic constraint.[51] Neither variable is statistically significant, and, most important, neither affects our key variables of interest (TV access, ENPP, and the interaction between the two). Because the N in this model is quite small (thirty-two countries, with two dropped due to missing data), we consider these results only suggestive. However, it is worth noting that our key variables, and the interaction term, remain robust even with the reduced N.

Given the limited statistical leverage in this analysis, and to keep our robustness testing at a manageable length, we do not report additional models that include the clarity of responsibility variables. Yet, it is worth noting that neither the number of parties in the cabinet nor the number of days between elections is statistically significant or substantively influences troop contributions when interacted with TV access in place of the effective number of parties. The same holds true for the number of days from the last prewar election until the start date of the conflict, or from the start date of the conflict to the next election, when included as separate controls. All of these patterns, in turn, remain comparable when we employ ENEP in place of ENPP. Last, though ENPP and the number of parties in the cabinet are positively correlated at .46 in our data, they are oppositely signed in our models (when we exclude the interaction term for an "apples-to-apples" comparison). While a larger effective number of parties is associated with reduced conflict involvement, more parties in the cabinet is positively (albeit insignificantly) associated with *increased* troop contributions to the coalition. This further suggests that the two variables are to some extent capturing distinct phenomena. Regardless, based on this limited analysis of OECD countries and these relatively crude operationalizations of clarity of responsibility, we find no evidence that, at least with respect to the Iraq War and as measured in our data, the latter factors either trump or otherwise condition the effects of the effective number of parties on democratic constraint, either alone or in interaction with media access.

To maximize illustrative clarity and brevity, figure 5.2 presents scenarios where TV access is a standard deviation above or below the mean. However, it

---

[50] ParlGov is available at http://parlgov.org/stable/index.html (accessed May 26, 2014).
[51] Results from this test are shown in model 9 in table 5.A.4.

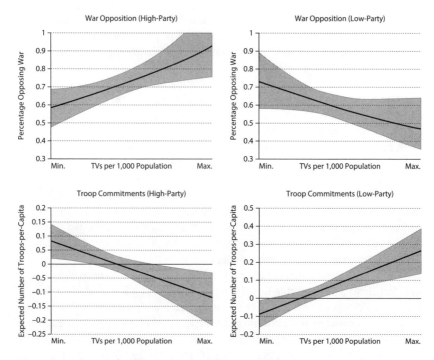

Figure 5.A.1. Expected public opposition and troop contributions to Iraq coalition as TV access increases from minimum to maximum levels, high versus low ENPP

is also helpful to observe the full range of predicted outcomes, as TV access varies. Hence, in figure 5.A.1 we present four such graphics, illustrating the expected levels of war opposition and troop commitments when ENPP is a standard deviation above or below the mean, as TV access varies from its minimum to maximum values in the data set. The graphic, derived from the same regressions as figure 5.2, includes 95 percent confidence intervals surrounding the mean expected values.

6

Downs Meets the Press: How Party Systems Shape the News

More parties → more policy, criticism, diversity in news coverage.

The theory and findings we have developed thus far partially rest on an untested foundation, which we have termed the Downsian Premise (DP for short). Recall that the DP represents our extension of Downs's well-known argument that multiparty systems tend to yield more policy and ideologically oriented political debates than two-party systems. Our argument is simply that news coverage will tend to reflect the nature of a nation's political debate. Consequently, given Downs's argument, and per our DP, high-party democracies should tend to engender political coverage that is more diverse, more policy-centric, and more prone to challenge the government's preferred line than coverage in low-party democracies.

Scholars often do not test the assumptions underlying their theories. If the evidence supports your theoretical expectations, the argument goes, then it does not matter how reasonable or unreasonable the assumptions are that led you to those conclusions. To paraphrase a prominent political scientist (who shall remain nameless) from one of our graduate school courses, "you can assume that pigs fly, so long as the evidence supports your conclusions." That said, notwithstanding the wisdom of drawing conclusions from untested assumptions about flying pigs, we believe that the DP is so central to our argument that it is prudent to establish its plausibility. This is the task we undertake in the present chapter.

If multiparty systems actually cover politics and foreign policy differently than their counterparts in two-party systems then our conclusions follow logically from an empirically valid premise. If not, then some might reasonably question whether the empirical patterns we have outlined thus far do, in fact, meaningfully support the theory, or whether they are spurious—that is, consistent with the theory yet attributable to some *other* causal mechanism we have overlooked. To answer this question we assess data from four multilateral conflicts: Kosovo (1999), Afghanistan (2001), Iraq (2003), and Libya (2011). We compare newspaper coverage of these interventions between high- and low-party democracies.

News coverage, of course, appears in various forms of electronic and print media. Yet, we primarily focus on newspapers due to their international prevalence as primary sources of information on political, economic, and social events. While the Internet is rapidly growing into a critical news source in many countries, even as the revenues and readership of print media have declined in recent years, a disproportionate share of online news originates with newspapers. For instance, as of March 2013, seven of the ten most popular Internet news sources either were online versions of print newspapers or featured either links to or aggregated content from online newspapers.[1] In 2011, in turn, there were three times as many daily newspaper readers worldwide as broadband Internet users—1.7 billion to 580 million.[2] Fraile empirically reinforces this notion, finding that newspapers have a larger marginal (if not total) effect on political knowledge than other types of media, like television.[3] We replicate Fraile's finding in our own analysis of a distinct, cross-national data set in the appendix to chapter 3.

Ideally, we would also investigate television news since, as we argue throughout this book, TV access is the best indicator of mass media *access*. Worldwide, large majorities of people report primarily relying on television as a news source. Moreover, research has shown that broadcast television has an important positive effect on both political knowledge and political participation.[4] Unfortunately, TV transcripts are unavailable on a sufficient scale, making such a replication implausible. That said, the greater information diversity in newspapers—due to a combination of larger numbers of outlets per country, better country coverage, and a larger news hole (that is, more stories per day) for each outlet—makes newspapers in some ways a better vehicle for testing the DP. For instance, according to a study of the news ecosystem in Baltimore, Maryland, by the Pew Center's Project for Excellence in Journalism, general interest newspapers accounted for about half of all new information reported in the news.[5] If specialty, or niche, newspapers (e.g., papers focused on business or law) are included, this figure jumps to 63 percent. This compares to 28 percent for local television news, 7 percent for radio, and only 4 percent on average across nine new media outlets the study investigated.

With these concerns in mind, we identified one data set, collected by the European Election Study (EES), that includes content analyses of both newspaper and television coverage during the 2004 and 2009 European elections by the top news outlets in all EU member states. These data allow us to assess the extent to which television news content also follows patterns anticipated by the DP while directly comparing television and newspaper coverage of the same events, based on identically coded data.

[1] http://www.ebizmba.com/articles/news-websites (accessed June 1, 2014).
[2] WAN-IFRA World Press Trends Database (http://www.wptdatabase.org/, accessed June 1, 2014).
[3] Fraile (2011).
[4] Prat and Strömberg (2006).
[5] Pew Research Center for the People and the Press (2010).

MAPPING NEWS CONTENT ONTO
THE DOWNSIAN PREMISE

Our newspaper analyses focus on three aspects of coverage for which the DP offers clear implications: diversity, valence, and focus. *Diversity* refers to the number of distinct topics or frames included in news stories. Simply stated, the greater the number of topics or frames included in news stories, the greater the likelihood that one or more of them will either contradict or compete with the government's most preferred frame or topical focus. Greater topical diversity implies a greater risk of challenges to the government's preferred policy frame and hence an increased perception of domestic political risk. All else equal, this ought to make leaders more risk averse in foreign policy.

Valence refers to the tone of news coverage; that is, the extent to which such coverage is supportive or critical of the government's policies. Presumably, more critical coverage reduces the government's capacity to sustain public support. This in turn raises the domestic political risks to leaders of pursuing a policy, thereby presumably reducing their inclination to do so.

Finally, *focus* refers to the emphasis on hard news (e.g., stories addressing substantive policy) relative to soft news (e.g., personality- or human-interest-oriented stories). Harder news—that is, news with greater emphasis on issues of public policy relative to entertainment—ought to produce better-informed citizens. More knowledgeable citizens, in turn, are better situated to hold their leaders accountable for policy failures. Once again, this ought to make leaders more risk averse.

In chapter 2 we argued that differences in media coverage either raise or lower the perceived domestic political risks to the government of pursuing a policy like military intervention. Many of our predictions in chapter 2 follow from the presumed differences on this dimension between high- and low-party democracies. This means that for our theory to be valid, it is important that these patterns actually emerge. In this chapter we subject these expected relationships in media content to systematic empirical testing.

To estimate coverage focus, in the Iraq case we compare the volume of personality- or human-interest-oriented coverage (soft news) with that of policy-oriented (hard news) coverage by measuring policy coverage as a proportion of all three types of coverage combined. For the other three cases (Libya, Afghanistan, Kosovo), we measure the average amount of policy focus (with larger values indicating more and lower values less policy focus in coverage). Turning to valence, for the Iraq case we calculate the probability that a story includes progovernment coverage as a proportion of the combined probabilities of all types of coverage (progovernment policy, antigovernment policy, or neutral).[6] For the other three cases, we compute the average level of support for the gov-

---

[6] Since news reports may contain multiple types of valenced coverage, the total combined probability of positive, negative, or neutral coverage exceeds 100 percent (see the codebook in the appendix to this chapter).

ernment's policy (where larger values indicate more pro- and smaller values more antigovernment coverage).[7]

Finally, to measure diversity of coverage, for all four cases we compare the number of distinct topics included in the news.[8] It is in all likelihood the case that the diversity of news coverage will increase at least to some extent with the overall volume of coverage. After all, more stories about a conflict means a wider news hole that needs filling. Even given a party system that tends to produce relatively narrow coverage, more news means more opportunities to cover more angles on a story. The implication is that in order to undertake a proper test of the relationship between party system and frame diversity, it is necessary to account for the magnitude of the news hole in a given country, as represented in our data set. All else equal, countries with more newspapers in the data set tend to have more articles on a given conflict, simply by virtue of having a larger presence in the data.

We can correct for this bias by weighting the number-of-topics indicator with some empirical measure of potential coverage intensity. The most obvious such indicator for which we have data is the total number of newspapers in our data set for a given country. The number-of-topics variable represents the sum of the probabilities of each individual topic appearing in a typical article in a given country. Weighting this by the number of newspapers accounts for the baseline increase in the size of the news hole as the number of newspapers available for coding increases.

While the presence of a newspaper in the LexisNexis or ISI Emerging Markets databases is presumably unrelated to countries' policies toward a given conflict, it is nonetheless positively associated with other factors that may be systematically related to the party system. For instance, in the Iraq case, per capita GDP and the number of troops per capita contributed to the coalition correlate positively with the number of newspapers from a given country

---

[7] The focus indicator for the Iraq case differs from the others due to the somewhat unique manner in which the global media covered that war, which was far higher in profile than the others. In that case, the most noteworthy difference between low- and high-party states emerged somewhat less in the simple level of policy-oriented coverage than in the relative contrast between different types of coverage (that is, policy vs. personality and human interest orientation). This is presumably attributable to the extended and highly public deliberations of the major decision makers in the run-up to the Iraq War, including President Bush and his senior cabinet, as well as, in Europe, Tony Blair, to name only two. So, to a greater extent than in the other cases, the differences emerge in the extent of personality- and human-interest-oriented coverage, rather than a simple tally of the amounts of policy coverage. For Iraq, we thus employ a ratio that compares the amount of policy coverage to the amount of personality and human-interest coverage, the latter two of which should, per the DP, be more prevalent in low-party states. We also employ a ratio for coverage valence in the Iraq case, though in this instance the reason, in addition to maximizing internal consistency within the case, is simply that we calculated the summary valence variables in a slightly different manner for the Iraq case relative to the others.

[8] Given the difficulty of achieving acceptable intercoder reliability when counting unique frames included in the news, we employ the diversity of substantive topics as a "best available" proxy.

within our data (at around .42 and .77, respectively, depending on the specific indicators we employ). The number of papers, in turn, is inversely correlated (at around –.26) with having more than the mean effective number of parliamentary parties in the data set (our primary definition in this chapter of a high-party state). To reduce any potential effect of this sort of skew in the data, we divide the topical diversity indicator by the number of newspapers in our data set from a given country.

Given the relatively small numbers of cases for these country-level analyses, we employ a series of simple difference of means tests to compare countries above and below the mean number of parties, based on the ENPP indicator.[9] Finally, it is important to note that all variables employed in this chapter meet or surpass standard levels of intercoder reliability across a variety of tests (see the appendix to this chapter for a detailed discussion of intercoder reliability tests and results).

Because these three variables (valence, focus, and diversity) are each measured quite differently both within and across cases, it is difficult to define a single nomenclature to describe the magnitudes of the differences between low- and high-party states. The most common practice employed in the social science literature for standardizing the reporting of results in such circumstances is to describe effects relative to standard deviations in the variable of interest.[10] We adopt this convention. In other words, we describe the magnitudes of differences between low- and high-party states in terms of standard deviations on the pertinent news characteristic variable. For instance, if the mean valence score for the Iraq analysis across the forty-three countries included in that case is two and the standard deviation is one, then we would describe a difference between low- and high-party states of, say, .50 on the valence scale as equivalent to one half of a standard deviation. We also list the statistical significance of that difference. While we do report the absolute differences on the several unique scales, we present the standard deviation and its statistical significance in an effort to characterize the substantive magnitudes of the differences across party systems in a relatively straightforward manner that is common across all media content indicators.

Our primary goal in this chapter is to empirically test the theoretical link we have drawn between differences in conflict decision making across party systems and the effects of party systems on the content of news coverage. Thus far we have tested all stages of our logical argument save one: the effects of party

[9] In order to limit the volume of statistical results presented in this chapter and enhance readability, we do not report results employing the effective number of *elective* parties (ENEP). However, nearly all results reported throughout the chapter replicate—in some instances producing even stronger relationships—when we substitute ENEP for ENPP. Results from replications employing ENEP are available from the authors upon request.

[10] Mathematically, a standard deviation is the positive square root of the variance of a distribution of values. In a normally distributed data sample, 68 percent of observations lie within one standard deviation of the mean.

systems on news content. The content analyses presented below substantiate this final untested link in our theoretical argument.

In the remainder of this chapter, we begin by introducing the cases and describing our data for each case. We then report the results of our difference of means tests and their implications for the DP. Finally, we undertake a series of robustness checks, using the aforementioned 2004 and 2009 EES television and newspaper content analytic data, which we describe in greater detail in the sections that follow.

CASES AND DATA

Case 1: Iraq (Operation Iraqi Freedom)

Our Iraq data set includes all newspaper articles (311,921 in total) available through the LexisNexis and ISI Emerging Markets database that included the word "Iraq" between December 20, 2002, and April 28, 2003.[11] The data cover sixty-three countries and include 2,310 newspapers (or an average of nearly 37 papers per country).[12] Of these, 478 papers (or 21 percent)—including 424 papers in democratic countries—published at least one story on Iraq. Forty-one of the sixty-three countries are democracies for which we have the necessary party system data. For all news stories, we coded a variety of dimensions, including the aforementioned three factors that we employ to test the DP: *valence* (positive, negative, neutral), *focus* (personalities, human interest, or policy orientation), and *diversity* (distinct topics covered, out of seventeen possible topics).[13]

Case 2: Libya (Operation Unified Protector)

The 2011 Libyan Civil War offers a unique opportunity to further test the DP. The popular uprising against the entrenched regime of Colonel Muammar Gaddafi and subsequent NATO intervention represent the type of unexpected turn of events that media organizations typically find newsworthy. Nineteen countries contributed troops, including sixteen NATO members and three Arab states (Jordan, Qatar, and United Arab Emirates). The relatively short duration of the Libyan crisis (less than one year, from the beginning of regional

[11] As noted in chapter 5, we define democratic countries as those that score 6 or higher on the Polity IV DEMOC-AUTOC scale.
[12] Comparable multicountry TV transcripts were inaccessible. As noted in chapter 5, given that we do not know the criterion for inclusion in these databases, this could potentially be an unrepresentative sample of newspapers, though, as we also noted in chapter 5, there is no *ex ante* reason to anticipate that this should work in favor of our predictions.
[13] See the appendix to this chapter for a detailed description of all content analyses investigated in this chapter, including lists of all countries and newspapers covered in the several analyses.

protests to the overthrow of Gaddafi) enabled us to track news coverage over the full course of the uprising, with less contamination by coverage fatigue than we might expect in more protracted conflicts like the Iraq and Afghanistan invasions or the more recent civil war in Syria.

As with the Iraq case, for each country we conducted a census of all daily and weekly newspapers listed in the electronic databases LexisNexis and ISI Emerging Markets. For each newspaper, we collected every unique article containing the term "Libya" (again, in English or the newspaper's source language). We ultimately identified 215,537 pertinent articles published by 2,322 unique and active (i.e., currently in press) newspapers in 115 countries (an average of over 20 newspapers per country), 65 of which are democracies. Our coverage included the period from December 18, 2010, through October 23, 2011. These dates mark, respectively, the day of the first protests in Tunisia following Mohamed Bouazizi's self-immolation—generally accepted as the beginning of the Arab Spring—and the National Transitional Council's declaration of the liberation of Libya.[14] Of these newspapers, 1,468 (or 63 percent)—and 1,140 papers in democracies—published at least one story on Libya. We have ENPP data for 56 democracies, which form our universe of cases for this analysis.[15]

Case 3: Afghanistan (Operation Enduring Freedom)

Beginning in 1996, the Taliban regime in Afghanistan permitted al-Qaeda and its leader Osama bin Laden—who had recently been expelled from his prior base of operations in Sudan—to operate freely in its territory. Consequently, the United States resolved to remove the Taliban regime from power in Afghanistan following the 9/11 attacks. As we outlined in chapter 5, on October 7, 2001, the United States, along with Great Britain, launched an aerial attack on Taliban and al-Qaeda targets. Though initially involving only US, UK, and Afghanistan resistance forces, the operation subsequently expanded as the United States formed a broad international coalition both to fight the Taliban and rebuild the nation. By 2003, forty-three nations, under NATO leadership, were participating as part of the ISAF (International Security Assistance Force) in Afghanistan. Thirty-seven of these contributed troops to the coalition.

For this analysis, we employed identical data gathering techniques as those described above, in this case coding every published unique article in Lexis-Nexis or ISI containing the term "Afghanistan" (as before, in English or the newspaper's source language). In total, we identified 77,534 pertinent articles published by 2,189 currently in press newspapers in fifty-two countries (or an average of nearly 35 papers per country) between September 9 and October 27, 2001. Out of this universe of newspapers, 1,468, or 67 percent (and 1,140 news-

---

[14] We exclude weekend supplements, inserts, evening editions, and similar associated materials.

[15] As with Iraq, democracy is defined as a country with a polity DEMOC-AUTOC score greater than or equal to 6.

papers in democratic countries) published at least one story on Afghanistan. Of the fifty-two country cases, forty-three are democracies, among which missing data on ENPP limits our t-tests to forty countries.

Case 4: Kosovo (Operation Allied Force)

Our final case is the US-led NATO air war against Bosnian Serbs in Kosovo, known as Operation Allied Force. The operation began on March 24, 1999, and concluded on June 10, 1999, when the Yugoslav government agreed to withdraw its military forces from Kosovo. While the United States unambiguously dominated Operation Allied Force, which involved about one thousand aircraft and thirty-eight thousand combat missions, all NATO countries participated in one form or another. Our data span December 18, 1998, through April 24, 1999, or from roughly four months prior to the conflict initiation to a month following initiation. During that time period, we identified 43,000 newspaper articles mentioning "Kosovo" across 1,813 newspapers from thirty-three countries, twenty-two of which are democracies for which we have party system data. Out of this set, 256 newspapers, or 14 percent, published at least one story on Kosovo (241 of these papers are located within democracies). Consequently, this data set is considerably smaller than the others, and readers should keep this limitation in mind when viewing results derived from it. That said, as we will see, all of the results obtained in the prior three investigations reemerge here, even in this more restrictive context.

Table 6.1 lists the countries included in each of the four original content analysis investigations discussed above. Following presentation of the country listings, we turn to our statistical results.

Table 6.1. Countries Included in Content Analyses

	Kosovo	Afghanistan	Iraq	Libya
Albania				X
Argentina		X	X	X
Australia	X	X	X	X
Austria	X	X		X
Belgium	X	X	X	X
Bolivia				X
Brazil			X	X
Bulgaria		X	X	X
Canada	X	X	X	X
Chile		X	X	X
Colombia		X	X	X
Costa Rica				X
Croatia		X	X	X
Cyprus				X
Czech Republic	X	X	X	X
Denmark	X	X	X	X
Ecuador		X	X	
Estonia		X	X	X

Table 6.1. (*continued*)

	Kosovo	Afghanistan	Iraq	Libya
France		X	X	X
Georgia				X
Germany	X	X	X	X
Ghana				X
Guatemala				X
Hungary		X	X	X
India	X	X	X	X
Indonesia		X	X	X
Ireland	X	X	X	X
Israel	X	X	X	X
Italy	X	X	X	X
Japan	X	X	X	
Kenya				X
Latvia		X	X	X
Lebanon				X
Liberia				X
Lithuania		X	X	X
Mauritius				X
Mexico		X	X	X
Nepal				X
Netherlands	X	X	X	X
New Zealand	X	X	X	X
Pakistan				X
Peru				X
Philippines	X			X
Poland		X	X	X
Romania	X	X	X	X
Russia			X	
Senegal				X
Sierra Leone				X
Slovakia		X	X	X
Slovenia				X
South Africa			X	
South Korea	X	X	X	X
Spain	X	X	X	X
Switzerland	X	X		X
Taiwan		X	X	X
Thailand	X	X	X	
Turkey		X	X	X
Ukraine		X	X	X
United Kingdom	X	X	X	X
United States	X	X	X	X
Uruguay				X
Venezuela		X	X	

RESULTS

Figure 6.1 presents the results from a series of *t*-tests investigating the DP across each of our three key indicators (valence, focus, and diversity). The figure includes all four country cases investigated in this chapter.[16]

---

[16] Readers interested in reviewing the numbers underlying the results shown in figure 6.1 should consult table 6.A.1 in the appendix to this chapter.

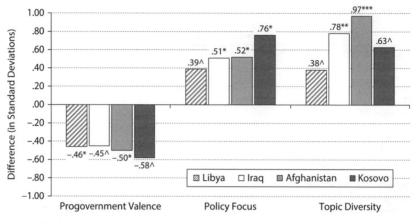

***p<.001, *p<.05, **p<.01, ^p<.10

Figure 6.1. Average differences (in standard deviations) in news coverage of multinational conflicts, high- versus low-party states

In figure 6.1, the results for Iraq are shown in the solid white bars, those for Libya in diagonally striped bars, those for Afghanistan in solid, light-gray bars, and those for Kosovo in solid, dark-gray bars. We summarize the results for each country case by variable. Beginning with valence, a series of t-tests indicates that relative to high-party states (above the mean in each respective data set), low-party states feature significantly more pro-government-policy war-related coverage in all four cases. The differences (that is, high-party minus low-party states) for Iraq, Libya, Afghanistan, and Kosovo—in standard deviations—are −.45 ($p < .08$), −.46 ($p < .04$), −.50 ($p < .05$), and −.58 ($p < .09$), respectively. In short, the substantive effects are substantial in magnitude—varying from 45 to 58 percent of a full standard deviation—and in the predicted directions. Despite the small Ns, in each instance they are also statistically significant at $p < .10$ or better.

We turn next to coverage focus. Once again, across all four cases, the results of a series t-tests, summarized in figure 6.1, indicate that, relative to low-party states, high-party states include relatively more policy-oriented coverage on average. Recall that for Iraq, this is operationalized as policy- minus personality- and human-interest-oriented coverage. For the other three cases it is operationalized as the level of policy-oriented coverage. The results once again support our expectations in each instance. In all four cases, the differences are in the predicted directions, substantial in magnitude, and statistically significant at $p < .10$ or better. Specifically, for Iraq, Libya, Afghanistan, and Kosovo, the differences—again, in standard deviations—are .51 ($p < .05$), .39 ($p < .07$), .52 ($p < .05$), and .76 ($p < .04$), respectively.

We turn finally to topical diversity. Figure 6.1 shows that across all four cases, relative to low-party states, news coverage in high-party states includes more distinct topics (per newspaper)—suggesting greater diversity of frames—and so once again supporting the DP. As before, the results in all four cases are in the predicted directions, substantial in magnitude, and statistically significant at $p < .10$ or better. To briefly summarize, the differences for Iraq, Libya, Afghanistan, and Kosovo—once again, in standard deviations—are .78 $(p < .01)$, .38 $(p < .07)$, .97 $(p < .001)$, and .63 $(p < .07)$, respectively.

Across all four cases and all three measures of media content, the results from our investigation support our assumption regarding the effects of party systems on news content (that is, the DP).[17] In every instance, media in states with relatively high numbers of parties presented *less* progovernment and *more* diverse war-related coverage, featuring *more* policy focused stories, compared to their counterparts in states with fewer parties.

2004 AND 2009 EUROPEAN
ELECTION STUDIES (EES)

Our final investigation employs a data set that we did not construct—the EES Longitudinal Media Study.[18] Because the time period (2004–9), variables (see below), coding methodology (all human coding), and purpose (investigating news coverage of European elections) all differ from ours in the analyses detailed above, replicating our findings in this data environment would further enhance our confidence in our results. These data have the added benefit of including both newspaper and television content, thereby presenting an opportunity to test the DP in a relatively broad and cross-national data context. It is to this task that we now turn.

As part of its general study, the EES undertook detailed content analyses of media coverage (television and newspaper) of the European elections in 1999, 2004, and 2009.[19] Our analysis focuses on the latter two years, which included variables pertinent to the DP. Specifically, we focus on four variables coded by the EES. These follow below. In each case, we list the variable, followed by what we consider the intuitive prediction following from the DP.[20]

1. Explicit mention of the presentation or style of the actor featured in the story (DP = high-ENPP associated with less focus on presentation/style)
2. Usage of games, sports, or war metaphors in stories (DP = high-ENPP associated with less usage)

[17] All reported results replicate when we exclude countries with only one newspaper in the data set.

[18] Schuck et al. (2010).

[19] For details concerning the study, see Banducci et al. (2010).

[20] While not all of these variables perfectly map onto our predictions derived from the DP, we believe they are sufficiently comparable to allow a reasonably valid set of tests. For instance, while we made no specific predictions about metaphors involving games, sports, and war, these particular metaphors are more commonly associated with *soft* news—sensationalized, entertainment-oriented—than hard news (Baum 2003).

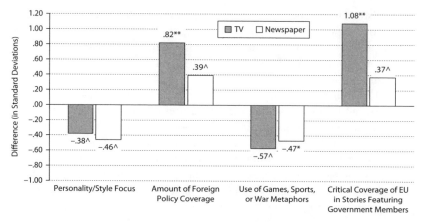

Figure 6.2. Average differences (in standard deviations) in news coverage of European elections, high- versus low-party states.

Note: Newspaper results for game-, sports-, and war-metaphors and television results for critical coverage exclude Spain.

3. Foreign policy focus in stories (DP = high-ENPP associated with more foreign policy stories)
4. The valence—supportive or critical—of stories featuring members of the incumbent government that pertain to the EU (DP = high-ENPP associated with more criticism of government)

We code all variables at the country-year level, meaning that there are two observations per country, one in 2004 and a second in 2009.[21] Figure 6.2 illustrates the results from a series of *t*-tests comparing the scores on each variable in countries above and below the mean level of ENPP at the time of the survey (2004 or 2009). As before, we focus on standard deviation differences between low- and high-party states.[22]

Overall, about 24 percent of stories in the data set were from television, with the rest from newspapers. Beginning with the newspaper results, in each case our results are consistent with expectations, given the logic of the DP. To begin with we find significantly less emphasis on presentation or style in news reports from high-party states ($p < .10$). This suggests that coverage in high-party states is less prone to focus on the personalities or styles of individual actors.

In high-party states, we also found less use of games, sports, or war metaphors ($p < .05$) and more foreign policy coverage, though this last difference is

---

[21] All reported results hold if we collapse the data to a single observation per country. However, we believe it is conceptually superior to treat observations five years apart as distinct, rather than averaging across them. Moreover, by employing the country-year, we are able to greatly increase our statistical leverage.

[22] In table 6.A.2 we present the data underlying figure 6.2.

not statistically significant at traditional levels ($p < .16$). However, even in this case, if we exclude one residual outlier (Spain), the results remain correctly signed, increase in magnitude, and become significant at the $p < .10$ level.

We turn finally to the valence of EU evaluations in news reports. In the context of a news content study focused on coverage of the Europe-wide elections of 2004 and 2009 in EU member states, we assume that critical or supportive coverage of the EU most directly represents a challenge to the government frame when it appears within reports focused on members of the incumbent government. We thus limit our analysis to this subset of all stories. Within this subset and consistent with the DP we find significantly more critical coverage of the EU in high-party states ($p < .10$). This suggests that coverage of the EU election in high-party states is more prone to challenge government officials, relative to such coverage in low-party states.

When we focus only on television, all results remain correctly signed and statistically significant. In fact, the difference is considerably larger and more highly significant for the volume of television coverage of foreign policy ($p < .01$), while remaining nearly identical in the other two cases. The only partial exception is the valence of EU coverage, which in the full data set falls short of standard levels of statistical significance ($p < .20$). However, in this case, excluding the same influential outlier as before (Spain) dramatically increases the magnitude and significance ($p < .01$) of the difference between high- and low-party states. Figure 6.2 illustrates these results.

Taken together, we interpret the results from these investigations as largely substantiating the DP. We find similar differences here between low- and high-party states—in both newspaper and television news coverage—as in the prior global newspaper analyses. Moreover, these data allowed us to test our predictions against a subset of data limited to television coverage, with consistently supportive results complementing those from our various analyses of newspaper coverage.

CONCLUSION

In this chapter we put the Downsian Premise—which serves as a core assumption underlying our theory—to the test, literally. Rather than simply assuming that the differences in party systems had the anticipated effects on news content, we explicitly tested whether this was in fact the case. We constructed four original news content analysis data sets, exploiting recent innovations in automated content analysis that allowed us to compare news coverage across many dozens of countries during four different multinational conflicts: Iraq (2003), Afghanistan (2001), Libya (2011), and Kosovo (1999). Though the particulars of the results predictably vary somewhat across cases—due to differences both in coding modalities and in the cases themselves—the bottom line remains the same: in all four cases we found clear support for all three elements of the DP as we have defined it. In each instance, newspapers in countries with more parion effortly

ties offered more policy-oriented news, more criticism of government policy, and more diverse coverage than their counterparts in countries with fewer parties. Our robustness test, based on the EES longitudinal media study, offered additional confirming evidence, in this case based on both newspaper and television data. This increases our confidence in the validity of the results from our own content analysis investigations. Taken together, these findings arguably constitute the final piece in our theoretical puzzle.

In the next chapter, we turn from large- and medium-N comparative analyses to in-depth case studies. Through a careful process-tracing exercise, we hope to demonstrate some of the processes explicated in this and previous chapters at work as particular countries contemplated becoming involved in a military coalition. The goal is to determine whether our key theoretical variables (parties, media access, media content, public opinion) played their "proper" roles (per our theory) as the governments under scrutiny weighed the pros and cons of intervention and ultimately determined whether or not to do so.

APPENDIX: STATISTICAL TABLES, ROBUSTNESS TESTS, AND CONTENT ANALYSIS CODEBOOK

Part I: T-tests Underlying Figure 6.1

Table 6.A.1. T-tests of Differences in News Coverage between Low- and High-Party States

	Difference (Low vs. High Parties)	Statistical Significance ($p < x$)	Difference (in Standard Deviations)
1. Iraq			
Valence	0.012	.08	0.45
Focus	−0.008	.05	0.51
Diversity	−1.286	.01	0.78
Observations	41		
2. Libya			
Valence	−0.076	.04	0.46
Focus	0.031	.07	0.39
Diversity	0.727	.07	0.38
Observations	56		
3. Afghanistan			
Valence	0.003	.05	0.50
Focus	−0.001	.05	0.52
Diversity	−1.660	.001	0.97
Observations	40		
4. Kosovo			
Valence	0.116	.09	0.58
Focus	−0.064	.04	0.76
Diversity	−1.115	.07	0.63
Observations	22		

Part II: *T*-tests Underlying Figure 6.2

Table 6.A.2. Differences in Newspaper and Television Content for States Below and Above Average ENPP, 2004 and 2009

	Low-ENPP	High-ENPP	Difference (High—Low)	Significance of Difference ($p < x$)	N
(A) Newspaper stories					
Explicit focus on presentation or style of actor featured in story (0 = no, 1 = yes)	0.248	0.182	−0.066	.09	49
Games, sports, or war metaphors used in story (0 = no, 1 = yes)	0.224	0.161	−0.063	.05	49
Foreign-policy-oriented story (0 = no, 1 = yes)[a]	0.071 0.067	0.081 0.081	0.010 0.014	.16 .09	47
Valence of EU evaluations in stories focused on members of incumbent government (1–5 scale, with 5 = most negative)	3.153	2.878	−0.276	.10	46
(B) TV stories					
Explicit focus on presentation or style of actor featured in story (0 = no, 1 = yes)	0.207	0.122	−0.170	.10	32
Games, sports, or war metaphors used in story (0 = no, 1 = yes)	0.203	0.104	−0.159	.06	32
Foreign-policy-oriented story (0 = no, 1 = yes)	0.089	0.138	0.049	.01	32
Valence of EU evaluations in stories focused on members of incumbent government (1–5 scale, with 5 = most negative)[a]	3.133 3.456	2.827 2.827	−0.305 −0.629	.20 .01	18 16

Source: EES Longitudinal Media Study (25 countries in 2004; 27 countries in 2009).
[a]First row includes all observations; second row excludes one influential outlier (Spain).

Part III: Newspaper Content Analysis Codebook

These data sets measure the diversity in the media coverage of foreign policy in various party systems, during four recent US-led military interventions (Kosovo, Afghanistan, Iraq, Libya). At the document level, we coded articles according to their topics and attributes. At the country level of analysis—the level of aggregation used in the book—variables capture the average levels and content of coverage within a given country.

Selection

The sample includes *all* newspaper articles available through the LexisNexis and ISI Emerging Markets databases, indexed by the terms "Kosovo," "Afghanistan," "Iraq," or "Libya," published in the weeks and months immediately preceding and following the initiation of military operations by the US-led coalitions. Below, we present the periods of observation and sample sizes for the full data set and for democracies only in tables 6.A.3 and 6.A.4, respectively. Table 6.A.5 presents the numbers of countries (overall and democracies only) with newspapers that covered the four conflicts. We employ the democracy-only data in this chapter.

Table 6.A.3. Data Summary (Full Data Set)

Conflict	Period Start	Intervention	Period End	Articles	Countries	Papers
Kosovo	December 18, 1998	March 24, 1999	April 24, 1999	43,000	33	1,813
Afghanistan	September 9, 2001	October 7, 2001	October 27, 2001	77,534	52	2,189
Iraq	December 20, 2002	March 20, 2003	April 28, 2003	278,361	63	2,310
Libya	December 18, 2010	March 19, 2011	October 23, 2011	215,537	115	2,322

Table 6.A.4. Data Summary (Democracies Only)

Conflict	Period Start	Intervention	Period End	Articles	Countries	Papers
Kosovo	December 18, 1998	March 24, 1999	April 24, 1999	41,141	23	1,507
Afghanistan	September 9, 2001	October 7, 2001	October 27, 2001	74,926	43	2,075
Iraq	December 20, 2002	March 20, 2003	April 28, 2003	267,269	43	2,085
Libya	December 18, 2010	March 19, 2011	October 23, 2011	185,710	65	1,828

Following convention, we define democracies as cases where the combined Polity DEMOC-AUTOC score is six or higher.

Table 6.A.5. Data Summary (Number of Newspapers That Published Conflict-Related Stories)

Conflict	Overall	Democracies
Kosovo	256	241
Afghanistan	406	393
Iraq	478	424
Libya	1,468	1,140

Coding

We classified the articles in the four text corpora into several dozen categories using automated text analysis. The analysis begins by conversion of a corpus of text documents into an $n \times k$ document-term matrix, where rows represent the set of n documents, and columns represent the frequencies with which the k terms (words or stems) appears in each document. We use stemming and stop-word removal for dimensionality reduction, and filter remaining terms such that each term appears in at least five documents. The reduced document-term matrix then serves as the feature set, which we can analyze using a variety of logical searches, unsupervised and supervised learning techniques. We identified the content of each article (i.e., coverage type, focus, and valence) through supervised machine learning techniques, which use a training set of predefined labels to classify texts according to their features. We ascertained the topic(s) of each article though dictionary-based coding. The text corpus in each of the four cases is multilingual, including articles in the native language and—where available—in English. Where the articles were in a language other than English, we used statistical machine translation (Google Translate API) to convert them to English.[23]

For each of the four cases, a team of three research assistants manually coded a randomly selected subset of training data, based on instructions and examples provided in a codebook—the relevant parts of which are provided below. The assistants coded three training sets of four hundred documents each, randomly selected from each corpus. We held constant the selected documents across the coders to assess intercoder reliability. The human coders classified texts along three dimensions of coverage focus (*policy, human interest, personality*) and three dimensions of valence (*foreign policy, execution, personality*). We then combined the disaggregated focus and valence variables in the

---

[23] Although Google Translate uses statistical methods based on bilingual text corpora (using a training set of 200 billion words from United Nations materials), rather that grammatical or rule-based algorithms, this approach is well suited for the automated content analysis techniques employed in this chapter and discussed below—which rely on natural language processing that discards grammar, stop words (e.g., "a," "the," "and"), and word order, producing an unordered array of terms (a "bag-of-words" model).

following manner: *focus* (for the Iraq case only) = *policy focus/(policy focus + human interest focus + personality focus)* and *valence* (for all four country cases) = *foreign policy valence + execution valence + personality valence*. This approach converts nominal variables to a 0 to 1 interval, where smaller values of *focus* indicate more personality-based coverage, and positive values indicate more policy-oriented coverage. For *valence*, the combined variable maintains the same positivity/negativity/neutrality as before, but permits negativity/positivity in one dimension to be offset by negativity/positivity in another. (In the other three country cases, several factors, such as coding differences, limited the practicality of employing the combined variables. Hence, we employ the amount of policy focus in news coverage.)

For each document, we asked the coders to indicate whether it was on a topic unrelated to the Iraq War (e.g., an apolitical article about the Iraqi soccer team), incomprehensible, or mistranslated (*other*). We further asked the coders to indicate if the article was ambiguously worded or otherwise difficult to classify into categories (*tough call*). We provide detailed descriptions of each measure in the next section.

Intercoder reliability

We assessed intercoder reliability using four measures: (1) percentage agreement, (2) Fleiss's kappa, (3) Kendall's *W*, and (4) Krippendorff's alpha, with bootstrapping. We based calculations on the evaluation set of one hundred documents, which overlapped between the coders' training sets. We used the first measure (percentage agreement) due to its intuitive interpretation as the proportion of documents in the evaluation set for which both coders gave the same value. Its obvious drawback is that it does not account for agreement that could be expected to occur by chance. The other three measures explicitly account for chance agreements among multiple coders, and test the null hypothesis that agreements can be regarded as random. Fleiss's kappa permits the assessment of agreement between two coders, but treats input data as categorical—such that each value on an ordinal or interval scale is treated as a distinct category, and the "closeness" of adjacent values (e.g., +1, +2) is discarded. We also included Kendall's coefficient of concordance (*W*), which is appropriate when the data are of ordinal measurement and do not meet the assumptions of parametric methods. Finally, we calculated Krippendorff's alpha statistic, which is highly flexible and can be used with multiple coders, as well as with ordinal-, interval-, and ratio-level variables. We obtained the alpha distribution by bootstrapping, using ten thousand samples of one hundred codings (same size as the evaluation set), and fit 95 percent confidence intervals based on the resulting distribution of the test statistic. In table 6.A.6 we present intercoder reliability statistics.

Table 6.A.6. Intercoder Reliability Test Results

Case	Variable	All Agree	Fleiss's Kappa	Kendall's W	Krippendorff's Alpha (95% CI)
Iraq[a]	FOCUS_HUM	.92	.76***	.84***	.76 (.57, .91)
	FOCUS_POL	.89	.74***	.84***	.73 (.55, .87)
	FOCUS_PER	.76	.6***	.75***	.59 (.43, .72)
	VALENCE[b]	.7	.42***	.81***	.66 (.39, .84)
Libya	FOCUS_POL[c]	.78	.71***	.81***	.71 (.55, .86)
	VALENCE[b]	.65	.60***	.84***	.77 (.67, .85)
Afghanistan	FOCUS_POL[c]	.89	.75***	.83***	.74 (.58, .88)
	VALENCE[b]	.47	.33***	.74***	.56 (.42, .67)
Kosovo	FOCUS_POL[c]	.89	.74***	.84***	.73 (.55, .87)
	VALENCE[b]	.51	.32***	.71***	.54 (.36, .69)

***$p < .001$.
[a]FOCUS = FOCUS_POL / (FOCUS_POL + FOCUS_HUM + FOCUS_PER). [b]VALENCE = VAL_FP + VAL_EX + VAL_PR. [c]FOCUS_POL = amount of policy focus.

Variable Definitions

ARTICLE LEVEL

Case Identifiers
  ID1: Unique identifier for each document.
  DATE: Format is YYYYMMDD.
  TID: Integer, indexing day of observation.
  Post intervention: Binary indicator of whether article was published after start of military intervention (see table 6.A.1).

Coverage Variables (Coded with Wordscores)
Let R be a set of reference texts included in the training set (e.g., a pair of news articles: one with a human interest focus and one without). Each text in $r \in R$ is assigned a position on dimension d (coverage type), denoted A_{rd}. For example, $A_{rd} = 1$ if article r has a human interest focus, and $A_{rd} = 0$ otherwise. Let F_{wr} be the relative frequency of word w in text r, as a proportion of the total number of words in the text. Let $P_{wr} = F_{wr}/\Sigma r(F_{wr})$ be the probability that we are reading text r, given the occurrence of word w. The wordscore is defined as the expected position of a text on dimension d, given that we are reading word w: $S_{wr} = \Sigma r(P_{wr} A_{rd})$. This statistic is an average of the a priori reference text scores A_{rd}, weighted by the probabilities P_{wr}. Let T be a set of texts included in the test set. The scores calculated for the training set are used to estimate the position of any new text $t \in T$ on dimension d: $S_{td} = \Sigma w(F_{wt} S_{wd})$, where F_{wt} is the frequency of scored word w in document t and S_{wd} is that word's score in the original training set.

FOCUS_HU_WS: Document score (S_{td}) of article t on dimension d = FOCUS_HU, where FOCUS_HU = 1 indicates human interest focus, and FOCUS_HU = 0 otherwise.

FOCUS_HU_RS: Rescaled document score.

FOCUS_PL_WS: Document score (S_{td}) of article t on dimension d = FOCUS_PL, where FOCUS_PL = 1 indicates policy focus, and FOCUS_PL = 0 otherwise.

FOCUS_PL_RS: Rescaled document score.

FOCUS_PR_WS: Document score (S_{td}) of article t on dimension d = FOCUS_PR, where FOCUS_PR = 1 indicates personality focus, and FOCUS_PR = 0 otherwise.

FOCUS_PR_RS: Rescaled document score.

VAL_FP_WS: Document score (S_{td}) of article t on dimension d = VAL_FP, where VAL_FP = 1 indicates positive foreign policy valence, and VAL_FP = −1 indicates negative foreign policy valence.

VAL_FP_RS: Rescaled document score.

VAL_EX_WS: Document score (S_{td}) of article t on dimension d = VAL_EX, where VAL_EX = 1 indicates positive execution valence, and VAL_EX = −1 indicates negative execution valence.

VAL_EX_RS: Rescaled document score.

VAL_PR_WS: Document score (S_{td}) of article t on dimension d = VAL_PR, where VAL_PR = 1 indicates positive personality valence, and VAL_PR = −1 indicates negative personality valence.

VAL_PR_RS: Rescaled document score.

Coverage Variables (Coded with SVM)

Support Vector Machine (SVM) fits a hyperplane to the feature space, separates data points from each other according to their labels, and finds the maximum marginal distance D between the points labeled $y_i = 1$ from those labeled $y_i = -1$. Given a training set of documents $(\mathbf{x}_i, y_i)$, $i = 1, \ldots, n_{ts}$, where $x_i \in \mathcal{R}^p$ and $y \in \{1,-1\}^{nts}$, SVM solves the optimization problem

$$\text{maximize } D, \text{ s.t. } y_i(\beta\varphi(\mathbf{x}_i) + \beta_0) \geq D$$

where $\varphi()$ is a function that maps the training data $\mathbf{x}_i$ to a high-dimensional space, and $\mathbf{K}(\mathbf{x}_i, \mathbf{x}_j) = \varphi(\mathbf{x}_i)'\varphi(\mathbf{x}_j)$ is a kernel function.[24]

To account for coder disagreement and uncertainty, we used a voting algorithm, where we used the training sets to estimate two separate SVM models (m_1, m_2), rather than a single model based on pooled training set data. We then calculated a weighted average of classifications from the two models, with

---

[24] For technical background on this class of models, see Joachims (2002). For recent applications in political science, see Yu, Kaufmann, and Diermeier (2008), Diermeier et al. (forthcoming), and Wilkerson, Purpura, and Hillard (2008).

weights corresponding to model accuracy rates ($a_k = [0,1]$, the proportion of outcomes correctly predicted in training set k by model m_k) calculated with a tenfold cross-validation.

$$\hat{y} = \sum_k^2 w_k y_k \quad w_1 = \frac{a_1}{\sum_k^2 a_k}$$

We intended the weighted average to address the concern that some codings may be more "accurate" than others. If labels are assigned to a training set in a consistent manner, predictions derived from an SVM model estimated with those data will be better able to replicate the original hand codings than in the case of data labeled in an ad hoc and contradictory manner. By weighting training models with higher accuracy higher than those with lower accuracy, we are able to account for this type of uncertainty in document classification.

FOCUS_HUM: Predicted probability of human interest coverage focus.
FOCUS_POL: Predicted probability of policy coverage focus.
FOCUS_PER: Predicted probability of personality coverage focus.
FP_VALENCE_POS: Predicted probability of positive foreign policy valence.
EXEC_VALENCE_POS: Predicted probability of positive execution valence.
PERS_VALENCE_POS: Predicted probability of positive personality valence.
FP_VALENCE_NEG: Predicted probability of negative foreign policy valence.
EXEC_VALENCE_NEG: Predicted probability of negative execution valence.
PERS_VALENCE_NEG: Predicted probability of negative personality valence.
FP_VALENCE_NEU: Predicted probability of neutral foreign policy valence.
EXEC_VALENCE_NEU: Predicted probability of neutral execution valence.
PERS_VALENCE_NEU: Predicted probability of neutral personality valence.

Coverage Variables (Aggregated from SVM)
FP_VALENCE: Higher values indicate more positive foreign policy valence (FP_VALENCE_POS—FP_VALENCE_NEG).
EXEC_VALENCE: Higher values indicate more positive execution valence (EXEC_VALENCE_POS—EXEC_VALENCE_NEG).
PERS_VALENCE: Higher values indicate more positive personality valence (PERS_VALENCE_POS—PERS_VALENCE_NEG).

Topic Variables

Topic variables are coded using Boolean logic, matching terms contained in each document against a custom dictionary. Formally, given a list of m_Y dictionary terms $d(Y) = \{d(Y)_1, d(Y)_2, \ldots, d(Y)_{m_Y}\}$ defined for variable Y, and given n documents indexed by $i \in \{1, \ldots, n\}$, each variable Y_i is defined as

$$Y_i = \{1 \text{ if document } i \text{ contains any of the terms in } d(Y)$$

$$0 \text{ otherwise}$$

We performed all automated topic classification in the R statistical language, using the *tm* (text mining) package developed by Meyer et al.[25]

MIL_TECH: Article describes technical military decisions or actions on the ground, e.g., a description of new military equipment or of a military operation/move on ground.

MIL_PERS: Article describes a personal military story, e.g., how a soldier or a division of soldiers showed courage, or the story of the loss of a soldier with a description of his personal characteristics.

MIL_CAS: Article mentions the loss of an individual soldier or the aggregate number of lost soldiers.

UN_INTL: Article mentions the United Nations or other international organizations.

CIV_SUFF: Article refers to any suffering among civilians on the ground: suffering, wounded or casualties.

HUM_AID: Article refers to any privately or publicly funded humanitarian aid concerns or initiatives.

DEMOC: Article refers to democracy or democratization.

WMD: Article refers to weapons of mass destruction.

TERROR: Article refers to terrorism.

FIN_ECON: Article refers to the cost of the foreign policy mission in the short, medium or long term.

RECONST: Article refers to any plans for reconstruction in the medium or long term.

POL_LEAD: Article refers to the character/leadership of a specific political leader regardless of country.

US_ALLIES: Article contains direct reference to an alliance with the United States—positive as well as negative.

OTH_ALLIES: Article contains direct reference to an alliance with any countries other than the United States—positive as well as negative.

ME_PEACE: Article contains direct reference to the Middle East conflict/peace process.

PUB_OPIN: Article contains direct references to public opinion.

---

[25] Meyer, Hornik, and Feinerer (2008).

MEDIA: Media coverage of foreign policy is explicitly discussed.

NUM_TOPICS: Sum of above topic categories. Ordinal variable indicating diversity of frames.

COUNTRY LEVEL

Case Identifiers

COW: Correlates of War three-letter country code for state in which article was published.

CNTRY: Alternate three-letter country code.

CCODE: Numerical country code (compatible with Correlates of War and Polity data sets).

CTID: Country-day identifier.

CNT_GTD1: Alternate country name.

Original Covariates

N_PAPERS: Number of newspapers in country sample.

N_ARTICLES: Number of articles in country sample.

Polity IV

DEMOC: Institutionalized democracy.

AUTOC: Institutionalized autocracy.

POLITY: Combined Polity score.

POLITY2: Revised combined Polity score (p4).

Party Systems Data[26]

ENEP: Effective number of elective parties.

ENPP: Effective number of parliamentary parties.

Below are coding instructions used by the research assistants in labeling the training data. (The instructions below focus on the Iraq case but are identical across the four cases.)

TRAINING SET (FOR IRAQ)

<u>Coverage Focus</u>

This category is divided into three subcategories that are not mutually exclusive: HUMAN INTEREST (issue is described from a general human interest perspective with emphasis on human needs, concerns or achievements), POLICY (any discussion of the content of a foreign policy, outside the other two categories), and PERSONALITY (article contains direct reference to the personality/personal story/motivation/feelings of a political, military or civilian person). Check all that apply.

(continued)

[26] Golder (2005); Bormann and Golder (2013).

(continued)

Focus

   [ ] HUMAN INTEREST
   [ ] POLICY
   [ ] PERSONALITY
   [ ] None of the above

Coverage Focus: Tough Call? Check box if text is ambiguous, or if you were otherwise uncertain about how to code it.

   [ ] TOUGH CALL

Coverage Focus: Good example? Check box if text is a particularly clear, unambiguous example of coverage focus.

   [ ] GOOD EXAMPLE

Valence

Valence is defined as the positivity/negativity/neutrality of the document with regards to (1) a government's foreign policy, (2) its execution thereof, or (3) the personalities involved in policy planning and execution. A POSITIVE evaluation would include direct praise of the official foreign policy/execution/personality such as "Blair has impressed the Americans with his commitment to the Coalition of the Willing" or "Secretary Powell has really mastered dealing with the United Nations." You may also count self-defensive statements as praise. For instance if a journalist asks whether US policy is based on faulty intelligence, and the White House Press Secretary says "that's not true" it would be coded as praise. Contrary, a NEGATIVE evaluation would include direct criticisms of the official foreign policy/execution/personality as in "Bush failed to grasp the costs of the Iraq War." NEUTRAL statements either raise the issue without making any explicit judgment, or feature a balance between positive and negative statements. As for all other coding, the coding for valence must be unambiguous and defensible. You should be able to point out the statement containing the praise and criticism to another person and have them agree.

Foreign Policy

Praise or criticism of a government's foreign policy goals, strategies, priorities.

   [ ] POSITIVE [article explicitly expresses support for a government's foreign policy.]
   [ ] NEUTRAL [article is either balanced between criticism and praise, or does not take a position.]
   [ ] NEGATIVE [article explicitly expresses opposition to a government's foreign policy.]

Execution

Assessments of the effectiveness or ineffectiveness of the conduct of diplomacy or military operations.

[ ] POSITIVE [article explicitly expresses praise for a government's execution of its foreign policy.]

[ ] NEUTRAL [article is either balanced between criticism and praise, or does not take a position.]

[ ] NEGATIVE [article explicitly expresses criticism of a government's execution of its foreign policy.]

Personality

Praise or criticism of a head of state, foreign minister, military commanders, or other senior public officials involved in foreign policy planning or execution.

[ ] POSITIVE [article explicitly expresses praise for specific personalities involved in foreign policy.]

[ ] NEUTRAL [article is either balanced between criticism and praise, or does not take a position.]

[ ] NEGATIVE [article explicitly expresses criticism of specific personalities involved in foreign policy.]

Valence: Tough Call? Check box if text is ambiguous, or if you were otherwise uncertain about how to code it.

[ ] TOUGH CALL

Valence: Good example? Check box if text is a particularly clear, unambiguous example of positive or negative valence.

[ ] GOOD EXAMPLE

Other

[ ] Gibberish / Incomprehensible / Mistranslated / Missing text

[ ] Topic is not foreign policy

Submit [ ]

Countries

Kosovo (1999): Australia, Austria, Azerbaijan, Belgium, Cambodia, Canada, China, Czech Republic, Denmark, France, Germany, India, Indonesia, Ireland, Israel, Italy, Japan, Korea South, Laos, Malaysia, Netherlands, New Zealand, Philippines, Romania, Russia, Singapore, Spain, Switzerland, Thailand, UAE, United Kingdom, United States, Vietnam

Afghanistan (2001): Argentina, Australia, Austria, Azerbaijan, Belgium, Brazil, Bulgaria, Cambodia, Canada, Chile, China, Colombia, Croatia, Czech Republic, Denmark, Ecuador, Estonia, France, Germany, Hungary, India, Indonesia, Ireland, Israel, Italy, Japan, Kazakhstan, Korea South, Laos, Latvia, Lithuania, Malaysia, Mexico, Netherlands, New Zealand, Philippines, Poland, Romania, Russia, Singapore, Slovak Republic, Spain, Switzerland, Taiwan, Thailand, Turkey, UAE, Ukraine, United Kingdom, United States, Venezuela, Vietnam

Iraq (2003): Algeria, Argentina, Australia, Bahrain, Belarus, Belgium, Brazil, Bulgaria, Canada, Chile, China, Colombia, Croatia, Czech Republic, Denmark, Ecuador, Egypt, Estonia, Fiji, France, Germany, Hungary, India, Indonesia, Iraq, Ireland, Israel, Italy, Japan, Jordan, Kazakhstan, Korea North, Korea South, Kuwait, Latvia, Lebanon, Lithuania, Malaysia, Mexico, Morocco, Netherlands, New Zealand, Oman, Papua New Guinea, Poland, Romania, Russia, Saudi Arabia, Serbia, Singapore, Slovak Republic, South Africa, Spain, Switzerland, Syria, Taiwan, Thailand, Turkey, UAE, Ukraine, United Kingdom, United States, Venezuela

Libya (2011): Afghanistan, Albania, Algeria, Argentina, Armenia, Australia, Austria, Bahrain, Bangladesh, Belgium, Benin, Bolivia, Bosnia, Botswana, Brazil, Bulgaria, Burkina Faso, Cambodia, Cameroon, Canada, Chile, China, Colombia, Congo Kinshasa, Costa Rica, Croatia, Cyprus, Czech Republic, Denmark, Ecuador, Egypt, Estonia, Ethiopia, Fiji, Finland, France, Gabon, Gambia, Georgia, Germany, Ghana, Guatemala, Hungary, India, Indonesia, Iran, Iraq, Ireland, Israel, Italy, Japan, Jordan, Kazakhstan, Kenya, Korea North, Korea South, Kosovo, Kuwait, Laos, Latvia, Lebanon, Liberia, Libya, Lithuania, Madagascar, Malaysia, Mauritania, Mauritius, Mexico, Morocco, Mozambique, Namibia, Nepal, Netherlands, New Zealand, Nigeria, Oman, Pakistan, Papua New Guinea, Peru, Philippines, Poland, Qatar, Romania, Russia, Rwanda, Saudi Arabia, Senegal, Sierra Leone, Singapore, Slovak Republic, Slovenia, South Africa, Spain, Sri Lanka, Switzerland, Syria, Taiwan, Tanzania, Thailand, Tunisia, Turkey, UAE, Uganda, Ukraine, United Kingdom, United States, Uruguay, Venezuela, Vietnam, Yemen, Zambia, Zimbabwe

SOURCES

Afghanistan: *Afghan Islamic Press, Daily Outlook Afghanistan*
Albania: *Tirana Times*
Algeria: *Algeria Press Service, Horizons, La Tribune, L'Expression*
Argentina: *Ambito Financiero, BAE Buenos Aires Econmico, Clarin, El Cronista, El Economista, Horizons, La Nacion, La Tribune, La Voz del Interior*
Armenia: *AZG Newspaper, Novoe Vremia, Noyan Tapan*
Australia: *Advertiser Mail Adelaide, Advocate Perth, Age* (Melbourne), *Ayr Advocate, Bowen Independent North Queensland, Brisbane News, BusinessWeek Magazine, Cairns Post, Cairns, Caloundra Weekly* (Queensland), *Canberra Times* (Australia), *Canberra Times, Canning Times Perth, Capricorn Coast Mirror* (Queensland), *Central and North Burnett Times* (Queensland), *Central Courier, Central Telegraph and Rural Weekly* (Queensland), *Centralian Advocate, Chronicle Australia, City North News Australia, Coffs Coast Advocate* (New South Wales), *Comment News Perth, Community Express, Cooloola Advertiser* (Queensland), *Coolum and North Shore News* (Queensland), *Countryman, Courier Mail, Cum-*

berland Newspapers Sydney, Daily Examiner (Grafton, New South Wales), *Daily Mercury and Rural Weekly* (Mackay, Queensland), *Daily Telegraph* (Australia), *Daily Telegraph and Telegraph Sydney, Darwin Palmerston Australia, Eastern Suburbs Reporter Perth, Echo* (Australia), *Fremantle Cockburn Gazette Perth, Gatton, Geelong Advertiser Victoria, Geelong News* (Free Suburban), *Gold Coast Publications, GT magazine, Guardian Express Perth, Gympie Times* (Queensland), *Herald* (Australia), *Herbert River Express, Hills Gazette Perth, Hobart Mercury* (Australia), *Home Hill Observer, Home Magazine Australia, Illawarra Mercury Australia, Inner West Courier, Innisfail Advocate, Ipswich News Queensland, Joondalup Times Wanneroo Perth, Kalgoorlie Miner, Leader Newspapers Melbourne, Lockyer and Brisbane Valley Star* (Queensland), *Mail Australia, Major Australian Newspapers, Mandurah Coastal Times Perth, Melville Times Perth, Mercury Tasmanian Australia, Messenger Newspapers Adelaide, Midland Kalamunda Reporter Perth, Morning Bulletin* (Rockhampton, Queensland), *MX, Newcastle Herald Australia, News Bites–Results, News-Mail and Rural Weekly* (Wide Bay, Bundaberg, Queensland), *North Coast Times Perth, Northern Miner, Northern Star and Rural Weekly* (New South Wales), *Northern Territory News Australia, Northside Courier, NT Business Review Australia, Observer* (Gladstone, Queensland), *Perth Communities Australia, Port Curtis Post* (Queensland), *Port Douglas and Mossman Gazette, Queensland Times* (Ipswich), *Quest Newspapers Brisbane, Range News* (Maleny, Queensland), *Rockhampton & Fitzroy News* (Queensland), *South Australia, South Burnett Times and Rural Weekly* (Queensland), *Southern Courier Australia, Southern Gazette Perth, Sportsman, Stanthorpe Border Post* (Queensland), *Stirling Times Perth, Sunday Herald* (Sydney), *Sunday Mail* (Queensland), *Sunday Territorian* (Australia), *Sunshine Coast* (Queensland), *Sydney Morning Herald Australia, Sydney MX, Tablelander, Tablelands Advertiser Australia, Tasmanian Country, Toowoomba's Mail* (Queensland), *Townsville Bulletin Townsville, TV Guide Australia, Tweed Daily News* (New South Wales), *Village Voice Balmain, WA Business News Australia, Wanneroo Times Perth, Warwick Daily News* (Queensland), *Weekend Australian, Weekend Courier Perth, Weekend Post Weekender Australia, Weekly Times, Wentworth Courier Australia, West Australian, Western Suburbs Weekly Perth, Whitsunday Times* (Airlie Beach, Queensland)

Austria: *Die Presse, Der Standard*

Bahrain: *Akhbar Al Khaleej, Al Ayam, Bahrain News Agency, Daily Tribune, Gulf Daily News*

Bangladesh: *Energy Bangla, Financial Express, New Nation, Weekly Blitz*

Belgium: *De Krant van West Vlaanderen, De Lloyd, De Tijd, Gazette of West Flanders, LEcho Belgium TE Briefing, TE Depeche*

Benin: *L'Autre Quotidien*

Bolivia: *La Razon, Los Tiempos Newspaper*

Bosnia: *B&H Business Daily, Bosnia Daily, Oslobodjenje, Poslovne Novosti*
Botswana: *Botswana Gazette News, Botswana Guardian News, Mmegi Daily*
Brazil: *A Notcia, AE Agronews, Agencia O Globo, Agncia IN Entrevista, Brasil
Economico, Brasilturis, Campinas Agncia Anhanguera de Notcias Correio
Popular, Daily Online–International, DCI Diario Comercio, Diario Ca-
tarinense, Diario de Santa Maria, Diario Gacho, Diario Grande ABC Sete-
cidades, Diario Online, Folhapress, Industria e Servicos, Jornal A Tarde
Bahia, Jornal Correio Braziliense, Jornal de Santa Catarina, Jornal do
Commercio, Jornal O Pioneiro, Jornal O Tempo, Jornal Pampulha, Meio
Mensagem, O Estado de S Paulo, Official Mail Braziliense, RAC Gazeta de
Piracicaba, Super Noticia, Valor Econmico, Zero Hora*
Bulgaria: *Banker Weekly, Capital, Dnevnik, Monitor Daily, Pari, Standart
Daily*
Burkina Faso: *Le Pays, L'Observateur Paalga, Sidwaya*
Cambodia: *Phnom Penh Post*
Cameroon: *Cameroon Tribune, Le Messager, Le Quotidien Mutations, Post*
Canada: *24 Hours* (Toronto), *Abbotsford Times British Columbia, Airdrie
Echo* (Alberta), *Alberni Valley Times British Columbia, Barrie Examiner*
(Ontario), *Belleville Intelligencer* (Ontario), *Brantford Expositor* (On-
tario), *Brockville Recorder and Times* (Ontario), *Calgary* (Alberta), *Cal-
gary Herald, Cambridge Reporter, Carstairs Courier Alberta, Chatham
Daily News* (Ontario), *Cochrane Times* (Alberta), *Collingwood Enterprise
Bulletin* (Ontario), *Cornwall Standard Freeholder* (Ontario), *Courier
Press* (Wallaceburg, Ontario), *Daily Gleaner New Brunswick, Daily
Herald-Tribune* (Grande Prairie, Alberta), *Daily Miner and News* (Ke-
nora, Ontario), *Edmonton* (Alberta), *Edmonton Journal, Financial Post
Investing, Fort McMurray Today* (Alberta), *Gazette Montreal, Globe and
Mail Canada, Guardian Charlottetown, Guelph Mercury, Halifax Daily
News, Hamilton Spectator, Hanover Post* (Ontario), *Kamloops Daily News
British Columbia, Kingston Whig-Standard* (Ontario), *Lawyers Weekly
News, Leader Post Regina, Lindsay Daily Post* (Ontario), *London Free
Press* (Ontario), *Melfort Journal* (Saskatchewan), *Nanaimo Daily News
British Columbia, National Post fka Financial Post, Nelson Daily News
British Columbia, Niagara Falls Review* (Ontario), *Nipawin Journal* (Sas-
katchewan), *North Bay Nugget* (Ontario), *North Shore News British Co-
lumbia, Northern News* (Kirkland Lake, Ontario), *Ontario Farmer* (Can-
ada), *Orillia Packet & Times* (Ontario), *Ottawa Citizen, Ottawa, Owen
Sound Times* (Ontario), *Pembroke Observer* (Ontario), *Peterborough Ex-
aminer* (Ontario), *Plastics News tm, Portage Daily Graphic* (Manitoba),
*Prince George Citizen British Columbia, Prince Rupert Daily News British
Columbia, Red Deer Express Alberta, Sarnia Observer* (Ontario), *Sault
Star* (Sault Saint Marie, Ontario), *Sherbrooke Record Quebec, Southam
Publishing Company, Southwest Booster Saskatchewan, St John's Telegram,
Star Phoenix Saskatoon, Telegraph Journal New Brunswick, Times Colonist*

Victoria, Times Transcript New Brunswick, Toronto Star, Vancouver, Waterloo Region Record, Western Standard Alberta, Windsor Star, Yukon News Yukon

Chile: *Copesa La Tercera, Diario Financiero, El Mercurio, Estrategia, La Nacion Newspaper, Santiago Times*

China: *21st Century Business Herald, CBN Daily, China Chemical Industry News, China Construction News, China Daily, China Education News, China Insurance News, China Knowledge News, China Nonferrous Metals News, China Petrochemical News, China Pharmaceutical News, China Railway Construction News, China Textile News, China Trade News, China Water Transport, Chinese Enterprises, Communications Industry Report, Communications News, Economic Information Daily News, Economic Observer, Education in China, International Business Daily, Investor Journal, MEB, National Power Grid Report, Shanghai Daily, South China Morning Post, State Grid News, Supermarket Weekly, China Insurance, China National Petroleum*

Colombia: *Diario El Espectador, El Tiempo, La Republica, Portafolio*

Congo Kinshasa: *Le Potentiel, La Prosperite*

Costa Rica: *Al Dia, El Financiero, La Nación*

Croatia: *Banka Prilozi, Jutarnji List, Poslovni Dnevnik, Privredni Vjesnik, Veernjihr, Vjesnik*

Cyprus: *Cyprus Mail, Financial Mirror*

Czech Republic: *Berounsky denik vyber zprav, Brnensky denik vyber zprav, Ceskobudejovicky denik vyber zprav, Dopravni noviny, E15, Euronews Euro Online, Hospodarske noviny, Hradecky denik vyber zprav, Jihlavsky denik, Karlovarsky denik vyber zprav, Liberecky denik vyber zprav, Lidove noviny, Mlada fronta Dnes, Moravskoslezsky denik vyber zprav, Olomoucky denik vyber zprav, Pardubicky denik vyber zprav, Plzensky denik vyber zprav, Pravo Vybrane rubriky, Prazsky denik vyber zprav, Sip vyber, Prague Post, Ustecky denik vyber zprav, Zlinsky denik digest*

Denmark: *Politiken, Politiken Weekly*

Ecuador: *Diario El Comercio, Diario El Financiero News, Diario El Universo, Diario Hoy*

Egypt: *Al Alam Al Youm, Al Gomhuriah, Al Messa, Al Seyassah, Al-Ahram, AmCham Egypt Tenders Alert Service, Daily News Egypt, Emirates News Agency, Le Progrès Egyptien, Nahdet Misr, Egyptian Gazette*

Estonia: *Baltic Business News Russian, Baltic Times*

Ethiopia: *Addis Fortune*

Fiji: *Fiji Times, Sunday Times*

Finland: *Kauppalehti*

France: *AFP RELAXNEWS, Aujourd'hui en France, Centre Presse, Charente Libre, Eastern Republican, InvestirJournal des Finances, Journal of Finance, L'Agefi Quotidien, L'Est Republicain, L'humanite, L'Indpendant, L'Yonne Republicaine, La Croix, La Montagne, La Nouvelle Republique du Centre*

Ouest, La Republique du Centre, La Tribune, La Voix du Nord, Le Berry
Republicain, Le Figaro, Le Havre Libre France, Le Journal du Centre, Le
Monde, Le Parisien, Le Populaire du Centre, Le Progress de Fecamp France,
Le Telegramme, Les Echos, Libration, Midi Libre, NA, New Republic Mid-
west, Ocean Press, Ouest France, Paris Normandie, Presse Ocean, Release,
Sud Ouest, Today in France

Gabon: *Infos Plus*

Gambia: *Daily Observer, FOROYAA Newspaper*

Georgia: *FINANCIAL, Georgia Today, Georgian Times, Messenger*

Germany: *Aachener Nachrichten, Aachener Zeitung, Aar Bote Germany,
Allgemeine Zeitung Germany, Berliner Kurier, Berliner Morgenpost, Ber-
liner Zeitung, Borstdter Zeitung Germany, Borsten-Zeitung, Central Ger-
man newspaper, Cologne Rundschau, Der Neue Kammerer, Der Tagesspie-
gel, Die Presse, die tageszeitung, Die Welt am Sonntag, Die Welt, Die ZEIT,
Duesseldorf Rheinische Post, Financial Times Deutschland, Frankfurter
Rundschau, Gazette Giessen Germany, Gelnhauser Tageblatt Germany,
General Anzeiger Bonn, Giessener Anzeiger Germany, haben, Hamburger
Abendblatt, HandelsZeitung, Hochheimer Zeitung Germany, Hofheimer
Zeitung Germany, Horizont, Idsteiner Zeitung Germany, Immobilien Zei-
tung Akll, In the Front, Indian J General, Jewish General, Judische Allgeme-
ine, Kolner Stadt Anzeiger, Kolnische Rundschau, Kreis Anzeiger Germany,
Lampertheimer Zeitung Germany, Lauterbacher Anzeiger Germany, Leb-
ensmittel Zeitung, Main Spitze Germany, Main Taunus Kurier Germany,
Mitteldeutsche Zeitung, Moneyclips Germany Stories, Oberhessische Zei-
tung Germany, Rheinische Post Duesseldorf, Sanktionen, SonntagsZeitung,
Stuttgarter Nachrichten, Stuttgarter Zeitung, Swisscontent Corp, Tages An-
zeiger, taz, Telecom Handel, Usinger Anzeiger Germany, Welt kompakt,
Wiesbadener Kurier Germany, Wiesbadener Tagblatt Germany, Wormser
Zeitung Germany*

Ghana: *Accra Mail, Ghanaian Chronicle*

Guatemala: *Noticias Financieras, Siglo Veintiuno*

Hungary: *Axel Springer Regionlis napilapok vlogats, Blikk, Delmagyarorszag,
Delvilag, Elet es Irodalom, Esztergomi Hdlap Selection, Hajd Bihari Napl,
Kelet Magyarorszg, Kisalfold, Lapcom Presztzs TOP 100, Magyar Hrlap,
Magyar Nemzet, Magyar Tkepiac, Metropol, Napi Gazdasg, Nepszava,
Npszabadsg, Pannon Lapok Trsasga Regionlis Napilapok vlogats, szak
Magyarorszg, Vasrnap reggel, Vasrnapi Blikk, Vci Napl, Vilaggazdasag,
World Economy*

India: *Accommodation Times Ht Media, Bharat Chronicle, Bihar Times India,
Business Today More, Columnists IndiaPak, Crest, DLA AM, DNA, DQ
Week, Early Times India, Economic Times, Financial Express, Frontier Post
Pakistan, Garhwal Post India, Health Daily Digest Ht Media, Herald Goa
India, Hindustan Times, Imphal Free Press India, Indian Express, IPR,
Kashmir Images India, Kashmir Monitor India, Kashmir Observer, Kash-*

mir Times, Mail Today, Medianama, MINT, Mirror Publications, New India Express, Northlines, Pioneer India, Political Business Daily India, Prevention, Siasat Daily India, Sikkim Express, South East Asian News India, Star of Mysore, Statesman India, Telegraph India, Times of India TOI, Today India Ht Media

Indonesia: *Jakarta Post*

Iran: *Iran News, Iranian Government News, Iranian Students News Agency, Mehr News Agency, Moj News Agency*

Iraq: *Al Rafidayn, Kurdish Globe, National Iraqi News Agency, Soma Digest*

Ireland: *Argus, Bray People, Carlow People, Corkman, Drogheda Independent, Dundalk Democrat, Enniscorthy Echo, Enniscorthy Guardian, Evening Herald Ireland, Fingal Independent, Gorey Echo, Gorey Guardian, Irish Examiner, Irish Independent, Irish News, Irish Post, Irish Times, Kerryman, Kilkenny People, Leitrim Observer, Limerick Leader, Longford Leader, Nationalist Munster Advertiser, New Ross Echo, New Ross Standard, Offaly Express, Sunday Business Post, Sunday Independent Ireland, Sunday Tribune, TCM Carlow Nationalist, TCM Down Democrat, TCM Kildare Nationalist, TCM Kingdom, TCM Laois Nationalist, TCM Newry Democrat, TCM Roscom Herald, TCM Sligo Weekender, TCM Waterford News Star, TCM Western People, TCM Wexford Echo, Tipperary Star, Wexford People, Wicklow People*

Israel: *Globes, Jerusalem Post*

Italy: *Corriere della Sera Italy, Il Giorno Italy, Il Resto del Carlino Italy, ItaliaOggi, La Gazzetta dello Sport Italy, La Nazione Italy, La Stampa, Milano Finanza*

Japan: *Daily Yomiuri Tokyo, Japan Times, Japanese World, Nikkei Weekly Japan*

Jordan: *Ad Dustour, Al Liwa, Al Watan, AmmanNet, Jordan Times, Shabab Shabab, Star*

Kazakhstan: *Business Daily Kapital, Caravan, Central Asia Monitor, Delovoi Kazakhstan, Express K, Gazeta Vremya, Juridicheskaja Gazeta, Kazakhstan Today, Kazakhstanskaia pravda, Kursiv, Liter, Megapolis, Novoe pokolenie, Panorama, Stroitel'nyj Vestnik, Vecherni Almaty, Zheleznodorozhnik Kazakhstana*

Kenya: *Africa Science, Business Daily, Coast Week, Daily Nation Kenya, FSD Kenya, IRIN, Nairobi Star, Nation*

Korea, South: *Korea Herald, Korea Times*

Kosovo: *KosovaLive News, Kosovapress News*

Kuwait: *Alam Alyawm, Al Seyassah, Arab Times, Kuwait News Agency, Kuwait Times*

Laos: *Thai News Service, Vientiane Times*

Latvia: *Baltic Business News Russian, Baltic Times, Dienas Business*

Lebanon: *Al-Akhbar, An-Nahar, As-Safir, Daily Star, Dar Al Hayat, Emirates*

News Agency, L' Orient-le Jour, Middle East Reporter, National News Agency Lebanon, tayyar.org

Liberia: *Analyst, Informer, Liberian Journal, New Democrat*

Libya: *Al Jamahiriya, MENA English Service, New Libya News, Tripoli Post*

Lithuania: *Baltic Business News Russian, Baltic Times*

Madagascar: *L'Express de Madagascar, Midi Madagasikara*

Malaysia: *Berita Harian, Business Times, Channel News Asia, Daily Star, Edge, Harian Metro, Malaysian Reserve, New Straits Times, NSTP Tech and U, SME News, South East Asian News, Star*

Mauritania: *Le Quotidien de Nouakchott*

Mauritius: *L'Express Port Louis*

Mexico: *Agencia EFE-Mexico, Andina-Newswire, APD-Political News, BAE-Last time, Bolsa Mexicana de Valores-Relevant Events, Cerigua-Daily News, Chronicle-Last Moment, Daily Delights, Diario de Juarez, Diario de Quertaro, Diario de Yucatan, Diario El Mundo, Diario La Hora, e-mid News, Ecos de Morelos La Unin de Morelos, El Diario de Chihuahua, El Diario de Delicias, El Diario de Nuevo Casas Grandes, El Diario de Parral, El Economista, El Financiero, El Mexicano, El Norte Newspaper, El Occidental, El Pais, El Panama America, El Sol de Mexico, El Sol de San Luis, El Sol Regional Newspapers, El Sudcaliforniano, El Universal, Excelsior, Express, High Level, Infocampo.com.ar-Agribusiness latest news, InformaBTL, Informational Efficiency, Infosel-News, intraday Scope, Journal Millennium City, La Cronica Diaria, La Jornada Newspaper, La Nacion, La Razon Newspaper, La Voz de la Frontera, Milenio Diario DF, Milenio, Ministry of Popular Power for Communication, Mural Newspaper, NA, Notimex, Observer-Newswire, Periodico AM, PGR-Press Releases, Post Digital-Business, Puntobiz-Companies, Radioprogramas of Peru, Reforma-Newspaper, Republic, Sun-Regional Newspapers, T21, Trade, ValorFuturo-Peru*

Morocco: *Agence Maghreb Arabe Presse, Agence Maghreb Arabe Presse, L'Economiste, L'Economiste, National Iraqi News Agency, National Iraqi News Agency*

Mozambique: *Agencia de Informacao de Mocambique*

Namibia: *Namibia Economist, Namibian, New Era*

Nepal: *Ekantipur, Himalayan Times, My Republica, Nepali Times*

Netherlands: *Agrarisch Dagblad, Algemeen Dagblad, Almere Vandaag, Alphencc, Amersfoortse Courant, BBC News, BN DeStem, Brabants Dagblad, Charleston Daily Mail Dutch Stories, Chicago Times Dutch Stories, Dag, Dagblad De Limburger, Dagblad De Pers, Dagblad Rivierenland, Dagblad van het Noorden, Dayton Daily News Dutch Stories, De Dordtenaar, De Gelderlander, De Gooi en Eemlander, De Stentor, De Telegraaf, De Twentse Courant Tubantia, De Volkskrant, Eindhovens Dagblad, Goudsche Courant, Groene Hart, Haagsche Courant, Haarlems Dagblad, Het Financieele Dagblad English, Het Financieele Dagblad, Het Parool, Ijmuider Courant,*

Leeuwarder Courant, Leidsch Dagblad, Limburgs Dagblad, Los Angeles Times Dutch Stories, Metro NL, Nederlands Dagblad, Noordhollands Dagblad, NRC Handelsblad, NRCNEXT, Pakblad, Provinciale Zeeuwse Courant, Reformatorisch Dagblad, Rivierenland, Rotterdams Dagblad, South China Morning Post Dutch Stories, Spits, Sportwereld Pro, Utrechts Nieuwsblad, Zeeland Provincial Courant

New Zealand: *Daily News New Plymouth, Dominion Wellington, Evening Post Wellington, Evening Standard Palmerston North, National Business Review New Zealand, Nelson Mail Nelson, New Zealand Herald, New Zealand Infotech Weekly Wellington, News Auckland, Press Christchurch, Southland Times New Zealand, Star Times Auckland, Timaru Herald, Truth Auckland, Waikato Times Hamilton*

Nigeria: *Leadership News, Vanguard Daily–Nigeria*

Oman: *Al Shabiba, businesstoday, Muscat Daily, Oman News Agency, Oman Today, SmartOman.com, Times of Oman, Week*

Pakistan: *Associated Press of Pakistan, Balochistan Times, Business Recorder, Daily Balochistan Express, Daily National Herald Tribune, Daily the Pak Banker, Daily Times, Education Watch Pakistan, Express Tribune, Financial Daily, Financial Post, Friday Times, Frontier Post, Frontier Star, Islamabad Dateline, Messenger, Nation, Pakistan Observer, Pakistan Today, Patriot, Regional Times, Right Vision News, Statesman, Sunday Times, Times Islamabad*

Papua New Guinea: *PNG Post-Courier, Weekend Courier*

Peru: *El Comercio*

Philippines: *Asia Times Online, Business World, Cebu Daily News, Freeman Newsletter, IT Matters Daily, Malaya, Manila Bulletin, Manila Standard Online, Manila Times, Media Corp News Asia, Philippine Daily Inquirer, Philippine Star News, Sun Star News*

Poland: *Codzienna Gazeta Nowiny, Dziennik Baltycki, Dziennik Gazeta Prawna, Dziennik Polski, Dziennik Wschodni, Dziennik Zachodni, Echo dnia, Express Ilustrowany, Gazeta Lubuska, Gazeta Polska, Gazeta Pomorska, Gazeta Wspolczesna, Gazeta Wyborcza, Gazetapl, Glos Koszalinski, Glos Pomorza, Glos Szczecinski, Journal Legal Newspaper, Kurier Poranny, Niezalezna Gazeta Internetowa, Nowa Trybuna Opolska, Nowe Zycie Gospodarcze, Parkiet, Polish News Bulletin, Puls Biznesu, Rzeczpospolita, Tygodnik Ostrolecki, Warsaw Business Journal, Warsaw Voice, Zycie Warszawy*

Qatar: *Al Raya, Gulf Times, Qatar Tribune, Peninsula*

Romania: *Adevarul, Cotidianul, Curentul, Economic Daily, Evenimentul Zilei, Jurnalul National, Nine Oclock, Romania Libera, Scholarships Newspaper, Ziarul BURSA, Ziarul Financiar*

Russia: *Air Transport, Altaiskaia pravda, Amurskaia pravda, Amurskii meridian, Argumenty Fakty, Argumenty i fakty Bashkortostan, Argumenty i fakty Mordoviia, Argumenty i fakty Samara, Astrakhanskaia pravda, Au-*

toreview, Birzha, Biznes i banki, Bogatei, Brianskaia uchitelskaia gazeta, Brianskii rabochii, Budni, Business Class, Chastnik, Cheliabinskii rabochii, Dagestanskaia pravda, Delovoe povolzhe, Delovoi Express Perm, Delovoi kvartal NNovgorod, Ekonomicheskii kurs, Ekonomika i vremia, Ekstra reklama, Evenkiiskaia zhyzn, Ezhednevnye novosti Podmoskovie PDF, Ezhednevnye novosti Podmoskovie, Finansovaia gazeta PDF file, Gazeta iuga, Grani, Gudok, Iakutiia, Iat, Ilken, Iuzhnyi federalnyi, Ivanovo Press, Ivanovo voznesensk, Ivanovskaia gazeta, Ivanovskaia zemlia, Izvestiia, Kaliningradskaia pravda, Karavan ros, Karelia, Karelskaia guberniia, Kazanskie vedomosti, Khakasiia, Khronometr, Kommercheskie vesti, Kommersant, Kommuna, Komsomolskaia pravda, Krasnaia zvezda, Krasnodarskie izvestiia, Krasnoiarskii rabochii, Krasnyi put, Krasnyi Sever, Kurer Karelii, Kurer, Kurgan i kurgantsy, Kursk, Kurskaia pravda, Kuzbass, Lipetskaia gazeta, Lipetskie izvestiia, Literaturnaia gazeta, Magadanskaia pravda, Mariiskaia pravda, Meditsinskaia gazeta, Miasskii rabochii, Mir novostei, MK Mobil, Moia informatsionnaia gazeta, Molodezh iakutii, Molodezh tatarstana, Molodezhnaia gazeta, Molodoi kommunar, Molodoi leninets, Moscow News in PDF, Moscow News, Moscow Times, Moskovskaia pravda, Moskovskii komsomolets, Narodnaia gazeta, Nedelia oblasti, Nedelia Podmoskovie, Nedelia v Podlipkakh, Nedvizhimost i stroitelstvo Peterburga, Nezavisimaia gazeta, Novaia gazeta, Novgorodskie vedomosti, Novye Izvestiia, Novyi mir, Omskii vestnik, Omskoe vremia, Orlovskii meridian, Orskaia khronika, Panorama okruga, Parlamentskaia gazeta, Perm Area Economics Press Digest, Perm Stock market, Petrovka,38, Poliarnaia pravda, Priamurskie vedomosti, Promyshlennyi ezhenedelnik, Prostory rossii, Pskovskaia gubernia, Rabochii krai, RBC daily, Rechnik Irtisha, Respublika molodaia, Respublika Tatarstan, Riazanskie vedomosti, Rossiiskaia biznes gazeta, Rossiiskaia gazeta, Rostov ofitsialnyi, Samarskaia gazeta, Selskaia zhizn, Sem verst, Severnyi krai, Shok, Simbirskie izvestiia, Simbirskii kurer, Smolenskie novosti, Sobesednik, Sovershenno Sekretno, Sovetskaia Chuvashia, St Petersburg Times, St Petersburg Vedomosti, Strana Kaliningrad, Svobodnyi kurs, Taimyr, Tambovskii meridian, TeRa press, Tikhookeanskaia zvezda, Tiumenskie izvestiia, Torgovaia gazeta, Transport Rossii, Tribuna, Trud, Tsentr Azii, Tulskie izvestiia, Tverskaia zhizn, Tverskaia,13, Ulianovsk segodnia, Uralskii avtomobil, Utro vechera mudrenee, Vash oreol, Vashe delo, Veche Tveri, Vecherniaia Kazan, Vecherniaia Moskva, Vecherniaia Riazan, Vechernii Ekaterinburg, Vechernii magadan, Vechernii Murmansk, Vechernii Novosibirsk, Vechernii Omsk, Vechernii Saransk, Vechernii Stavropol, Vedomosti, Versiia, Vesti St Petersburg, Viatskii krai, Vladimirskie vedomosti, Vladivostok, Voenno promyshlennyi kurier, Volga, Volkhonka, Volkhov, Vologodskie novosti, Voronezhskaia nedelia, Vostochno Sibirskaia pravda, Vremia i dengi, Yaik,

Yakutsk vechernii, Yuzhnyi ural, Zabaikalskii Rabochii, Zapoliarnaia pravda, Zolotoe koltso, Zolotoi Rog

Rwanda: *New Times*

Saudi Arabia: *Al Eqtisadiah, Al Riyadh, Arab News, Asharq Alawsat, Aswaq News, Majalla, Sabq News, Saudi Press Agency*

Senegal: *Le Soleil, Sud Quotidien, Wal Fadjri*

Sierra Leone: *Concord Times, Independent*

Singapore: *Business Times, Edge, South East Asian News, Straits Times, Today*

Slovak Republic: *Direction Today Magazine, Dnesok, Hospodarske noviny, Kosicky korzar vyber, Kysucke noviny, Liptov, Metro Manila Corsair* (select), *My Ziara, Nasa Orava, Nase Novosti, Nitrianske noviny, Noviny Juhozapadu, Novohradske noviny, Novy Cas, Novy Zivot Turca, Obzor, Plus jeden den vyber, Plus One Day* (select), *Prieboj, Rolnicke noviny vyber, SME, Smer Dnes Magazin, Trencianske noviny, Trnavske noviny, Tyzden na Pohroni, Tyzdennik pre Zahorie, Uj Szo vybrane clanky slovensky, Week at the Hron, wwwbratislavskenovinysk, Zilinske noviny, Zilinsky vecernik vyber, Zvolensko Podpolianske noviny*

Slovenia: *Delo, Dnevnik, Domus, Finance, Poslovni Dnevnik, Slovenia Times, Vecer, zalozba in trgovina doo Business Investment*

South Africa: *Algoa Sun, Business Day South Africa, Cape Argus Cape Town, Cape Times South Africa, Daily Dispatch South Africa, Daily News South Africa, Go Express, Herald South Africa, Independent South Africa, Mail Guardian, Mercury South Africa, Our Times, Post South Africa, Pretoria News, Representative, Sowetan South Africa, Star South Africa, Sunday Tribune South Africa, Sunday World South Africa, Talk of the Town, Times South Africa, Weekend Post, Weekender South Africa*

Spain: *ABC, Basque Journal, Cinco Dias, Diario Cordoba, Diario tanes, Diario Vasco, El Comercio, El Correo, El Mundo, El Norte de Castilla, El Pais, El Periodico de Aragon, El Periodico de Catalunya, El Periodico Extremadura, El Periodico Mediterraneo, Expansion Madrid, Hoy, Ideal, La Rioja, La Verdad, La Voz de Cadiz, Sur, tae Journal*

Sri Lanka: *Colombo Times, Daily Mirror, Daily News, Lanka Business Online News, Nation News*

Switzerland: *24 Heures, Appenzeller Zeitung, AWP SME Small and Medium Enterprises German, HandelsZeitung, La Tribune de Genve, Le Matin, Le Temps, NA, SonntagsZeitung, St. Galler Tagblatt, Swisscontent Corp, Tagblatt fur den Kanton Thurgau, Tages Anzeiger, Toggenburger Tagblatt*

Syria: *Syrian Arab News Agency*

Taiwan: *CENS Lighting, China Post, China Times, Commercial Times, Media Corp News Asia, South China Morning Post, Taiwan Economic News, Taiwan Export Express, Taiwan Furniture, Taiwan Hardware, Taiwan Machinery, Taiwan News, TTG Taiwan Autoparts*

Tanzania: *Arusha Times, Citizen*

Thailand: *Bangkok Post, Business Day Thailand, Nation Thailand*
Tunisia: *African Manager, Afrique Press, Agency Tunis, La Presse, Le Renouveau, Le Temps*
Turkey: *ANKA Gunluk Ekonomi Bulteni, Dunya Gazetesi Kobi, Dunya Iletisim, Ekonomik Cozum Gazetesi, Flight To Turkey, Gozlem Gazetesi, Haberturk, Hurriyet, Kobihaber, Kose Yazarlar, Made in Turkey, Milliyet, Radikal, Sabah Gazetesi, Turizm Gazetesi, Turkiye Gazetesi, Vatan Gazetesi, Zaman*
UAE: *7 Days, Al Ain Times, Al Ittihad, AlArabiya.net, Alaswaq.net, Alrroya, Andy McTiernan Property and Economy Bulletin, Business Traveller Middle East, Computer News Middle East, Emerging Markets Business Information News, Emirates News Agency, Gulf News, Khaleej Times, National, Sport360, UMCI News, XPRESS*
Uganda: *East African Business Week, New Vision, Monitor*
Ukraine: *Business Newspaper, Chas pik Newspaper, Delo, Delovaya stolitsa, Den, Ekonomicheskie izvestia, Investment Newspaper, Kommentarii Newspaper, Kommersant Ukrayina, Kreschatic newspaper, KYIV POST, Kyiv Weekly, Melitopolskie vedomosty News, ProVincia Newspaper, Rivne Newspaper, Rivne vechirne, Sevastopolski meridian, Ukraina moloda, Ukrainian Times, Uryadovy Kuryer News, Visti Pridneprovya Newspaper, Ytro newspaper, Zerkalo Nedeli*
United Kingdom: *ABC Magazine, Aberdeen Evening Express, Aberdeen Press and Journal, Abingdon Herald, Aca Today, Airdrie Coatbridge Advertiser, Andover Advertiser, Antrim times, Arbroath Herald, Argus, Arts Books Review, Ashbourne News Telegraph, Ashford Adscene, Asia Today, Asian Image, Bakewell Today, Ballyey Moyle Times, Ballymena Times, Baltic States Today, Banbridge Leader, Banbury Cake, Banbury Guardian, Barking Dagenham Post, Barry And District News, Basingstoke Gazette, Batley News, Bedfordshire on Sunday, Bedfordshire Times Citizen, Belfast News, Belfast Telegraph, Belper News, Berwick Advertiser, Berwickshire News East Lothian Herald, Beverley Guardian, Bexhill Observer, Bexley Times, Bicester Advertiser, Biggleswade Chronicle, Birmingham Evening Mail, Birmingham Post, Bishops Stortford Citizen, Blackmore Vale Magazine, Blackpool Citizen, Bognor/Chichester Midhurst Observers, Bolton News, Borehamwood Times, Boston Standard, Bourne Local, Bournemouth Echo, Bradford Telegraph and Argus, Braintree and Witham Times, Brechin Advertiser, Brentwood Gazette, Brentwood Weekly News, Bridgwater Mercury, Bridgwater Times, Bridlington Free Press, Bridport and Lyme Regis News, Brighouse Echo, Bromley Times, Bromsgrove Advertiser, Buchan Observer, Bucks Free Press, Bucks Herald, Burnham Highbridge Weekly News, Burnham Times, Burton Mail, Bury Free Press, Bury Times, Business, Business,7 UK, Buteman, Buxton Advertiser, Cambridge Evening News, Cambridge First, Cambs Times, Campaign Series, Canterbury Adscene, Carluke Lanark Gazette, Carmarthen Journal, Carrick Gazette,*

Carrick Times, Caterham Advertiser, Caterham Mirror, Central Asia This Week, Central Somerset Gazette, Cheadle Post and Times, Cheddar Valley Gazette, Chelmsford Weekly News, Chester Chronicle, Chichester Bognor Regis and Midhurst Petworth Observer, Chorley Citizen, City AM, Clacton and Frinton Gazette, Clevedon Mercury, Clitheroe Advertiser Times, Coleraine Times Series, Comet, Compact Traveller, Cornish Guardian, Cotswold Journal, Coulsdon and Purley Advertiser, Coventry Evening Telegraph, Craven Herald, Crawley News, Crawley Observer, Crewe Guardian, Croydon Advertiser, Croydon Guardian, Cumbernauld News Kilsyth Chronicle, Czech Republic This Week, Czech Republic Today, Daily Echo, Daily Mail and Mail on London, Daily Mail London, Daily Post Liverpool, Daily Record Mail, Daily Star, Daily Star, Daily Telegraph London, Dartford Messenger, Daventry Express, Deeside Piper Series, Derbyshire Times, Derry Journal, Dewsbury Reporter, Dinnington Guardian, Diss Express, DMNews, Docklands, Doncaster Free Press, Donegal Democrat, Donside Piper, Dorking Advertiser, Dorset Echo, Dover Express, Driffield Times, Droitwich Advertiser, Dromore Banbrige Leader, Dudley News, Dumfries Galloway Standard, Dundalk Democrat, Dunmow Broadcast, Ealing Times, East Anglian Daily Times, East Herts Herald, East Kent Gazette, East Kent Mercury, East London Advertiser, East Lothian News Series, Eastbourne Herald, Eastern Daily Press, Echo NewsQuest, Edinburgh News, Ellon Times, Ely Standard, Enfield Independent, England, Epping Sawbridgeworth Star, Epsom Guardian, Esk Valley Today, Essex Chronicle, Essex County Standard, Essex, European, EuroWeek, Evening Chronicle Newcastle, Evening Gazette, Evening News Norwich, Evening Standard London, Evening Star, Evening Times Glasgow, Evesham Journal, Express, Falkirk Herald, Falmouth Packet, Faversham Times, Fenland Citizen, Fife Free Press, FILEY, Financial Times, Focus, Folkstone Herald, Forester, Forfar Dispatch Kirriemuir Herald, Fosse Way Magazine, Fraserburgh Herald, Free Press Series, Frome and Somerset Standard, Future News Media Planner, Gainsborough Standard, Galloway Gazette, Garstang Courier, Gateshead Post UK, Gazette Blackpool, Gazette Essex, Gazette Series, Glasgow East News, Goole, Grantham Journal, Gravesend Messenger, Gravesend Reporter, Great Barr Observer, Guardian London, Guide and Gazette, Hackney Gazette, Halesowen News, Halifax Courier, Halstead Gazette, Hampshire Chronicle, Hampstead and Highgate Express Ham and High, Harborough Mail, Haringey Independent, Harlow Herald, Harlow, Harrogate Advertiser, Harrow Times, Hartlepool Mail, Harwich and Manningtree Standard, Hastings St Leonards Observer, Haverhill Echo, Havering Post, Hawick News Scottish Border Chronicle, Hayling Islander, Hebden Bridge Times, Hemel Gazette, Hemsworth South Elmsall Express, Hendon Times, Herald Glasgow, Herald Post UK, Herald, Hereford Times, Herne Bay Times, Hertfordshire Mercury, Herts Advertiser, Herts Essex Observer, Hillingdon Times, Horley Mirror, Horncastle News, Hounslow Guardian,

Hucknall Dispatch, Huddersfield Daily Examiner, Hunts Post, Hutton Cranswick, Hythe Herald, i Independent Print Ltd, Ilkeston Advertiser, Illford Recorder, Independent London, IntelliNews Reports ,from ISI Emerging Markets, Inverurie Herald, Irish News, Isle of Thanet Gazette, Islington Gazette Archant, ITN, Journal Newcastle, Keighley News, Kenilworth Weekly News, Kent and Sussex Courier, Kent Messenger, Kentish Express, Kentish Gazette, Kidderminster Shuttle, Kilkenny People, Kincardineshire Observer, Kingston Guardian, Kirkintilloch Bishopbriggs Herald, Knutsford Guardian, Lakeland Echo, Lancashire Evening Post, Lancashire Telegraph, Lancaster and Morecambe Citizen, Lancaster Guardian, Larne Times, LB News, Leamington Spa Courier, Leatherhead Advertiser, Ledbury Reporter, Leeds Weekly News, Leek Post and Times, Leigh Journal, Leighton Buzzard Observer, Leinster Express, Leinster Leader, Leitrim Observer, Leyland Guardian, Lichfield Mercury, Life, Limerick Leader, Lincolnshire Echo, Linlithgowshire Journal Gazette, Liverpool Echo, Llanelli Star, London Lite, Londonderry Sentinel, Longford Leader, Longridge News, Loughborough Echo, Louth Leader, Ludlow Advertiser, Lurgan Mail, Luton On, Luton Today, Lynn News and Advertiser, Maidstone Adscene, Mail on Sunday, Mail, Maldon and Burnham Standard, Malton Pickering Mercury, Malvern Gazette, Manchester Evening News, Manchester Guardian, Mansfield Chad Series, Market Rasen Mail, Matlock Mercury, Mearns Leader, Medway AdScene, Medway Messenger, Medway News, Medway Standard, Melton Times, Mercury, Messenger Newspapers, Messenger, Metro UK, Mid Devon Star, Mid Sussex Times, Mid Ulster Mail Series, Middlesbrough Evening Gazette, Middlewich Guardian, Midhurst and Petworth observer, Midland Independent Newspapers, Midlothian Advertiser, Milford Mercury, Milngavie Bearsden Herald, Milton Keynes Citizen, Mirror, MK News, Montrose Review, Morecambe Visitor, Morley Observer Advertiser, Morning Star, Morpeth Herald, Motherwell Times Bellshill Speaker, NA, Nafferton Today, Nationalist Munster Advertiser, New Addington Advertiser, New Review, Newham Recorder, Newmarket Journal, News Guardian Group, News of the World, News Post Leader, News Shopper, News, Newtownabbey, Normberland Gazette, North London Journal, North West London Times, Northampton Chronicle Echo, Northants Evening Telegraph, Northern Echo, Northwest Tabloid, Northwich Guardian, Nuneaton News, Observer, Oxford Mail, Oxford Times, Paisley Daily Express, Paisley Renfrew Extra, Pembrokeshire Farmer, Penarth Times, People, Peterborough Evening Telegraph, Peterlee Mail, Petersfield Post, Pink, Pocklington Post, Pontefract Castleford Express, Portadown Times, Prestwich and Whitefield Guide, Racing Post, Redditch Advertiser, Redhill And Reigate Life, Regional Independent Media, Reigate Mirror, Retford Guardian, Retford Times Series, Richmond and Twickenham Times, Ripley Heanor News, Robin Hoods Bay Today, Romford Recorder, Romney Marsh Herald, Romsey Advertiser, Royston Crow, Rugby Advertiser, Runcorn and Widnes

World, Rye Battle Observer, Saffron Walden Reporter, Salisbury Journal, Scarborough Evening News, Scotland on Sunday, Scotsman, Scotsman, Scottish Business Insider, Scottish Express, Scottish Farmer, Scottish Star, Selby Times, Selkirk Advertiser, Sheerness Times Guardian, Sheffield Telegraph, Sheppey Gazette, Shepton Mallet Journal, Shields Gazette, Sittingbourne and Seppey Adscene, Skegness Standard, Sleaford Standard, Sleights Today, Smallholder, Solihull News, Somerset County Gazette, Somerset Guardian, South Wales Argus, South Wales Echo, South Wales Guardian, South West Farmer, South Yorkshire times, Southern Reporter, Spalding Guardian Lincolnshire Free Press, Spenborough Guardian, Sports Argus, St Helens Star, Staffordshire Newsletter, Stage, Staines Guardian, Staithes Hinderwell Today, Stamford Mercury, Star Sheffield, Stirling Observer, Stornoway Gazette West Coast Advertiser, Stourbridge News, Streatham Guardian, Stroud News and Journal, Suffolk Free Press, Sun, Sunday Herald, Sunday Life, Sunday Mercury, Sunderland Echo, Surrey Mirror, Sussex Express County Herald Series, Sutton Advertiser, Sutton Guardian, Sutton Observer, Swindon Advertiser, Tamworth Herald, Tandridge Mirror, Target series, Tewkesbury Admag, Thame Today, Thanet AdScene, Thanet Extra, Thanet Times, This is Local London, Thorne and District Gazette, Thorne Howden Courier, Thurrock Gazette, Times London, Tivyside Advertiser, Todmorden News, Tyrone Times, UK Newsquest Regional Press This is Black Country, UK Newsquest Regional Press This is Bradford, UK Newsquest Regional Press This is Brighton and Hove, UK Newsquest Regional Press This is Buckinghamshire, UK Newsquest Regional Press This is Cheshire, UK Newsquest Regional Press This is Cotswold, UK Newsquest Regional Press This is Dorset, UK Newsquest Regional Press This is Eastbourne, UK Newsquest Regional Press This is Essex, UK Newsquest Regional Press This is Gwent, UK Newsquest Regional Press This is Hampshire, UK Newsquest Regional Press This is Herefordshire, UK Newsquest Regional Press This is Hertfordshire, UK Newsquest Regional Press This is Lake District, UK Newsquest Regional Press This is Lancashire, UK Newsquest Regional Press This is Local London, UK Newsquest Regional Press This is Ludlow, UK Newsquest Regional Press This is Mid Sussex, UK Newsquest Regional Press This is North East, UK Newsquest Regional Press This is Oxfordshire, UK Newsquest Regional Press This is Ryedale, UK Newsquest Regional Press This is Stratford Upon Avon, UK Newsquest Regional Press This is Trafford, UK Newsquest Regional Press This is West Country, UK Newsquest Regional Press This is Wiltshire, UK Newsquest Regional Press This is Wirral, UK Newsquest Regional Press This is Worcestershire, UK Newsquest Regional Press This is Worthing, UK Newsquest Regional Press This is York, UK, UK, Ulster Star, Uttoxeter Advertiser, Uttoxeter Post and Times, Wakefield Express, Wales on Sunday, Walsall Advertiser, Wandsworth Guardian, Warrington Guardian, Watford Observer, Wells Journal, Welwyn Hatfield Times, West Briton, West Sussex County Times,

West Sussex Gazette, Western Gazette series, Western Mail, Western Tele-
graph, Westmorland Gazette, Weston and Worle News, Wharfedale Ob-
server, Whitby Gazette, Whitstable Times, Wigan Today, Wilts and
Gloucestershire Standard, Wiltshire Gazette and Herald, Wiltshire Times,
Wimbledon Guardian, Winsford Guardian, Wirral Globe, Wishaw Press,
Witney Gazette, Worcester News, Worksop Guardian, Worthing Herald,
Yeovil Express, York Press, Yorkshire Post, Your Leek Paper, Your Local
Guardian

United States: *Advertising Age, Advocate Baton Rouge Louisiana, Alameda
Times Star Alameda, Alamogordo Daily News New Mexico, American
Banker, Anchorage Daily News, Argus Fret, Arizona Capitol Times, Arkan-
sas Democrat Gazette, Atlanta Journal and Constitution, Augusta Chroni-
cle, Austin American Statesman, Automotive News, Baltimore Sun, Bangor
Daily News Maine, Banner Bernice, Bay City Times Michigan, Bedford
Journal, Berkshire Eagle Pittsfield, Birmingham News Alabama, Bismarck
Tribune, Bluff Country Reader Spring Valley, Bond Buyer, Bonney Lake,
Boomerang Palouse, Brattleboro Reformer Vert, Buffalo News, Business In-
surance, Cabinet Milford, California Energy Climate Report, California,
California, Capital Annapolis, Capital Times Madison, Cardiology News,
Chapel Hill Herald, Charleston Daily Mail, Charleston Gazette, Chatfield
News Minnesota, Chattanooga Times Free Press Tennessee, Chicago Daily
Herald, Chicago Times, Chico Enterprise Record California, Christian Sci-
ence Monitor, Chronicle of Higher Education, Chronicle of Philanthropy,
City Pages Minneapolis-St Paul, CityBusiness North Shore Report New Or-
leans, Clatskanie Chief Oregon, Clinical Endocrinology News, Clinical
Neurology News, Clinical Psychiatry News, Clovis Livestock Market News,
Colorado Springs Business Journal Colorado Springs, Columbia Star South
Carolina, Columbian Vancouver, Conexion, CongressNow, Connecticut
Post Online, Contra Costa Times, Crains Cleveland Business, Crains De-
troit Business, Daily Deal, Daily Journal of Commerce Portland, Daily
News New York, Daily News of Los Angeles, Daily Record Baltimore, Daily
Record of Rochester, Daily Reporter Milwaukee, Daily Review Hayward,
Daily Variety, Dallas Morning News, Dallas Observer Texas, Dayton Daily
News, De Baca County News, Delhi Express California, Deming Headlight
New Mexico, Denver Post, Denver Westword Colorado, Deseret Morning
News Salt Lake City, Digital Archives, DMNews, Dodge County Indepen-
dent News, Dolans Virginia Business Observer Norfolk, East Bay Express
California, Eastern Express Times Pennsylvania, Edds Beacon Washington,
Education Week, El Nuevo Dia Puerto Rico, El Paso Times Texas, Enter-
prise Record Chico, Enumclaw Courier Herald Washington, Eureka Times
Standard California, Evening Sun, Fairbanks Daily News Miner Alaska,
Family Practice News, Farmington Daily Times New Mexico, Feather River
Bulletin Quincy, Finance Commerce Minneapolis, Flint Journal Michigan,
Florida Times Union, Forward, Free Press, Fresno Bee, Gloucester County*

Times New Jersey, Grand Rapid Press Michigan, Hartford Courant, Haxtun Fleming Herald Colorado, Herald News Passaic County, Herald Rock Hill, Hill, Hollis Brookline Journal, Hollywood Reporter, Holmes County Herald, Home Textiles Today, Hospitalist News, Houston Chronicle, Houston Press Texas, Huntsville Times Alabama, Idaho Business Review Boise, Idaho Falls Post Register, Illinois Legal Times, Indianapolis Business Journal, Inland Valley Daily Bulletin Ontario, Inside Bay Area California, Intelligencer Journal, Internal Medicine News, Investors Business Daily, Iowa, Island Packet, Ivanhoe Times Minnesota, Jackson Citizen Patriot Michigan, Jersey Journal New Jersey, Journal of Jefferson Parish Louisiana, Journal Record Legislative Report Oklahoma City, Journal Record Oklahoma City, Kalamazoo Gazette Michigan, Kansas City Daily Record Kansas City, La Opinion, LA Weekly, Lake Tapps Courier Herald, Las Cruces News New Mexico, Las Vegas Review Journal, Latah Eagle, Lawyers USA, Lebanon Daily News Pennsylvania, Ledger Lakeland, Legal Ledger St. Paul MN, Lewiston Morning Tribune, Lincoln Journal Star Nebraska, Long Beach Press Telegram Long Beach, Long Island Business News Long Island, Los Angeles Times, Louisiana, Lowell Sun Lowell, MabelHary News Record Minnesota, Maine, Marin Independent Journal Marin, Maryland Gazette, Massachusetts Lawyers Weekly, Mattawa Area News Washington, McClatchy Tribune Business News Most Recent,2 Weeks, McClatchy Washington Bureau, McKenzie River Reflections McKenzie Bridge, Mecklenburg Times Charlotte, Medical Device Daily, Merced Star California, Merrimack Journal New Hampshire, Metropolitan Corporate Counsel, Metropolitan News Enterprise, Miami New Times Florida, Michigan Lawyers Weekly, Minneapolis Star Tribune, Minnesota Lawyer Minneapolis MN, Mississippi Business Journal Jackson, Mississippi Press, Missouri Lawyers Media, Missouri, Mobile Register Alabama, Modesto Bee, Monterey County Herald CA, Morning Call Allentown, Mukilteo Beacon Washington, Muskegon Chronicle Michigan, Network World Biographical Stories, New Hampshire, New Orleans CityBusiness New Orleans, New Times Broward Palm Beach Florida, New York Observer, New York Post, New York Times, New York, News and Observer, News Lancaster Pennsylvania, News Lancaster, News Tribune Tacoma, Newsday New York, North Carolina Lawyers Weekly, Oakland Tribune Oakland, ObGyn News, OC Weekly, Oklahoman, Omaha World Herald, Orange County Register, Oregon, Oregonian Portland Oregon, Original Irregular Kingfield, Oroville Mercury Register California, Palm Beach Post, Pantagraph, Pasadena Star News Pasadena, Patriot Ledger, Patriot News Harrisburg Pennsylvania, Pediatric News, Pennsylvania, Pensions and Investments, Philadelphia Daily News PA, Philadelphia Inquirer, Phoenix New Times Arizona, Pittsburgh Post Gazette, Pittsburgh Tribune Review, Plain Dealer Cleveland OH, Plastics News tm, Portland Press Herald, Post and Courier Charleston SC, Post Standard Syracuse NY, Providence Journal Bulletin, Public Opinion Chambersburg, Pueblo Busi-

ness Journal, Raleigh Extra, Raton Range New Mexico, Record Bergen County, Republican Leader Preston, Republican Springfield Massachusetts, Rheumatology News, Rhode Island Lawyers Weekly, Richmond Times Dispatch, Riverfront Times St. Louis, Roanoke Times Virginia, Rochester, Roll Call, Rubber Plastics News, Ruidoso News New Mexico, Sacramento Bee, Saginaw News Michigan, Salt Lake Tribune, San Antonio Express News, San Bernardino San Bernardino, San Francisco Chronicle, San Gabriel Valley Tribune San Gabriel Valley, San Jose Mercury News California, San Mateo County Times San Mateo, Santa Fe New Mexican, Sarasota Herald Tribune, Seattle Post Intelligencer, Seattle Weekly, Sentinel Enterprise Fitchburg, SF Weekly California, Silver City News New Mexico, Sioux County Index Reporter Hull, Skin Allergy News, South Bend Tribune, South Carolina Lawyers Weekly, Spokesman Review, Sporting News, Spring Grove Herald Minnesota, Spring Valley Tribune Minnesota, SqueezeOC, St. Charles County Business Record St. Charles, St. Louis Countian St. Louis, St. Louis Daily Record, St. Louis Post Dispatch, St. Paul Pioneer Press Minnesota, St. Petersburg Times, Star Ledger Newark New Jersey, Star News Wilmington, Star Tribune Minneapolis MN, State Journal Register Springfield, Staten Island Advance New York, Tampa Tribune, Taos News, Telegram Gazette Massachusetts, Telegraph Herald Dubuque, Times of Trenton New Jersey, Times Picayune New Orleans, Times Union Albany, Tire Business, Today's Beam New Jersey, Topeka Capital Journal, Tri City Herald, Tri Valley Herald Pleasanton, Tribune Review, Trinidad Times Independent Colorado, Tulsa World, Union Leader, USA Today, Vallejo Times Herald California, Variety, Vida en el Valle Spanish Language, Village Voice, Virginia Lawyers Weekly, Virginian Pilot Norfolk, Wall Street Journal, Washington Post, Washington Times, Washington, Washington, Westbrook Sentinel Tribune Minnesota, Whittier Daily News California, Winston Salem Journal North Carolina, Wisconsin State Journal, Wyoming Tribune Eagle, York Dispatch York

Uruguay: *Diario El Pais, El Observador*
Venezuela: *Cadena Global National News, Diario El Nacional, El Universal*
Vietnam: *Vian Macroeconomic News, Vietnam Business Forum News, Vietnam Industry News, Viet Nam News*
Yemen: *Al Sahwa, Yemen News Agency, Yemen Observer, Yemen Post, Yemen Times*
Zambia: *Times of Zambia*
Zimbabwe: *Financial Gazette, Herald, Zimbabwe Independent, Zimbabwe Standard*

7

Coalition Stories: Cases from the Iraq Coalition

In the preceding empirical chapters we found consistent evidence that partisan opposition and media access play important roles in a wide variety of conflict behaviors, ranging from initiation, to reciprocation, to coalition formation. These patterns consistently track our theoretical expectations. That said, aggregate empirical analyses are better suited to identifying general relationships rather than tracing the nuances of causal processes in action. Consequently, however robust our empirical findings thus far—and the sheer variety of tests all pointing to the same conclusion are compelling—they remain subject to the critique that they might possibly arise from some omitted but consistently correlated mechanism or a misidentification of the true causal relationships. This is particularly true given that the nature of our inquiry means that opportunities for quasi-experimental treatments or truly exogenous (but sufficiently powerful) instrumental variables are unlikely to arise.

To better elucidate the causal processes behind out findings, we turn to qualitative analyses of four countries' decisions to either join or forego joining the 2003 coalition against Iraq. This is, of course, the same policy decision that we explored in one of the aggregate analyses presented in chapter 5. Digging more deeply into the stories behind these decisions, however, allows us to better balance generalizability and causality. Our general tests (particularly the cross-national, time-series analyses in chapters 3 and 4) are ideal for identifying systematic relationships between our proposed ingredients for democratic constraint and actual conflict behavior, but are relatively less well suited to rooting out the underlying mechanisms driving the observed relationships. The case studies that we undertake here better address causal identification and the data-generating mechanism, but are inevitably less generalizable. However, when taken together, the evidence converges on our contention that it takes both robust opposition and well-functioning media institutions to constrain executive preferences over foreign policy.

CASE SELECTION

This chapter presents examples of (and exceptions to) our theory of democratic constraint. That said, there is no perfect example that illustrates every facet of our argument. Each country we profile presents elements of our theory combined with its own idiosyncrasies that influence the interplay among partisan opposition, media, and information. The point is that the aggregate findings elucidate broad patterns (chapter 5) or long-standing trends (chapters 3 and 4). But case studies, even with their deficiencies and limitations, can provide additional insight into how and why these trends emerge.

Given the lack of "smoking gun" examples, case selection becomes critical. To facilitate comparison, we limit ourselves to Europe so as to hold constant the possible effects of regional distinctions or vast differences in development or regime type that might disproportionately influence the key relationships in a particular case. Moreover, it only makes sense to assess countries that plausibly could have joined the coalition, a condition that holds throughout much of Europe given the continent's relative wealth and close strategic, economic, and cultural ties with the United States.

In addition, we have attempted to select cases that vary meaningfully on the dimensions that we argue are key to democratic constraint: partisan opposition and a robust and accessible media. The conditional nature of this argument means that we anticipate that when either (or both) of these conditions is lacking, it will be possible for leaders to discount public opinion and pursue their independent policy preferences, if they have them. Only when both are present will public opinion truly constrain leaders. Table 7.1 locates our cases, in relative terms, along these two key structural dimensions: opposition and media access.[1]

Due to its centrality in the war on Iraq, we turn first to the United Kingdom as a relatively low-opposition state with high access that, as our theory would anticipate, joined the coalition. The United Kingdom has a history with the United States unlike any other.[2] The ties of heritage, language, politics, and common values have led to a "special relationship" that arguably reached its post–World War II zenith in the lead-up to the Iraq War, first through Prime Minister Tony Blair's close personal relationship with Bill Clinton and subsequently through his similarly intimate relationship with George W. Bush. Blair aligned himself with the United States to strengthen Britain's position in the world, to become a trusted second to the one remaining superpower and, he asserted, to end the dictatorship of Saddam Hussein and restore Iraq to its peo-

---

[1] Focusing on Europe, while helpful in many ways, comes at the cost of limiting variation in media access, as virtually all European nations exceed the global average on this dimension. Consequently, while our cases vary widely in their party systems, in terms of media access, they range from moderate (less than a standard deviation above the global mean) to high (more than a standard deviation above the mean).

[2] Russett (1963).

Table 7.1. Distribution of Cases on Key Structural Dimensions

| | | Media Access | |
		Low/Moderate[a]	High[b]
Opposition	Low[c]	Spain	UK
	High[d]	Poland	Germany

[a]Less than one standard deviation above global mean
[b]More than one standard deviation above global mean
[c]ENPP < 3
[d]ENPP > 3

ple. However, to the extent the US- and UK-led coalition ultimately achieved these goals—a hotly contested assertion in its own right—it did so in the face of fierce opposition among the British electorate and even within Blair's own party.

This raises an important point that our aggregate analyses cannot address. The core elements of our theory that focus on electoral and media institutions describe circumstances that provide an *opportunity* for heads of states to diverge from public preferences in foreign policy. However, leaders are unlikely to exploit this opportunity absent some *motive* to do so. Our aggregate analyses, by their nature, smooth out this distinction because the systematic variation on opportunity alone is enough to produce an aggregate pattern of unconstrained leaders behaving differently, on average, from constrained ones. However, in practice, leaders, even when unconstrained, will buck public opinion only when they expect to gain some personal, strategic, or political advantage by doing so. This is because even when the institutional and political climate combine to minimize democratic constraint, capitalizing on the loosening of one's political shackles carries its own political risks. After all, even an *ex ante* unconstrained leader can face *ex post* political punishment at home for a policy failure abroad.[3]

The case of the British role in Iraq bears this out. Blair's political decline and the eventual return of the Conservatives to power were both tinged with references to the Iraq "debacle." Observers noted that "Iraq, and Iraq only . . . defines Blair. . . . [T]he conventional wisdom in Britain [is] . . . that he and his government tweaked and twisted weak intelligence in order to strengthen their case for going to war on grounds that were dubious and possibly illegal under

[3] Baum (2004a); Bueno de Mesquita and Siverson (1995).

international law."[4] Many observers recognized at the time that though Blair was able to buck public opinion on Iraq, doing so was enormously costly. The *New York Times* noted that "New Labour falls into two halves: pre- and post-Iraq, . . . Iraq destroyed a lot of trust with the voters."[5] Though Mr. Blair won the election in 2005, he won just 35 percent of the vote and was eventually ousted in 2007 over these same concerns about his handling of Iraq. Nor did the costs end there. The Conservatives used Iraq as an issue in their successful 2010 campaign, threatening to reopen inquiries and re-releasing Blair's March 18, 2003 video right before the election. However, because the Conservatives had advocated joining the coalition, they did not push the issue too hard. Instead, it was the Liberal Democrats who arguably benefitted most, and Nick Clegg nearly became prime minister because of that point of Conservative weakness.[6]

The key question for us, however, was how Blair was able to prioritize his objectives over strong public opposition, elite criticism, and even dissent within his own party. We argue that part of the answer lies in the particular institutional structures of the UK system, which features relatively few parties and a correspondingly compliant media. In addition, it turns out that the specific set of contemporaneous circumstances that Blair faced, combined with his significant strategic aptitude, were also important because they allowed him to exploit these institutional opportunities. Blair had media savvy far beyond that of the other leaders profiled here, and his party won reelection in the midst of large-scale controversy over Britain's involvement in Iraq. Though he faced opposition from within his own party, he had the support of the main opposition party, giving him enough parliamentary votes to win approval to join the coalition against Iraq.

The key insight is that the macro-scale institutional features we highlight in the aggregate empirical analyses in chapters 3 to 5 can influence the probability that public opinion will constrain a given leader to a greater or lesser degree, but they cannot be determinative. This illustrates the extent to which systems that are structurally low or high in political opposition (that is, those tending to have many or few parties) do nonetheless vary internally over time on this dimension. The short-term circumstances must be right, and leaders must choose to take advantage of these circumstances. But such opportunities to buck public opinion are systematically more likely to arise in states with the electoral and media features that we identify than in states lacking them.

---

[4] http://www.newsweek.com/tony-blairs-fall-grace-75237 (accessed June 15, 2004). This sentiment is echoed throughout the British media analyses of these events. "For some he is the disgraced leader who misled parliament and plunged the country into an illegal war; for others he remains that tantalizing figure of a great reforming prime minister whose early potential was consumed by Iraq" (Fairweather 2011).

[5] Castle (2010).

[6] The Spanish case shares this same attribute. There were eventually electoral consequences for the decision to join an unpopular coalition.

Next we assess Spain as a European state that differs substantially from the United Kingdom with regard to wealth, political history, and its relationship with the United States. Spain presents an interesting contrast as a relatively young democracy with a history of political patronage in the press. At the same time, its population has somewhat lower levels of media access when compared to the rest of Europe. It also had a relatively low-opposition party system in 2003, when compared with the global mean.

Despite these differences between Spain and the United Kingdom, however, our theory predicts that there should be similarities in the extent to which the executive is shielded from public opinion in foreign policy making. That is, given the relative weakness of access and opposition, our theory leads us to anticipate that Spanish leaders would also be in a position to contribute troops to the coalition of the willing should they be so inclined. In fact, this was indeed the case. Spain, despite having arguably the most antiwar electorate in Europe, had at that time a powerful ruling majority party with a charismatic leader, José María Aznar, who saw an opportunity to use foreign policy engagement to stake out a hawkish position on domestic terrorism, potentially creating a legacy of support for his party for years to come.

Spanish support, however, collapsed in the face of a terrorist attack just prior to the 2004 election, badly undermining Aznar's political strategy, restoring the opposition, and culminating in a hasty departure from Iraq. As was true in the UK example, insulation from democratic constraint can buy a leader time and space to make and pursue unpopular foreign policies, but it is not a free pass. If the conflict drags on, goes poorly, and remains unpopular, the political costs will mount.[7] Moreover, while fleeting political circumstances can result in momentary constraint in relatively low-party/low-access systems and a lack thereof in relatively high-party/high-access systems, our aggregate analyses indicate that the broader trends tend to result in a reversion to the mean over the long term.

We next assess Poland as an example of a high-opposition and moderate media access state. The conditional nature of our argument again suggests that leaders in a state with this institutional arrangement would be well situated to join the coalition, and indeed that is what happened. Even with opposition in a position to blow the whistle, without sufficient media access the public will not reliably hear it. Interestingly, as the Polish case demonstrates, when the information transmission mechanisms are limited, there is little reason for the opposition to object since it will not likely result in electoral gain. Thus in Poland we see a surprisingly compliant opposition (considering their size and diversity) when it comes to Iraq,

While public opposition to the war in Iraq was more muted in Poland than in Western Europe, at no point did a majority of Poles support the conflict. In

---

[7] This "catching up" process is the key insight of figure 2.3 and the accompanying discussion in chapter 2.

December 2002 fewer than 15 percent of Polish citizens supported unilateral action by the United States against Iraq.[8] Another relevant, albeit somewhat idiosyncratic, attribute of this case is the recent political history surrounding the end of the Cold War. Political elites in Poland strongly prioritized the relationship with the United States—the nation's comparatively numerous parties were in relative agreement on this point—and saw Iraq as an opportunity to strengthen strategic relations, particularly given Poland's emerging role in NATO. The media were poorly positioned to contest that decision. As we noted in chapter 3, the end of the Cold War led to an influx of democracies into the international system. But in many of these states, robust, independent, and accessible media lagged. This was certainly the case in Poland, and the legacy of this lag is media institutions that are tightly linked to elite preferences and, by extension, a relatively politically unengaged and compliant populace. Thus, as Radziszewski and Wolfe note, "Polish leaders pursued a policy that contradicted public preferences because the political costs of doing so were minimal in comparison to the benefits they believed the policy was likely to deliver."[9]

Finally, we assess Germany as an example of a high-party system with high media access, which our theory suggests would be particularly unlikely to be able to buck domestic public opinion. That prediction holds true, as German public opinion strongly opposed joining the US-led coalition in Iraq and German leadership never seriously considered doing so. One interesting element of this relationship is the extent to which systems such as this disincentivize divergence from public opinion. While the institutional structure in Germany provided no opportunity for leaders to turn a blind eye to public opinion and join the coalition, there is also no meaningful evidence that they ever wanted to do so. In such a political environment, leaders' preferences (and the actual leaders who are selected to begin with) become much more aligned with public preferences, meaning that the presence of constraint often coincides with electoral outcomes, thereby ensuring that there is little need for it.

Together, these four cases illustrate the extent to which electoral and media institutions play an important role in the timing and extent of democratic constraint. They also usefully demonstrate the limitations of our argument, which we will address both here and in the concluding chapter.

THE UNITED KINGDOM

As we noted in the outset of this book, it is somewhat counterintuitive that the United Kingdom became the most stalwart US ally in Iraq given the extent of public opposition to becoming involved the conflict in the first place. Figure 7.1 presents the trend in public opinion regarding intervention in Iraq from

---

[8] http://www.cer.org.uk/sites/default/files/publications/attachments/pdf/2011/back_brief_springford_dec03-3848.pdf (accessed June 10, 2014).

[9] Radziszewski and Wolfe (2012: 69).

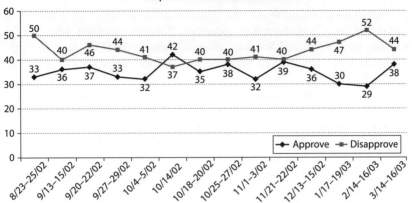

Figure 7.1. British public opinion on intervention in Iraq, August 2002–March 2003.
Source: ICM Research Poll (2002).

August 2002 up to the initiation of the actual conflict and shows that opposition consistently outweighed support. Indeed, a majority of the public in the United Kingdom opposed US military action in Iraq as early as March 2002, with 51 percent against and only 35 percent in favor.[10]

A critical piece of the explanation for why Tony Blair was so willing to go against the tide of public opinion is that most of the political opposition to the war came from within his own Labour Party. The Conservative Party strongly supported the war as early as August 2002, and was ultimately more reliable in supporting the pro-coalition stance in Parliament. After a meteoric rise through the House of Commons, success in media management during his years as an opposition leader in the Labour Party and the historic electoral victories that brought his party to power left Blair feeling politically invulnerable. As a result, he was confident in his ability to eventually win the media campaign for going to war. When combined with Conservative Party support, Blair's confidence emboldened him to commit to a military partnership with the United States even as public opinion seemed to be stacked against him.

Why was support for the United States such a strategic priority for the Blair administration? The answer lies in his long-standing understanding of the centrality of the United Kingdom's special relationship with the United States. The strength of this relationship originates in the countries' shared history, the aftermath of World War II, and fallout from the 1956 Suez Canal invasion by Britain and France.[11] As US international influence grew, Britain found "that it could no longer project influence in the world without the support, or at least

[10] Travis (2002).
[11] Pickering (1998). For more on the origins of this special relationship, see Russett (1963: 5). He argues that the United States and United Kingdom developed a security community, which in

the acquiescence, of the United States."[12] Harold McMillan, Britain's Conservative prime minister from 1957 to 1963, developed a post-Suez doctrine that prioritized the relationship with the United States as an avenue for maintaining British influence.[13] While still in opposition, Tony Blair defined Britain's relationship with the United States as "essential," and spoke of the need to maximize UK influence through partnerships with the United States and with Europe.[14]

While Blair's prioritization of the US relationship is an important part of the explanation, he also was a long-standing supporter of action against Iraq. This position dated back to at least 1998, when Saddam Hussein expelled United Nations Special Commission (UNSCOM) and International Atomic Weapons Agency (IAEA) weapons inspectors in defiance of UN mandates put in place in the aftermath of the Persian Gulf War. On November 12, 1998, Blair sent a briefing to the UK House of Commons designed to influence public opinion by detailing British intelligence on Saddam and Iraq's weapons of mass destruction (WMD) program.[15] The United States and Britain then undertook a four-day bombing of Iraq on December 16, during which Britain flew 15 percent of total missions.[16] The primary justification for this action was to degrade Iraq's military capabilities. But almost half of the one hundred targeted sites were bureaucratic in nature, leading to speculation that regime destabilization was also a goal.

Interventionism in general was a key element of Britain's foreign policy under Blair. An outspoken advocate of NATO's intervention in Kosovo, Blair explained in a 1999 speech at the Chicago Economic Club: "This was a just war, based not on any territorial ambitions but on values. We cannot let the evil of ethnic cleansing stand. We must not rest until it is reversed. We have learned twice before in this century that appeasement does not work. If we let an evil dictator range unchallenged, we will have to spill infinitely more blood and treasure to stop him later."[17] During this speech, Blair introduced the Doctrine of the International Community. Later known as the Blair doctrine, it emphasized the need for international cooperation among partners in economic and humanitarian matters and outlined the path by which the international community should decide on whether or not to intervene in other nations.

---

turn meant that "the last serious threat of war between the two powers passed" and deep cooperation on security affairs developed.

[12] Stephens (2004: 146).

[13] Bentivoglio (2009).

[14] Stephens (2004).

[15] Coughlin (2006: 69).

[16] Youngs and Oakes (1999).

[17] Interestingly, these engagements were comparatively popular. A December 18 MORI online poll showed 56 percent of the British public supported the bombings, while 33 percent were against and 11 percent were uncertain (*PBS NewsHour* 1999).

The question remains as to how Blair was able to pursue his policy preferences despite public opposition. The beginnings of an answer lie in the extent of his electoral strength. The United Kingdom is an archetypal low-party system in which two parties, Conservative and Labour, have shared between 70 and 90 percent of the popular vote since the 1920s. By the logic we have laid out in previous chapters, this type of system is associated with a less robust and diverse opposition, and with it a less knowledgeable and engaged public and a less independent media. Indeed, consistent with this expectation, the coalition frame dominated media coverage of the Iraq War. An analysis of UK media content from March 18 to April 17, 2003, found that coalition media management efforts succeeded in focusing the story on the war's progression, narrowing the window of opportunity for the public to hear dissent.[18]

During this period, however, the opposition in the United Kingdom was in disarray even by these standards. After eighteen years of Conservative Party rule, Tony Blair's Labour Party was elected on May 1, 1997, garnering 43.2 percent of the vote and winning 418 parliamentary seats (to Conservative's 165), the most the party had ever held. The next general election took place in 2001. Dubbed the "quiet landslide" by British media, Labour was reelected, losing only 6 seats overall and holding 40.7 percent of the vote. Conservatives collected about 31 percent of the vote in each election, holding 165 and 166 seats, respectively, and the Liberal Democrats held not-insubstantial margins of 16.7 percent and 18.3 percent, giving them nearly 50 seats in each sitting of Parliament.

These electoral landslides left Blair with an unusually free hand to prioritize relations with the United States. However, although this wave of Labour support provided substantial insulation from public opinion, Blair's early discussions with US President George W. Bush on Iraq included a request for enough time to convince the public of the need to go to war.[19] Thus, in spite of private guarantees that came as early as April and July 2002 that the United Kingdom would join the United States on any military action in Iraq, the two leaders delayed preparations for both engagement and postwar reconstruction in favor of continuing to build the case for war. This prioritization of public opinion over planning resulted in Ministry of Defence orders for body armor being delayed and the British ambassador to Turkey receiving insufficient information to warn his government about the "massive opposition" they would face in the Muslim world.[20] The key point is that though Blair possessed the political strength to ignore public opinion, he still recognized that doing so was potentially costly and something to avoid if possible—even at the potential expense of strategic priorities related to the conflict itself.

[18] Robinson et al. (2009).
[19] Fairweather (2011).
[20] Fairweather (2011: 14).

Blair held a secret meeting on July 23, 2002, attended by the foreign secretary, the defence secretary, the head of MI6, the head of the Joint Intelligence Committee, the attorney general, military chiefs, and three of Blair's closest advisors. In minutes not released until leaked to the press in May 2005, Attorney General Jack Straw described the case for going to war as "thin," voicing a strong level of doubt as to the legality of the now clearly imminent war. At the same time, Blair declared that "[i]f the political context were right, people would support regime change," and a plan was laid to create cause for the war by forcing weapons inspectors on the Iraqi regime. It was irrelevant whether the inspectors were denied entry or were allowed in and found WMDs; either outcome would justify regime change through military action.[21]

The fact that most of the political opposition to the war came from within his own Labour Party, and not from the rival Conservatives, further enhanced Blair's opportunity to buck the tide of public opinion. This effectively muted the partisan opposition that is so important in these situations because partisan media outlets index their coverage to interparty discord and debate.[22] Intraparty strife, by comparison, while newsworthy by traditional media standards, has less built-in "infrastructure" to allow it to reach voters via the United Kingdom's numerous partisan news outlets.

Iain Duncan Smith, leader of the Conservative Party, supported preemptive strikes on Iraq because he believed the United Kingdom would soon be within range of Iraqi missiles and therefore that Iraq would have a credible means of delivering any WMD capability it might develop or already have. Duncan Smith went so far as to accuse Blair of moving too slowly by allowing the campaign to gain public support for action against Iraq to drift over the summer months of 2002. He thus commented, "It is now time for the prime minister to explain to the British people what he already knows—that Iraq is a clear and growing danger to Britain."[23] The chair of the Conservative Party, Theresa May, promised Blair the support of her party should he decide to act against Iraq. In some sense this is unsurprising given that the potential political price of bucking public opinion was more likely to accrue to Labour—as the party in power—than the Conservatives regardless of their outspoken support.

Blair's government publicly released another key element of the campaign to win over public opinion in September 2002. The September Dossier, officially titled "Iraq's Weapons of Mass Destruction: The Assessment of the British Government," presented the work of the Joint Intelligence Committee and detailed the alleged state of Iraq's chemical and biological weapons programs, including the suggestion that Iraq's nuclear program had been reconstituted. BBC analysis of the dossier stated, "It is even clearer now that if Saddam Hussein does not

[21] Smith (2005).
[22] Baum and Groeling (2010).
[23] BBC News (2002b).

comply with the demands to disarm and allow unlimited inspections, the pace of diplomacy will become a torrent of war."[24]

On the same day as the dossier's release, Blair called for an emergency parliamentary session. During the resulting debate, more than fifty Labour MPs voiced opposition to action in Iraq without UN backing, thereby signaling growing opposition within the general public as well as within the Labour Party itself.[25] An August 2002 poll found 52 percent of voters indicating that Bush's Iraq policy was wrong and that Blair should not support it. Over half (52 percent) of Labour voters were also opposed, up from 46 percent in March.[26] The protest in London four days later drew more than 150,000 people, at that time one of the largest antiwar protests ever held in Europe.[27] During this period, polls consistently suggested that more than half the public opposed a strike in Iraq and that Blair should not support American policy on Iraq.[28]

The September Dossier included a foreword by Tony Blair, in which he highlighted the extraordinary nature of the public release of such an intelligence document. However, the document contained very little new information—most of which eventually proved to be inaccurate—and came to be seen as part of the campaign to win over the British public.[29]

In spite of Blair's extended efforts, by January 2003 more than two-thirds of the British public opposed going to war in Iraq without a UN mandate.[30] Support for the war continued to fall, reaching its lowest levels by February 2003. By the time of the February 15 antiwar protests in London—which drew between one and two million people, making them the largest ever held in the city—Tony Blair's personal standing had fallen dramatically. Yet Blair, even having failed to win the populace over, was resolute in his decision to contribute to the coalition of the willing.

The March 18, 2003, debate in the House of Commons began with Labour and Conservative parties agreeing to back the measure sending UK troops to Iraq. However, 139 Labour "rebels" and 15 Conservatives voted against their own party's positions, saying they still found no "moral justification" for going to war.[31] In the days surrounding the vote, three of Blair's cabinet ministers resigned in protest of their government's Iraq policy: Junior Health Minister Lord Hunt, Home Office Minister John Denham, and House of Commons leader and former Foreign Secretary Robin Cook. Cook's resignation speech to

[24] BBC News (2002a).

[25] BBC News (2002c).

[26] Travis and Watt (2002).

[27] BBC News (2002d).

[28] ICM Research (2002).

[29] With early polls having shown strong opposition to British participation in Iraq, Blair was widely believed to have given British support to US action in Iraq on condition of being allowed time to conduct a public relations campaign.

[30] Hummel (2007).

[31] BBC News (2003a).

the Commons received an unprecedented standing ovation as he detailed the reasons he could not support the move to go to war. BBC News Online said of Cook's speech, "The anti-war rebels have finally got what they have so far been lacking—a leader with the ability to scare the socks off the prime minister."[32]

Iraq dominated news coverage in the United Kingdom from March 17 through April 18, 2003, with almost half of newspaper stories during this time addressing the issue.[33] Yet despite the prior state of public opinion regarding Iraq, according to Robinson, Goddard, and Parry, the coalition message so dominated coverage that potentially dissenting views were "effectively crowded out." They note that most reports that drew on the WMD justification reinforced the coalition argument by "relaying the coalition's claims regarding Iraq's WMD capability in unproblematic terms." They further find that "less than 15% [of Iraq stories] actually challenged official narratives in this respect."[34] The same was true for the humanitarian justifications, which they find overwhelmingly reflected official narratives, with more than 80 percent of Iraq-related stories mirroring the government position and less than 12 percent challenging it. Overall, more than 80 percent of newspaper stories on the conflict during this period mentioned coalition officials, who were also responsible for 45 percent of all direct quotations.[35]

Another study, examining television coverage in the period between March 20 and April 14, 2003, found coalition actors present in over 85 percent of Iraq-related stories and responsible for over 50 percent of direct quotes.[36] Daily newspapers reach less than half of adults in the United Kingdom, but there are almost two radio receivers per person, and 97.5 percent of British households have televisions. However, the partisan structure and the way in which media indexed their coverage to it led to a situation in which the media contributed to a rally rather than giving a prominent voice to opposition.

This dynamic means that, in many regards, Blair was right about what would happen if he ignored public opinion and went ahead with the Iraq invasion. Within two weeks of the intervention, disapproval had dropped to 44 percent while approval had risen to 47 percent, a shift Ipsos MORI called "one of the most dramatic turnarounds" they had ever measured. Whether due to media coverage or a more traditional "rally-round-the-flag" effect, British opinion had swung even further by mid-April 2003, when an ICM/*Guardian* poll showed support for the war rising to 63 percent. An April/May Gallup poll found that over 50 percent of Britons believed the war had been justified, compared to around only 30 percent who felt it had not been.[37] The largest shifts

[32] BBC News (2003b).
[33] Robinson et al. (2009).
[34] Robinson et al. (2009: 545).
[35] Robinson et al. (2009).
[36] Robinson et al. (2009).
[37] Springford (2003).

came from women and young people, two groups that were initially strongly antiwar.

The above discussion demonstrates just how important institutional constraint can be. If the war had gone better—and Blair, though it is clear in hindsight that he was wrong, had reasons to think that it would—Iraq might have become an electoral bonus rather than a liability. In other words, this is not merely something that he was able to get away with because he was powerful and popular. In low-opposition situations, the media and whatever opposition exists disproportionately tend to rally around the use of force once it occurs, and the public tends to follow. Even beyond the immediate rally, Blair in general had reason to expect a positive outcome from the war and to be confident that given a good outcome he would receive a political bounce regardless of prior public opposition. The reason for this confidence was weak opposition, a compliant press, and, as a consequence, a pliable electorate.

SPAIN

Spain in 2003 was a relatively low-party system with one dominant party. This led Spanish Prime Minister José María Aznar (as it did Blair) to believe that he could win the framing war—that is, the contest with political opponents to control the framing of the Iraq conflict. In doing so, he believed public opinion would move to his position given a good outcome, which the Bush administration doubtless promised. Unfortunately for him, as the coalition's fortunes soured in Iraq, cracks appeared in this strategy and the opposition was able to rise up and topple him.

In the months from December 2002 to April 2003, the Spanish public consistently opposed the war in Iraq and especially the prospect of sending Spanish troops to participate in it. By December 19, 2002, Spain was the European country that most strongly rejected the war, with six in ten Spaniards believing that the United States should not invade Iraq. In a January 2003 EOS-Gallup Europe poll, 78 percent of Spanish respondents opposed participation in a military intervention in Iraq. February 2003 polls by Intergallup and the Center for Sociological Investigation "Opinion Barometer" showed opposition to military intervention at over 90 percent. Two-thirds of Spanish citizens felt that involvement in the Iraq War was illegal, according to an Intergallup poll of April 2003, while 71 percent opposed the use of Spanish air bases by coalition forces.

Mass demonstrations took place several times during this period. On February 15, fifty thousand Spaniards gathered in Seville for a protest. On March 2, as many as ten thousand antiwar protestors gathered near the Spanish-US base in Morón de la Frontera. On April 1, about thirty thousand university students staged protests in Barcelona. This popular unrest was not without political consequences. By March 17, the Popular Party, or Partido Popular (PP), which led the government and rhetorically supported the impending war effort, had suffered a five-point drop in electoral support.

While continuing to voice support for the Bush administration during these months, the PP's rhetoric reflected a clear awareness of the prevailing antiwar sentiment in Spain. The government consistently emphasized its position as an uninvolved party in the war, presumably in order to appease the public. On December 3, 2002, Defense Minister Federico Trillo said that war with Iraq was "not imminent." On January 20, 2003, he repeated the same sentiment, stating that military intervention in Iraq was "further away today than 10 days ago." In February, Prime Minister Aznar denied that Spain had offered any commitment or made any decision about militarily supporting the United States. Alejandro Sintes, army chief of staff, went even farther, saying that Spanish troops would not go to Iraq. In March, Prime Minster Aznar again assured Parliament that Spain was not sending combat troops to Iraq, but had agreed to send a fixed number of troops for humanitarian purposes only. During this time, Spain also supported a second UN resolution, which would give Iraq a deadline to comply with previous resolutions. By March 16, however, the United States, the United Kingdom, and Spain withdrew the resolution after it became clear that it was doomed to failure.

Even within the party, antiwar sentiment emerged. On March 23, Manuel Pimentel, former secretary general of the PP, announced his resignation from the party due to disagreement with the Iraq War. On April 9, PP deputy Luis Boned gave up his seat in the Congress of Deputies and resigned from the party, also over the war. While the government party faced opposition from within, it also encountered resistance from nongovernment parties who staunchly opposed the war. Prime Minister Aznar was the main target of criticism, which steadily increased over time. On December 20, the Socialist Party called on Aznar to appear before Congress and report on any commitments he made to the United States. By mid-March, the United Left Party (Izquierda Unida) was threatening Aznar with lawsuits, and by March 21 the Green Party had filed two lawsuits against him in the National High Court (Audiencia Nacional).

Thus, with public (and even elite) opinion set against the war, it appeared at first glance highly improbable that Spain would subsequently participate in the coalition of the willing. However, the outright majority won by the PP in the 2000 elections resulted in a power imbalance, thereby short-circuiting the constraint we would generally expect to see in a medium party system such as Spain's and creating the opportunity for President Aznar to discount public opposition and join the Iraq coalition. Though two major political parties won almost 80 percent of the vote in Spain's 2000 elections, this was the first time the incumbent PP had won an absolute majority in a general election. As a result, no coalition was necessary to elect Aznar to a second term.

But why would Aznar align Spain with US policy in Iraq despite a domestic environment characterized by the strongest antiwar sentiment in Europe? One likely explanation is that he anticipated a longer-term domestic political benefit from connecting already existing domestic efforts against the Basque separatist organization Euskadi Ta Askatasuna (ETA) with the US-led war on terror. Aznar was also motivated by a desire to raise Spain's international profile and increase its power on the world stage.[38] Thus, while Spain's objective differed from that of the United Kingdom, its leadership thought that there was something important to be gained by contravening public opinion and that they could politically afford to pursue that goal. Strong political influence over domestic media made this a realistic possibility. Indeed, the PP's gamble may well have paid off had it not been for the March 11, 2004, terrorist attacks in Madrid that preceded the general election by three days.

Having survived a 1995 assassination attempt by ETA—widely considered a domestic terrorist organization—Aznar and his government took a hard-line approach to dealing with the ETA from the moment they took office in 1996. The aftermath of the terrorist attacks in the United States on September 11, 2001, had brought new levels of coordination and focus to international antiterrorism efforts. Aznar exploited this new momentum in global antiterrorism efforts, using ongoing domestic efforts against ETA as an opportunity to align himself with the United States in the global war against terrorism and present the PP as the party best positioned to make a strong stand against terrorism.[39] In this frame, only the PP would have the insight and leadership capabilities to lead Spain toward its nationalist destiny, thereby cementing its political success for years to come.[40]

Aznar also saw the alliance with the United States as an opportunity to increase Spain's standing on the international stage. He spoke of ending Spain's medium-nation status,[41] of improving Spain's posture in the EU, and of using Spain's tenure in a rotating position on the UN Security Council to "combine his moral convictions with the goal of a more prominent role for Spain."[42]

Spain's participation in the coalition was therefore a balancing act between wanting support from the United States and the United Kingdom, on the one hand, and the need to appease the public and acknowledge widespread antiwar sentiment, on the other. Spain's foreign minister, Ana Palacio, announced on January 23, 2003, that Spain would permit the United States to use its military bases should it go to war in Iraq, acknowledging that Spain had discussed the

---

[38] Heywood (2003).

[39] Ordeix i Rigo (2005).

[40] Pujante and Morales-Lopez (2008).

[41] http://www.economist.com/node/1599099 (accessed May 29, 2014).

[42] http://www.businessweek.com/stories/2003-03-30/aznars-risky-gamble-on-iraq (accessed May 29, 2014).

possibility of participation in an international military action against Iraq.[43] On January 30, Spain and the United Kingdom led the group that signed the controversial "letter of the eight," which urged the EU to stand together with the United States in opposition to Saddam Hussein's rule. On February 12, Prime Minister Aznar denied that Spain had made any commitment or decision about militarily supporting the United States.[44] Nonetheless, just over a month later, on March 17, Aznar announced that US forces would be using two Andalusian military bases under existing bilateral defense accords.[45] The following day he added that Spanish troops would not be deployed to fight in Iraq, but that Spain "would offer warplanes to defend Turkey and send military personnel and equipment in a noncombat, support capacity."[46] The White House publicly announced Spain's commitment and support for the coalition on March 20, 2003.[47] A week later, on March 27, the US Senate passed a resolution acknowledging and expressing gratitude for Spain's participation in the Iraq coalition.[48]

By February, the PP's prowar stance had caused it to fall behind the social-democrat, center-left Spanish Socialist Workers' Party (PSOE) in polls for the first time since the 2000 elections.[49] Aznar claimed that joining the fight against terrorism would garner American support in Spain's efforts against Basque separatists. But opposition groups rallied around the immorality of using an attack on Iraq to gain support for a domestic issue. Mid-February protests, the largest ever seen in the country, drew almost three million Spaniards,[50] who expressed opposition to the war and anger at "the government's open contempt for the will of the broad mass of the population."[51] Observers credited the protests with limiting initial Spanish involvement in the Iraq War to humanitarian assistance, which in the short term prevented the use of Spanish combat troops.[52] Regional and local elections held on May 25 were widely viewed as a referendum on Aznar's prowar stance, and against expectations Aznar's PP re-

[43] "Aznar Rules Out Participation of Spanish Troops in Iraq Attack," Associated Press Worldstream, March 18, 2003.

[44] "Spanish Premier Denies Preparations for War Under Way," Madrid EFE, Madrid, February 12, 2003.

[45] "No Spanish Troops to Take Part in Attack on Iraq—Premier," Madrid RNE Radio 1, Madrid, March 18, 2003.

[46] http://paks.uni-duesseldorf.de/Dokumente/paks_working_paper_7_rev.pdf (accessed May 4, 2014).

[47] "The White House: Operation Iraqi Freedom. Coalition Members," http://web.archive.org/web/20030329185914/http://www.whitehouse.gov/news/releases/2003/03/20030320–11.html (accessed May 29, 2014).

[48] United States Senate 180th Congress 1st Session, Senate Concurrent Resolution 30 (S.Con. Res.30), Congressional Record, March 27, 2003, https://www.govtrack.us/congress/bills/108/sconres30/text/es (accessed May 29, 2014).

[49] http://www.economist.com/node/1599099 (accessed May 29, 2014).

[50] http://www.guardian.co.uk/world/2003/feb/17/politics.uk (accessed May 19, 2014).

[51] http://www.wsws.org/en/articles/2003/02/barc-f17.html (accessed May 19, 2014).

[52] http://www.guardian.co.uk/world/2003/mar/29/spain.iraq (accessed May 19, 2014).

ceived only "the mildest of rebukes" by voters.[53] *El Pais,* a center-left paper, speculated that the election results were as much a failure of PSOE to capitalize on antiwar sentiment as they were an endorsement of Aznar's policies.[54]

The weakness of Spanish media institutions made this a plausible strategy because these factors combined to limit the extent to which a disorganized opposition appeared capable of leveraging Aznar's Iraq policy for electoral gain. Though ranked as free by Freedom House in 2003, Spain's media has not completely freed itself from its tradition of political patronage. The state still appoints the heads of public television and radio, as well as the national news agency EFE. Television is the main source of information for the populace; in 2003, Spaniards had just over one television for every two people.[55] RTVE and Antena 3, two of the three most popular television stations with a combined 44.2 percent audience share, had clear prowar and pro-Aznar stances, in obvious opposition to public opinion.[56] RTVE, the public station, showed old films instead of covering antiwar protests, and ran programming emphasizing the horror of chemical weapons—a not-so-subtle nod to the central argument for going to war—to counteract the public's doubts about Saddam Hussein's actual arsenal.[57]

Less influential than television, Spain's print media tend to be regional, with a limited market for national newspapers. Spain's two most widely circulated national papers, *El Pais* and *El Mundo,* were strongly antiwar, and even center-right *ABC* criticized Aznar's approach to the war, if not his actual policies.[58] Readership is much lower than in most of Western Europe, however, with about a hundred papers distributed per one thousand readers—a number that includes highly popular sports papers.[59] Consequently, antiwar stances by prominent newspapers were largely drowned out by prowar coverage in the far more widely consumed television news. Given Spain's strong institutional relationships between media and government, Aznar had reason to believe that success in Iraq and increased Spanish influence internationally could turn public opinion around in the longer term.

In sum, Spain in 2003 was a moderate-party state where the leader had enough institutional (and short-term political) insulation to be willing to buck the public and go to war, with television boosterism backing him up. However, as was the case in the United Kingdom, the political viability of this strategy depended almost entirely on a relatively quick, positive outcome in the conflict. When that failed to materialize, the public's bill soon came due, and Aznar's government was ousted from power. Once again, the constellation of

[53] http://www.economist.com/node/1817707 (accessed May 19, 2014).
[54] http://www.economist.com/node/1817707 (accessed May 19, 2014).
[55] Albarran (2009).
[56] http://www.economist.com/node/1683729 (accessed May 19, 2014).
[57] http://www.economist.com/node/1683729 (accessed May 29, 2014).
[58] http://www.economist.com/node/1599099 (accessed May 29, 2014).
[59] http://news.bbc.co.uk/2/hi/europe/4470002.stm (accessed May 29, 2014).

institutions opened up a window of opportunity, but could not obviate entirely the political risks of acting contrary to the will of the people in an electoral democracy.

POLAND

Poland presents an interesting case of a relatively high-opposition system with relatively weak media institutions, low media access, and an electorate that is correspondingly less politically knowledgeable and engaged than those of most European nations. The last point is evident in figure 7.2, which compares political knowledge scores across EU member countries surrounding the 2009 European election, employing the same knowledge scale derived from the 2009 European Election Study (EES) utilized in chapter 2.

In figure 7.2, the cases investigated in this chapter, including Poland, are highlighted with darker bars. The figure reveals political knowledge in Poland (at least with respect to the six factual knowledge questions on the EU included in the survey) to be fourth lowest out of twenty-seven EU member states. Coincidentally, this places Poland just above two of our other country cases—Spain and the United Kingdom—that the theory predicts should be located near the low end of the scale due to their relative weakness in either access (Spain) or opposition (both Spain and the United Kingdom). (This stands in sharp contrast to Germany, our only high-party, high-access case, where political knowledge, also as predicted, lies near the high end of the scale.)

Our expectation is that such a system, despite the presence of partisan elites to act as whistleblowers, would be relatively fertile ground for a leader interested in conducting foreign policies counter to public preferences. The reason is that there would be at best a limited opportunity for opposition elites, regardless of their robustness, to reliably connect with the public. Moreover, such unreliable information transmission makes it unlikely that opposition elites would bother trying to "blow the whistle" to begin with since the costs (magnified by the high probability of failing to attract a critical mass of public attention) would likely outweigh any potential benefits. This was precisely the scenario in Poland in the lead-up to the Iraq War, and consequently Poland was among the largest troop contributors to the American-led coalition in Iraq.

Interestingly, Polish leaders never paid an appreciable price for ignoring public opinion in part because, unlike their counterparts in the United Kingdom and Spain, the Polish opposition was never able to translate public opposition to the war into a significant electoral issue. As a result, despite relatively consistent opposition, the issue remained relatively low in salience for the Polish electorate. This paradox gave opposition parties relatively little incentive to break rank over the issue for electoral gain.

While unambiguously opposed to the war in Iraq prior to its onset, Polish opinion was nonetheless more closely divided than in the other cases in this chapter. In January 2003, an EOS-Gallup Europe poll showed that 72 percent of

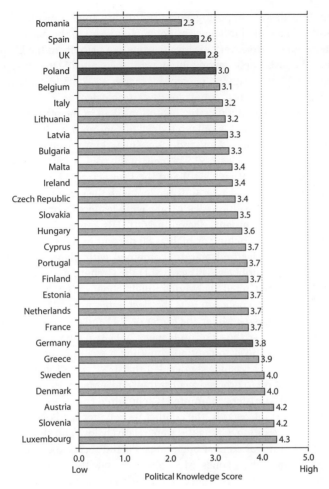

Figure 7.2. Average political knowledge scores of EU member countries, 2009.
Source: European Election Study (2009).

Polish citizens opposed Polish participation in a military intervention in Iraq absent UN authorization.[60] Though domestic polls showed slightly lower levels of opposition in January (still with clear majorities opposed, however), they also showed opposition rising through February and March. Antiwar demonstrations were correspondingly smaller and more muted in Poland than in the other countries we assess here (and, for that matter, compared to most countries in Europe). The same worldwide demonstrations on February 15 that drew millions of protestors in London attracted only about ten thousand in Warsaw. By February 2003, a majority of Poles actually favored supporting US

---

[60] Hummel (2007).

efforts in Iraq despite opposing Poland's military involvement, seeing economic and international influence as potential upsides to the partnership with the United States.[61] However, this loyalty came at a price from the US perspective—overall Polish public favorability toward the United States dropped from 86 percent in 2000 to only 50 percent by March 18, 2003. American foreign policy toward Iraq mostly accounts for this sizeable decline.[62]

With much younger democratic institutions than in the other countries explored in this chapter, dating only to the fall of communism, Poland's political parties are less entrenched. Aleksander Kwaśniewski was elected to his second term as president in 2000, with 53.9 percent of the vote. A founding member of the Social Democratic Party (SDP) and the Democratic Left Alliance (SLD), Kwaśniewski was reelected as an Independent with the support of SLD, but also occasionally formed coalitions with right-wing leaders in opposition to SLD and its coalition government, elected in 2001. His approval ratings generally exceeded 50 percent, reaching as high as 80 percent in the summer of 2001.[63] Kwaśniewski's high electoral margin, combined with high approval ratings, made early elections unlikely. This gave SLD the strength to prioritize Poland's relationship with the United States and brought about the emergence of a more assertive Polish foreign policy despite the electorate's ambivalence.

Prime Minister Leszek Miller, the leader of SLD and a Kwaśniewski appointee, signed the "letter of the eight" in January 2003, two days after Kwaśniewski urged US President Bush to continue building a coalition before going into Iraq.[64] By March 12, Kwaśniewski decided that UN resolution 1441 provided sufficient justification to proceed against Iraq, and a March 19 statement by the Polish Council of Ministers committed two hundred troops to the coalition.

In some important regards, the conflict went better for Poland than it did for others in the coalition. Casualties were relatively low, and shortly following the May 1 end of major combat operations, Poland received command of one of Iraq's four stabilization zones. Most observers saw this as a reward for loyalty. But this US decision also reflected humanitarian concerns, past Polish investment in Iraq, and Poland's experience in peacekeeping.[65] A multinational force of 7,000, including 2,200 Polish troops and under Polish command, deployed to Iraq in June 2003. As a result, by June, 40 percent of Poles felt the country's actions in Iraq had improved its standing internationally and 70 percent felt the Polish economy would improve as a result of contracts awarded

---

[61] http://www.cer.org.uk/sites/default/files/publications/attachments/pdf/2011/back_brief _springford_dec03–3848.pdf (accessed May 29, 2014).

[62] http://www.pewglobal.org/2003/03/18/americas-image-further-erodes-europeans-want -weaker-ties/ (accessed May 29, 2014).

[63] http://www.economist.com/node/709814 (accessed May 29, 2014).

[64] http://paks.uni-duesseldorf.de/Dokumente/paks_working_paper_9_rev.pdf (accessed September 6, 2014).

[65] http://mesharpe.metapress.com/app/home/contribution.asp?referrer=parent&backto =issue,1,6;journal,57,57;linkingpublicationresults,1:110914,1 (accessed May 29, 2014).

due to the nation's Iraq involvement. This prevented the backlash that leaders experienced in the United Kingdom and Spain and caused Iraq to remain a low-salience issue for the electorate. Notably, this is more akin to the outcome that Blair and Aznar thought that they would be able to engineer and subsequently use to bring their voters around to their positions.

Correspondingly weak media institutions and relatively lower levels of media access exacerbate the lack of constraint stemming from the somewhat underdeveloped (though diverse) party system. Though ranked as free by Freedom House in 2003, Polish media face considerable political constraints, a likely vestige of communism. Libel and political defamation suits against reporters are not uncommon, and the government has utilized passport seizure to exert political influence over journalists.[66] Government-owned radio and television stations have the greatest national reach; print media are largely privatized and reach less than 30 percent of the population.[67]

Moreover, for a developed European democracy, Poland has relatively low levels of media access, with media under strong political influence. For instance, out of 116 democracies (according to Polity IV) in our 2003 TV access data, Poland ranks 70th. This suggests that any criticism of the government's policies that may have appeared in privately owned newspapers would likely be overwhelmed by progovernment coverage in publicly owned television and radio. The implication is that there was little chance that an opposition party could break ranks in hopes of leveraging residual antiwar sentiment for electoral gain. The result was the outward appearance of elite consensus, though it is important to note that this is observationally equivalent to the absence of elite opportunity to challenge the government line.

Thus, government elites seemingly agreed on the advantages of alignment with the United States. They faced fairly strong public opposition (at least prior to committing troops) but comparatively mild intensity of antiwar opinion or demonstrations. Messages of the potential economic and political advantages to Poland's involvement in Iraq, transmitted by a compliant media, eventually swayed public opinion to favor the engagement in Iraq, in spite of a decline in overall favorable attitudes toward the United States.

GERMANY

Germany is a classic high-party system with robust opposition. Since World War II, three political parties have consistently bid for power in the German Bundestag, either alone or in coalitions, and they have done so in the context of a large number of smaller parties. This long-standing environment of political contestation is reflected in a vibrant media that are highly accessible to a

[66] http://www.freedomhouse.org/report/freedom-press/2003/poland (accessed May 29, 2014).
[67] http://news.bbc.co.uk/2/hi/europe/country_profiles/1054681.stm#media (accessed May 29, 2014).

knowledgeable and politically engaged public. In this sense, Germany is the prototypical high-opposition, high-media access state that we envisioned in chapter 2. Our theory suggests that German leaders should be much more responsive to public opinion than their counterparts in the other countries that we have outlined in this chapter, each of which is deficient in either opposition or media access (or both). Again, this is precisely the pattern we observe in German behavior in the lead-up to the Iraq War.

The center-right Christian Democratic Union (CDU) is Germany's strongest party. The conservative Bavarian party Christian Social Union (CSU) is frequently referred to as CDU's sister party due to a power-sharing arrangement at the national level, though the two parties have been known to disagree, particularly on social issues. The oldest party in Germany, the center-left Social Democratic Party (SDP), was founded in 1875. A frequent junior party in coalitions, the Free Democratic Party (FDP) began in the aftermath of World War II and promotes free trade and economic liberalism. Also in the mix, however, are a number of smaller but still robust parties that maintain autonomy and meaningful political voices. For instance, part of a larger European movement, Germany's Green Party was formed in the 1970s to support causes such as social justice and environmentalism.

The German system tends to generate new partisan opposition with relative ease when existing parties fail to reflect important segments of public opinion. For example, the 2007 merger of the offspring of East Germany's ruling Social Unity Party and Labour and Social Justice, which consisted mainly of disenfranchised SDP members, created the new Left Party, a staunchly pacifist party that demanded an immediate withdrawal of troops from Afghanistan. In general, this is a polity that is accustomed to small and sometimes highly idiosyncratic opposition. To take a colorful example, the Piratenpartei (Pirate Party) emerged in 2011 to take legislative seats in Berlin and three other states with a platform that included calls for Internet freedom and a liberal social agenda.

The peculiarities of the German system extend partisan competition over foreign policy even beyond what we would anticipate from a typical system with comparable partisan opposition. The German system of strong parties and weaker executive powers means that "parties play a much more central role as an interpreter and channel for public attitudes on policy issues."[68]

The challenges of Germany's recent political history have produced a system that is resistant in general to unilateral executive authority in foreign policy, and particularly so when it comes to the use of force. It was only in 1994 that a court decision granted the German military authority to participate in out-of-area missions. However, the criteria for such participation are strict. Deployments must be multilateral, conducted within collective security arrangement such as NATO, and, crucially, approved by the parliament. These constraints mean that even if motivated to do so, a hypothetical German leader would have

---

[68] Johnson (2012: 252).

a great deal of trouble following a path similar to that of the leaders we have already profiled.

As we laid out in detail in chapter 6, multiparty systems tend to engender political coverage that is more diverse, more policy-centric, and more prone to challenge the government's policy line than coverage in two-party democracies. In fact, the media environment in Germany has indeed come to reflect the impressive diversity of elite, partisan opinion. Five major newspapers crowd the national print market, each with widely recognized political leanings that tend to align with the nation's diverse partisan structure. The television media mirror this structure. As anticipated by our theory, coverage by these outlets tends to index to the diverse positions of the various parties. For example, working in the context of the 2001 Afghanistan conflict rather than Iraq, Pohr assesses the comments of five news sources for their depiction of the deployment of German or other military personnel and finds that coverage closely reflects the spectrum of opinion across the German Bundestag.[69]

The distinctiveness of the German media, arising from the country's institutional structure, was on full display in early 2003, prior to and immediately following the March initiation of the war in Iraq. According to Media Tenor, a media research firm focused on news content analysis, the focus of German media stories on Iraq differed substantially from those in the United Kingdom and the United States.[70] Whereas in the United States and the United Kingdom approximately 8 percent of total media coverage of Iraq focused on the political aspects of the conflict, and 2 percent on the challenges faced by journalists attempting to provide independent coverage (due, primarily, to the embedded journalist program), the corresponding percentages for the German media are more than twice as high. Across multiple measures, the introspective nature of the German media during the early days of the Iraq War—that is, the extent to which journalists write stories assessing the working conditions of journalists during the war—is consistently evident. This is indicative of a broad commitment to independent reporting and a mission to inform. It also makes for an interesting contrast with the timing of the *New York Times* self-critique of its own role in the conflict, particularly its failure to challenge the justifications that leaders provided for the conflict. This self-critique emerged many months after the early euphoria had soured and was replaced with recognition of the harsh realities of rebuilding Iraq.[71]

Another Media Tenor analysis notes that in the German media—again in direct contrast to media in the United Kingdom and the United States—criticism of the Iraqi government declined substantially as a coalition attack on Iraq became increasingly certain.[72] This again demonstrates the extent to which

[69] Pohr (2005).
[70] Kolmer and Semetko (2004). Their analysis was based on 54,223 media statements from March 20 to April 16, 2003.
[71] *New York Times* (2004).
[72] Media Tenor (2004).

German media are responsive to diverse opposition and public opinion. This is in stark contrast to media in two-party systems which are more prone to fuel public opinion rallies by indexing coverage to the preferences of foreign-policy decision makers (particularly the executive) with access to the most authoritative information.

German media were also distinctive in their framing of the conflict. Again in significant contrast to the United Kingdom, German media primarily painted the conflict as an American war against Iraqi civilians. In general, coverage of the United States in this period was notably negative, and this slant was particularly severe from RTL—Germany's largest private, "free to air" broadcaster. All German stations focused much more strongly on Iraqi civilian casualties than on allied casualties. Finally, German media gave much more coverage (3–5 percent) to protests against the war than did the BBC (1.5 percent).[73]

This independence with regard to the war in Iraq reflects a broadly independent German media. Pohr argues that across issue areas the German media are less tied to the opinions of the political elite than in the United States because German journalists possess a fundamentally more critical understanding of their profession than their American counterparts, who act more as a mediator between the political elite and the public. Erbring underscores this notion, observing that especially in the European continental area of news journalism, the foundation that news and opinion should be separated is in no way self-evident.[74] This is particularly the case among German journalists who, unlike their American counterparts, tend to associate objectivity with ignorance or at least a lack of worldliness.[75] Again, these tendencies may arise as long-term reflections of the deeper electoral and media institutional environment in which they are situated.

As a consequence of the extent of opposition, the quality of news coverage, and the high level of media access (e.g., Germany was 13th highest out of 180 countries in TV household penetration in 2003), the German system fosters a public that is both engaged and informed. Consequently, citizens are generally well positioned to hold their leaders to account. As we have noted in explicating our theory, these attributes tend to arise in systems with extensive opposition because opposition fosters an active, watchdog media and, through that mechanism, citizen knowledge and engagement.

To illustrate the point that the German public is unusually politically informed, we return to figure 7.2, introduced in our discussion of Poland. In those data, Germany rated seventh out of twenty-seven EU member states in political knowledge regarding the EU, far higher than the other three country cases investigated in this chapter. For additional evidence in this regard, in figure 7.3 we revisit the data on economic knowledge that we also introduced in chapter 2. (Recall that in this figure lower values indicate higher knowledge.) In

---

[73] Media Tenor (2004).
[74] Erbring (1989).
[75] Erbring (1989).

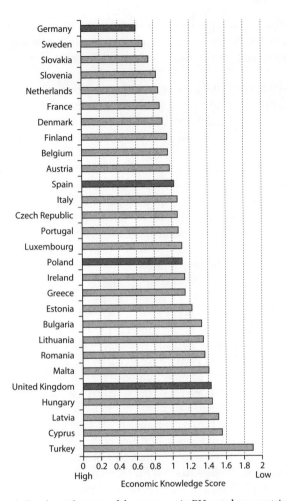

Figure 7.3. Knowledge about the state of the economy in EU member countries, 2007. Lower values indicate higher knowledge.
Source: European Election Study (2009).

these data, Germany places first in economic knowledge out of twenty-eight EU countries in 2007.

Given this status as a high-party, high-media access state with a correspondingly vibrant media and knowledgeable electorate, our theory anticipates that Germany's foreign policy would much more closely adhere to the public's preferences than a state of, say, the United Kingdom's profile. The Iraq case certainly bears this expectation out. The German public unequivocally opposed involvement in the Iraq War coalition from the earliest days of its discussion on the world stage and in spite of the potential (and in fact eventual) negative repercussions for Germany's relationship with the United States. The country's leadership reflected this preference by remaining at the vanguard of opposition to the conflict. Unlike the United Kingdom, according to Johnson, in Germany public opinion defines the outer parameters of what is possible in foreign policy.[76]

Germany's normally high baseline for partisan opposition and competition was accentuated ahead of a close election in September 2002. Given this political environment, and facing a deficit vis-à-vis the CDU in the polls, Gerhard Schröder and his SDP launched their reelection campaign in August 2002 with a promise that Germany would not go to war in Iraq, regardless of UN support.[77] The center-left coalition, composed of SDP and the Green Party, had trailed in the polls for almost three weeks before this announcement, primarily due to domestic issues. But foreign policy dominated the final weeks of the campaign. Thanks in no small part to his staunchly antiwar stance (which closely matched the public's preferences), Schröder was reelected on September 22, 2002. This illustrates the extent to which such issues can be pivotal in high-party systems, even though they tend not to be in low-party systems such as the United States and the United Kingdom.

The main political opposition, a conservative coalition of the CDU and the CSU, had publicly voiced support for US policy in Iraq but also promised to not involve German troops in the conflict. The CDU/CSU coalition received 38.5 percent of the vote in the 2002 election, exactly the same percentage as Schröder's SDP. The Green Party's 8.6 percent of the vote was therefore critical to putting the center-left coalition into power. Among the other smaller parties, the FDP received 7.4 percent of the vote and the Party of Democratic Socialism, the successor to East Germany's ruling party, gained only 4 percent.

Lehmann argues that media coverage in Germany between September 2002 and March 2003 tended to focus on the pros of the weapons inspection process and the cons of going to war, reporting frequently on Iraqi and other international perspectives. She suggests that the German media did not distance itself from the growing anti-Americanism in German public opinion, but rather embraced it as a commercial opportunity.[78] As a result, while some isolated voices criticized Schröder's foreign policy—particularly the risks associated with alienating close allies—the majority did not challenge the government's antiwar frame. In aggregate then, as the Iraq conflict loomed in July 2002, more than 60 percent of television news stories on Iraq opposed the conflict.[79]

German opposition to the use of force in the "war on terror," which subsequently informed attitudes on the war in Iraq, was unusually long-standing and developed. Even in 2001, Germans were already decidedly skeptical of US/NATO action in Afghanistan, despite the fact that most countries supported

[76] Johnson (2012).
[77] http://www.theguardian.com/world/2002/aug/06/iraq.johnhooper (accessed May 29, 2014).
[78] Lehmann (2005).
[79] Haumann and Petersen (2004).

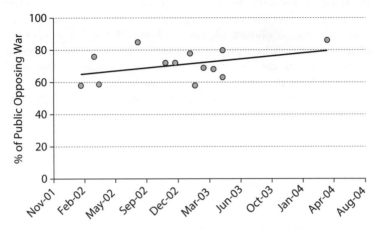

Figure 7.4. German public opinion on intervention in Iraq, 2002–3.
Source: Data compiled from Johnson (2012) and various polls by Pew, IPSOS, and Gallup.

US intervention as an appropriate response to the 9/11 attacks. When Chancellor Schröder pledged "unrestricted solidarity" with the United States in the days immediately following the 9/11 attacks, 47 percent of Germans already had no confidence in President Bush and felt Schröder's remarks had gone too far.[80] By November 2001, a majority of citizens felt Germany should avoid becoming involved with military operations such as those occurring in Afghanistan. A few months later, in March 2002, only 8 percent felt Germany should cooperate with the United States in future military endeavors.[81]

As figure 7.4 illustrates, these attitudes further solidified as the extent of US commitment to intervention in Iraq became increasingly clear. In early 2002, 64 percent of Germans opposed a military attack even if Iraq were found to have WMDs, and over half felt Germany should not go to war in Iraq under any circumstances (even with a UN Security Council authorization).[82] A January 2003 EOS-Gallup poll found 89 percent of Germans indicating that participation in military action in Iraq would be unjustified, and 61 percent characterizing it as "absolutely unjustified."[83] Public opinion remained strongly against the war throughout the conflict, and Germany never sent any military or logistical support to Iraq.

Germany paid a price for its strategic rift with the United States, which Johnson describes as precipitating the worst crisis in bilateral relations in nearly fifty years. Schröder's vow that Germany would not participate in any

[80] Haumann and Petersen (2004).
[81] Haumann and Petersen (2004).
[82] Haumann and Petersen (2004).
[83] Hummel (2007).

"adventure" in Iraq, regardless of the outcome of the quest for a UN resolution authorizing the use of force, led to a strong, negative response from the United States and led the Bush administration to isolate the German government.[84]

Despite these costs abroad, the costs at home of bucking public opinion would almost certainly have proven too much to bear. Within the opposition CDU/CSU there was some private support for the American position, particularly if the UN backed the mission. However, given the state of public opinion, party members were unwilling to publically challenge their candidate, Edward Stoiber, over his 2002 shift to opposing the war in Iraq. The result is that the party's positions barely differed from those of the incumbent government and the SPD/Green coalition squeaked out the tightest victory in German electoral history.

CONCLUSION

The key lesson from these case studies is that democratic constraint is fragile and elusive. These cases point to a variety of means by which policy makers outmaneuvered a consistently antiwar European public. Citizens in the United Kingdom enjoyed widespread media access to it, but a lack of serious opposition left Prime Minister Tony Blair with a strong hand. The extensive opposition in Poland meant relatively little in the context of a compliant media with less access to the public. This combination made it unlikely that an attempt by opposition elites to rally public opposition to the war for electoral gain would succeed. As a result, none of the parties even tried. Rather, constraint reliably arises only when both media and electoral institutions are robust—as they were in Germany. Echoing this theme, strong opposition to the war by Spanish citizens meant little when partisan opposition was weak, especially in the context of stunted media institutions. Spanish policy came to reflect long-standing popular preferences only after circumstances empowered the opposition.

Even though many factors are at play in these cases besides the institutional features that are our focus, media and partisan opposition are clearly an important part of the overall story and, more significantly, are among the few factors that hold steady from case to case and can therefore give us predictive insights. That said, we have chosen these cases primarily as illustrations of our theory. There are others in Europe that arguably fit less well, at least upon casual inspection.

The Netherlands, for example, was a high-access and high-opposition state that nonetheless contributed to the coalition. At first glance, this seems inconsistent with our theory. However, their participation was unusual. After much internal back and forth, the stated policy evolved into one of "political support: yes, military support: no," and this stance was very much a response to public opinion. Substantial evidence suggests that until the public took notice and

---

[84] Johnson (2012).

voiced its displeasure in polls and by taking to the streets, government elites were inclined to contribute militarily in deference to perceived alliance obligations to the United States.[85] However, confronted by strong public opposition—ranging from about 60 percent to nearly 90 percent, depending upon whether or not a given poll question stipulated that the UN Security Council had authorized the intervention—the Netherlands' leaders decided against sending troops for the first phase of the war to topple Hussein. Subsequently (and somewhat quietly), they contributed eleven hundred personnel to the stabilization effort in hopes of patching things up with the United States while limiting the potential public backlash. Thus, while at the most basic level this represents an exception to what we argue is the prevailing trend, when one more closely examines the details it appears to be the sort of exception that, while perhaps not "proving" the rule, is nonetheless seemingly supportive of it.

[85] Everets (2012).

8

Conclusion: Information, Constraint, and Democratic Foreign Policy

As we noted at the outset of this book, one of the relatively few places in which academic theories of international relations have substantially informed American grand strategy in the post–Cold War period concerns the distinctiveness of democracies. As President George W. Bush put it, "Democracy and the hope and progress it brings are the alternative to instability and to hatred and terror. Lasting peace is gained as justice and democracy advance."[1] In 2005, two years into the Iraq War, President Bush was still making much the same point: "History has proven that free nations are peaceful nations, that democracies do not fight their neighbors." Time and the war have undercut this rhetoric, but the actual deficiencies of the academic theories in question have remained opaque.

The answer, we have argued and sought to establish, is insufficient attention to the informational mechanisms that vary across democracies. In our view, a key element of what makes democracies distinctive from their autocratic counterparts is the role of information—who has it and where it comes from. However, this is not a dichotomous attribute that all democracies share equally. Rather, there are some with relatively weak information sharing between leaders and the public, and the result is poor accountability and constraint that may not fundamentally differ from that which holds in some autocracies. Others, specifically those with extensive partisan opposition (to blow the whistle on poor executive foreign-policy performance) and a robust and accessible media (to get that message to the public), excel at democratic constraint. Obviously, this means little if citizens lack the power to hold leaders accountable. But holding leaders to account is, after all, an essential aspect of democratic elections; indeed, it is the attribute that ties democracies together as a class. The murkier part of the democratic process is the extent to which voters are able to use this power to effectively constrain their leaders. This is the focus of our theory of information generation and transmission.

Rather than rehash this argument at length, in this concluding chapter we assess three key points that situate our work for both the policy and academic

[1] Bush (2003).

communities, and by doing so facilitate further conversation. Our analyses in the preceding chapters are necessarily highly stylized. As a result, some translation may help to take the arguments through to the next steps, be they in application to foreign policy or expansion into new academic questions. We begin by assessing the policy implications of our arguments and pointing out one way in which some of the constraining forces we outline might be fostered—through media ownership laws. We then address the nagging possibility that essential elements of our story are presently in flux given the emergence of the Internet and satellite television. Here, we argue that while these forces are transformative in some regards, they do not undercut the validity of out theory to the period in which we have applied it and are unlikely to do so in the foreseeable future. Finally, we consider the normative implications of fostering greater democratic constraint and point toward several potentially productive avenues for future research.

POLICY IMPLICATIONS

Initiation

Given the extent to which leaders' misperceptions of the nature of the democratic peace have led them to pursue potentially misguided policies of democratization, it is crucially important to develop a more coherent understanding of which democracies are relatively conflict-prone and which are not. Such an understanding could be useful to policy makers, both to help predict the future behavior of other states and to guide their own actions. The position that we have developed throughout this volume, particularly in chapter 3, is that robust democratic institutions do indeed constrain leaders in foreign policy, but that many (if not most) of the states that we think of as democracies fall short of these lofty standards.

Indeed, relatively few states in the international system possess both extensive partisan opposition and robust and accessible media. Those that do are heavily concentrated among well-established and generally developed states with strong, durable political institutions. In our view, this reality calls into serious question the efficacy of prodemocratization policies, especially to the extent that they are predicated on the notion that the resulting states will be more peaceful. While policies that encourage organic, domestically driven democratization may be fruitful over the longer term and may be desirable from a normative standpoint, there is little reason to believe that when it comes to matters of war and peace, imposed democracy will lead to an immediate decline in interstate conflict.

While arrived at in the context of coalition joining rather than initiation, the case of Poland, as discussed at length in chapter 7, clearly illustrates this point. At the time it joined the Iraq coalition, Poland had extensive political opposition, but the voters, media, and leaders still maintained many of the attributes inherited from the nation's authoritarian past. As a result, there was very little constraint on executive actions in foreign policy.

It is also worth considering the extent to which it is normatively desirable that all democracies be constrained from intervention when public opinion is opposed (even if the means by which we might generate such constraint is unclear). For instance, our theory, findings, and discussion all point to the United States as a relatively unconstrained actor in the international system, owing in part to a two-party system that limits the diversity of opposition. Yet the international system arguably relies on the United States as a stabilizing hegemon. It is at least debatable whether or not it would be preferable that US foreign policy be constrained by, say, a self-paralyzing coalition government.

Reciprocation

While the obsession with credibility and audience costs has remained the domain of scholars and only rarely and indirectly filters into policy discussions, leaders must always consider the possibility of having an adversary reciprocate (and by extension escalate) a provocation in a dispute. By more clearly outlining the mechanism by which audience costs actually function, as we have done here, we offer policy makers a guide for gauging their adversaries' credibility and for better understanding how their own credibility is perceived abroad.

Such an understanding might, for instance, have benefited President George H. W. Bush when he drew his famous line in the sand two days following Saddam Hussein's August 3, 1990, invasion of Kuwait. Though it is impossible to know with certainty, it seems reasonable to presume that President Bush expected Hussein to believe his unambiguous threat that "[T]his will not stand, this aggression against Kuwait." Yet Hussein reacted as if he did not. On this question, Donald Rumsfeld writes in his biography, "[F]or his part, Saddam Hussein came to believe that the United States lacked the commitment to follow through on its rhetoric."[2]

As with conflict initiation, we have established with regard to reciprocation that for most democracies credibility is hard to come by. Weak opposition and an inaccessible or cowed media often run together. When they do, information fails to flow consistently from leaders to the public, political knowledge and attention wane, and the resulting system produces very little constraint. No constraint means no credibility.

The implication is that democratic leaders must tie their own hands twice before they can credibly signal to a foreign adversary: first when they allow the independent media to develop as an institution, and second when they invoke audience costs. The latter step depends upon the former; only when the press is an effective independent actor are the actions of leaders transparent to citizens. This is why some democracies can generate audience costs more effectively

---

[2] Rumsfeld (2011: 413–14).

than others. More to the point, this independent, watchdog press is likely to arise only in conjunction with electoral institutions that foster it.

There is an essential paradox in the role of the opposition and media in the foreign policy of democracies. Leaders gain political benefits at home by controlling the framing of their policies and holding off political adversaries. Yet, the greater their capacity to control the domestic political debate, the less their capacity to persuade foreign leaders that their hands are truly tied. Their success at home, in this regard, compromises their capacity to send credible signals abroad. This means that they are less able to generate audience costs and signal credibility. On the other hand, to the extent that they lose control of the press and the opposition, this ironically enhances their capacity to generate audience costs and hence the credibility of their signals abroad. The bottom line is that, as Robert Putnam famously explained through the metaphor of two-level games, factors that *help* domestically can *hurt* internationally, and vice versa.[3]

Interestingly, this paradox appears to be an important underlying cause of the frustrations of American leaders who are repeatedly surprised when their threats—for example, against Iraq in 1990 and 2002 and more recently in Syria in 2013—are seemingly not taken seriously by adversaries, even those that are much weaker in conventional military strength. It is possible that, as Donald Rumsfeld asserts was the case with Saddam Hussein in 1990, these leaders fail to see American threats as credible. The reason, in part, is that the relative insulation of the US foreign policy apparatus means that US presidents have trouble manufacturing sufficient credibility simply by going public.

Coalition Joining

Our findings on coalition joining touch on a clearly pressing policy concern. In an era when states increasingly employ military force internationally through coalitions of various structures, it becomes vital for policy planners to understand who is likely to be politically able to contribute and who is not. One need look no further than the chaotic process that characterized the pulling together of the coalition of the willing against Iraq to recognize that leaders are essentially flying blind when it comes to this crucial task. The need has repeatedly recurred since the end of the Cold War—for example, in Bosnia, Kosovo, Libya, and most recently in Syria and (once again) Iraq.

Our analysis suggests a complex interplay between public opinion and constraint that could guide future coalition builders. If policy makers and the public agree on the proper course of action (either for joining a coalition or abstaining from it), then there is little to puzzle about—the state in question will almost certainly pursue that policy course. However, when there is disagreement either in terms of decision makers in favor of joining and the public op-

---

[3] Putnam (1988).

posed, or vice versa, then the mechanisms that we have delineated come to the fore in anticipating the policy outcome. Our view is that those attempting to cobble together an international coalition might still find allies where leaders support but citizens oppose involvement in a coalition. But this is likely only if such leaders are relatively insulated from public opinion due to limited opposition and a compliant media. Conversely, promises of support from leaders facing intense public opposition should be viewed circumspectly in contexts of robust opposition and widely accessible, watchdog-oriented media. That said, even in the former, more favorable environment, such leaders would be inclined only toward missions that they view as likely to be both short and successful.

This last caveat suggests a key element of this process that we have touched on throughout this book—most notably in chapter 2, in the context of figure 2.3—but have not developed in great detail. This is simply that even insulated leaders will face repercussions for bucking public opinion if they pursue a foreign policy action that ends catastrophically or drags on for an extended period of time while remaining unpopular. Such was arguably the case in the United States with the 2003 Iraq War. By the fall of 2006, roughly three and a half years after the war began, the public had turned strongly against the conflict and President Bush's Republican Party lost control of the Congress in the midterm election. This is, in an important way, what separates even relatively unconstrained democracies from their autocratic counterparts. We have not focused on this distinction because our goal has been to shine light on the differences *among* democracies, but it is important to recognize that in all democracies the public remains in the background; the question is *how far* in the background.

RECIPE FOR A WATCHDOG PRESS: SOME PRESCRIPTIONS FOR MEDIA OWNERSHIP

We have demonstrated in this book that whistleblowers, press freedom, and media access play important and interrelated roles in shaping the nature of information about foreign policy available to democratic citizens. Yet these variables are, in the parlance of institutional scholars, quite sticky. It is unlikely that states will rush out to reform their political institutions in order to achieve the foreign policy effects that we have described. One reason for this is that leaders at any given time typically lack the personal incentives to sacrifice their power and independence to provide their citizens with a more responsive democracy.[4] Even if leaders *want* such reforms, concerns over domestic powers and objectives often trump normative concerns over democratizing governance. Moreover, in new democracies that are designing institutions from scratch, history tells us that politicians are much more likely to shape these institutions to address pressing domestic considerations—such as the roles of existing fac-

---

[4] Baum (2011).

tions or ethnic groups, or the protection of particular economic interests—than to facilitate anything having to do with foreign policy, let alone constraining executive preferences over it.

In other words, the institutions that lie at the heart of our theory are not easy for policy makers to alter, at least not in the short or even medium term. Consequently, even if we make the arguably heroic assumption that a democratic government would *want* to enhance citizen influence on its foreign policy decisions, it is unclear how they might actually do so, at least in the near term.

That said, there are steps policy makers can take to promote both whistle-blowing and access, which we argue would contribute to better representation. Arguably, among the most pressing policies are those concerning rules and regulations surrounding media ownership. External influence or repression can indeed stifle the quality and content of media, but the internal institutional incentives of media actors also matter. For instance, Baum and Zhukov find that media are subject to ownership structures that can, for reasons having more to do with market incentives than ideological preferences, either undermine or enhance the press's watchdog function.[5] The implication is that some of the same advantageous (from an informational perspective) media properties that we argue can arise from a multiparty, high-opposition political system can also be possibly realized by policies governing media ownership.

The potentially stifling effect of concentrated private ownership on public debate has long concerned communication scholars.[6] Consistent with this literature, Baum and Zhukov argue that independently owned newspapers are relatively freer than their conglomerated counterparts to pursue the interests of their individual or family owners, which may be driven by profit, ideology, a sense of civic duty, or other factors.[7] While they might hesitate to criticize a particular government for personal or ideological reasons, their profitability is mostly locally determined, and hence relatively insulated from national policy. This frees them to set their own reporting priorities, with limited concern for the government's interests. Larger networks of media outlets, however, are subject to the same sorts of bottom-line pressures facing other corporate conglomerates.[8] For instance, large media conglomerates, like Rupert Murdoch's Sky TV Network, have consented to modify their news content to satisfy China's media censorship laws in exchange for limited broadcast rights in China.[9]

Additional research suggests that editorial content tends to follow the economic interests of media ownership.[10] For instance, Snider and Page found that, without exception, every newspaper they investigated that editorialized

---

[5] Baum and Zhukov (2013b).
[6] E.g., Bagdikian (2000); McChesney (2000); Herman and Chomsky (2010); Kellner (2005).
[7] Baum and Zhukov (2013b).
[8] DiMaggio (2008); Jenkins (2004); Kellner (2005).
[9] Flitton (2011).
[10] Snider and Page (2003a, 2003b); Gilens and Hertzman (2000).

either in favor of or in opposition to the 1996 Telecommunications Act did so consistently with the economic interests of their parent companies.[11]

The empirical implication is that larger media conglomerates are more likely than their independently owned counterparts to emphasize relatively less controversial topics (that is, entertaining, personality- and human-interest-driven stories) over more potentially controversial stories on public policy topics, and are less likely to criticize government policy.[12] Such companies are particularly beholden to government officials for favorable market policies and authoritative information.[13] Hence, the interests of ownership within larger media networks are more likely to reflect an emphasis on entertainment over politics,[14] and avoidance of conflict with powerful governmental interests.[15] The upshot is that alongside party institutions, media ownership also influences whether and to what extent a nation's press corps is likely to function as a watchdog of government.

Baum and Zhukov employ the same data and content-analysis techniques described in chapter 6 to empirically test the relationship between media ownership structures and news content surrounding the same multinational military interventions that we investigated in chapters 5 and 6, including Libya (2011), Iraq (2003), Afghanistan (2001), and Kosovo (1999).[16] Among their key findings is that, consistent with the above argument, newspapers within smaller ownership networks, and especially independent papers, offered significantly more hard news (that is, policy-oriented) coverage, and more coverage of conflict stories, than their counterparts within larger ownership networks.

These patterns indicate that the larger the network, the less the conflict coverage or hard news focus. They also suggest that policy makers are not without recourse to influence the nature and extent of democratic constraint in foreign policy. The reason is that to a much greater extent than with respect to party systems, governments have well-defined policy instruments available to them—via regulatory policy—for influencing the market shares of media enterprises. In recent decades, governments have used these instruments to facilitate the influence of market forces, rather than regulatory regimes or national policy preferences, in shaping media ownership structures. The driving force behind this movement toward media deregulation has been the idea that liberalization (that is, deregulation) maximizes market growth, while the resulting increase in competition benefits consumers via enhanced innovation, content

---

[11] Snider and Page (2003b).
[12] Kellner (2005); DiMaggio (2009); Jenkins (2004); Herman and Chomsky (2010).
[13] Bennett (1990); Baum and Groeling (2010).
[14] Baum (2003); Zaller (1999); Davis and Owen (1998).
[15] Herman (2002).
[16] Baum and Zhukov (2013b). While testing our hypotheses led us to employ countries as our unit of analysis, Baum and Zhukov by necessity focused on daily reporting decisions by individual newspapers as their primary unit of analysis.

diversity, and reduced prices. For purposes of this book we are agnostic on most of these questions. Yet it is clear that global media deregulation has ushered in a broad trend toward consolidation of traditional media enterprises. For instance, in 1983, fifty companies together controlled 90 percent of American media; in 2011 the corresponding number of companies was six.[17]

The above patterns represent a potentially important and unanticipated consequence of such consolidation, owing to the quite different economic incentives of corporate media conglomerates relative to their smaller network or independent counterparts. As media conglomerates control ever-larger networks of outlets, relatively more profitable and less risky entertainment increasingly trumps coverage of public policy. To the extent that democracies value a public informed about issues of public and foreign policy, policy makers may be wise to consider the role of regulatory policy in shaping the media environment. Ownership consolidation appears to result in less public affairs or policy content and less overall coverage of foreign policy crises, like the Libya and Iraq interventions. This suggests that policies aimed at reducing the market shares of media conglomerates, while fostering robust, independent media outlets, could enhance democratic constraint.

TECHNOLOGICAL CHANGE, THE INTERNET, AND SATELLITE TELEVISION

An additional question is the extent to which the mechanisms that we have outlined are likely to hold in a future dominated by technological change, particularly when it comes to media production, distribution, and consumption. More precisely, is the Internet qualitatively different in ways that might alter the relationships described in this book between media access and democratic constraint? Does satellite television break down the linkage between national boundaries (and politics) and media content and consumption?

Starting with the Internet, to begin to grapple with these questions, in our empirical chapters we accounted for Internet access in most of our statistical models. The results in every case showed that the Internet performed poorly and did not undermine the key relationships between media access (measured in terms of television and radio access) and conflict behavior. The question becomes why this is the case.

Our answer is twofold. First, to paraphrase and adapt Mark Twain, is that while a popular discussion point with pundits and technology enthusiasts, reports of the death of broadcast television as the world's dominant media conduit—especially for news and political information—have been exaggerated. Internet access is indeed rising worldwide, particularly via mobile platforms,[18]

[17] http://owni.eu/2011/11/25/infographic-media-consolidation-the-illusion-of-choice/ (accessed September 12, 2014).
[18] International Telecommunication Union (2013).

but as of 2013 global Internet penetration still lags far behind television. The International Telecommunication Union (ITU) estimates that in 2013, 41.3 percent of the world's households had Internet access. The corresponding figure for television was nearly double, 79 percent. The same report estimates that 38.8 percent of the world's roughly seven billion people use the Internet in some fashion. Of course, the percentages vary widely between the developed and developing world, with 77.7 percent of households in the developed world having Internet access, compared to only 28 percent in the developing world. Africa has the lowest level of Internet household penetration, at 15.6 percent. The next lowest regional penetration rate appears in Asia, at 27.5 percent.[19]

For television, the variance between the developed and developing worlds is considerably less stark, with TV ownership ranging from a low of 72 percent in developing countries to a high of 98 percent if developed countries. As with the Internet, Africa remains an outlier in television access, with only about 30 percent of the population having a TV in their household (though it is worth emphasizing that this is roughly double the rate of Internet penetration in the region). The corresponding figure for the next lowest region, again Asia, is about 73 percent.

With respect to our second indicator of media access, radio penetration, according to the ITU the overall average percentage of the world's population having access to radio closely mirrors that for television, with nearly 100 percent penetration in the developed world. The most noteworthy difference is that the radio penetration gap between the developing and developed worlds is far smaller. In developing countries in general and the least developed countries (LDCs) in particular, more people have radio than television. For instance, out of thirty-seven developing countries (excluding the LDCs) for which the ITU presents radio penetration data, an average of over 75 percent of the populations had access to radio; in only four countries was the figure below 50 percent. In a second ITU analysis focused on thirty-seven LDCs, about 55 percent of the populations, on average, had access to radio.[20]

Second, and equally important, despite its many unique characteristics, the Internet remains comparable to more traditional media in key respects that relate to our theory. Due to its seemingly ubiquitous, global architecture, it is tempting to assume that consumers seeking political information on the Internet would not be constrained by national boundaries. Indeed, with the exception of a small number of authoritarian states, most notably China, they are largely free to seek out news from any locale on the planet, limited only by their curiosity (and in some cases language barriers). The key implication for our purposes is that if Internet news consumers are not restricting themselves to domestic information sources, then the domestic institutional factors we

[19] International Telecommunication Union (2013).
[20] International Telecommunication Union (2010).

emphasize in our argument—the extent of domestic political opposition and media access—would not matter for the nature of information consumed. This, in turn, could break the link between the domestic information environment and democratic constraint.

As it turns out, however, to date Internet consumers largely appear to be eschewing the opportunity to behave as global news-consuming citizens in favor of diets of overwhelmingly domestically sourced news content. According to Google data from mid-2010 collected by Ethan Zuckerman, across the ten nations with the largest Internet consuming populations, domestic sources accounted for an average of over 97 percent of all news page views, with the percentages ranging from a low of 93.9 percent in the United States to a high of 99.9 percent in China.[21] Across the fifty most popular news sites in *each* of the top ten Internet consuming nations, a maximum of 7 percent of the content viewed by citizens was international in origin.[22]

Turning to satellite television, several of the same concerns (and rebuttals) as those we have just discussed with regard to the Internet apply equally to satellite television technology. The concern in this case is that satellite technology has the potential to divorce content from elite messages because it can so easily cross borders. However, as was the case for the Internet, in most developed democracies satellite technology relays the same news content as other domestic outlets and therefore lacks the substantial cross-border component that would undermine our theoretical link between partisan elites and the media's transmission of information. Most countries with very high satellite penetration rates, however, are authoritarian. Table 8.1 demonstrates this trend among the ten countries with the highest satellite penetration rates according to 2010 data from the International Telecommunication Union.

Among others, Iran and Iraq also are thought to have very high rates of satellite television penetration, but are not reported in the data due to either government restrictions or security issues.[23] What many of these countries have in

[21] Zuckerman (2013).

[22] There are, of course, different metrics one might employ to estimate the extent of domestic orientation of Internet consumption. For instance, by some estimates over 80 percent of Google searches seek local search results. Unsurprisingly, Google searches within any given country privilege domestic over international sources in search results. After all, if an individual in Los Angeles searches for an auto mechanic, that individual is unlikely to benefit from a search result listing auto mechanics in Europe. (See http://www.genealogyintime.com/GenealogyResources/Articles/genealogy_guide_to_google_country_search_engines_page2.html, accessed May 29, 2014.) Still another way of thinking about the extent of local emphasis in Internet consumption is to look at trends in language diversity online. One study (Bruegge et al. 2011) investigated the proportion of the top ten languages utilized in Wikipedia articles from 2001 to 2011 and found the proportion dropping from 100 percent in 2001 to 20 percent in 2011. In other words, locally oriented content—here proxied by language diversity—appears to be rapidly on the rise.

[23] http://www.global.asc.upenn.edu/fileLibrary/PDFs/FindingaWay.pdf (accessed June 5, 2014).

Table 8.1. Top Ten Counties by Satellite Penetration Rate

Country	Percentage of Homes with Satellite TV
Algeria	92.2
Palestine	86.1
Burkina Faso	83.3
Bahrain	65.3
Saudi Arabia	64.3
Austria	48.0
Lebanon	45.0
Syria	44.8
Slovenia	43.5
Jordan	40.1

common, of course, are very weak media and electoral institutions. Austria is the only highly functioning democracy on the list, and in that country satellite television carries the same domestic channels as broadcast television.

This raises a broader point about the variable nature of satellite television. In some countries it merely represents an alternative means of delivery. In the United States, for example, there is very little difference in content between cable providers such as Comcast and satellite providers such as Dish Network or DIRECTV. This, in turn, stands in direct contrast with Iran where satellites deliver over one hundred Persian-language channels into the country from abroad.[24] Even in authoritarian contexts, however, the vast majority of the content citizens consume is entertainment.

In instances where there is little difference in content between broadcast and satellite providers—primarily in advanced democracies—even pervasive satellite penetration has no meaningful impact on our television access measure. Satellite television primarily offers *alternative* content in countries where limits on media incentivize imported programming. As we have noted, such countries fall outside our theory.

MOVING FORWARD

In this study, we have assessed whether and how democratic citizens can constrain their leaders in foreign affairs. However, we have thus far not considered an equally important normative question concerning the extent to which they *should* be able to do so. After all, as we have described, a great deal of research shows that democratic citizens typically are ill informed about foreign policy. Indeed, the framers of the American Constitution worried as much about the tyranny of the masses as they did the tyranny of kings. One of the core purposes of the republican institutions they devised was thus insulating govern-

---

[24] http://www.global.asc.upenn.edu/fileLibrary/PDFs/FindingaWay.pdf (accessed June 5, 2014).

ment and political leaders from popular passions. In *Federalist 10*, for instance, Madison writes of the dangers from the mischief of faction and the incapacity of pure democracy to constrain it:

> [A] pure Democracy, by which I mean, a Society, consisting of a small number of citizens, who assemble and administer the Government in person, can admit of no cure for the mischiefs of faction. A common passion or interest will, in almost every case, be felt by a majority of the whole; a communication and concert results from the form of Government itself; and there is nothing to check the inducements to sacrifice the weaker party, or an obnoxious individual. Hence it is, that such Democracies have ever been spectacles of turbulence and contention; have ever been found incompatible with personal security, or the rights of property; and have in general been as short in their lives, as they have been violent in their deaths.[25]

In foreign affairs, an overly constrained leadership can have severe consequences. For instance, the Western democracies, including the United States, were arguably inhibited by widespread popular antiwar passions from more rapidly challenging a rising Nazi Germany in the 1930s. Our point is not that constraining leaders in foreign affairs is necessarily bad, only that it is not necessarily always good. Where and when to draw such lines represents an important and long-standing project of democratic theorists from Aristotle to Madison. Our findings add several new wrinkles to this very old question, by identifying several previously undertheorized implications of democratic institutional design.

There are also several empirical extensions of this project that are ripe for future work. First and foremost, the way people seek news and information is rapidly changing. This is potentially crucial because some have argued that media reliance on elite framing has declined in recent years as a direct result of these changes. Livingston and Bennett, for instance, assess whether new technology renders news producers less dependent on government officials to cue and frame political content. They find technology has led to a rise in event-driven news stories, but that official sources remain important to media coverage.[26]

To address these concerns, and notwithstanding our results in the prior section, it would be ideal to replicate the findings uncovered here for more recent years while including a measure of Internet access, which would serve to assess the extent to which new media and online communication alter the relationship between individuals and the government. Unfortunately, the Internet as a means of political discourse was in its infancy in most of the years covered by our data. Along these lines, it is easy to forget that there were no social media at

---

[25] *Federalist 10:* 234–35.
[26] Livingston and Bennett (2003).

the time of the 2003 Iraq War. Facebook, for instance, debuted in 2004. Hence, during most of the years covered by our data, the Internet was highly unlikely to influence public knowledge of foreign policy events in any meaningful way.

In addition to the Internet, were one to investigate more recent periods it would be worth exploring the extent to which access to satellite television or mobile broadband may alter the equation. The data needed to accomplish these extensions are not readily available, but as they become so it may be possible to uncover important insights about shifts in the nature of media consumption and changes in the extent to which different nations and leaders are able to signal the credibility of their international actions and commitments.

The relative disinterest among international relations scholars regarding the role of the mass media in reducing or enhancing international conflict is unsurprising given the literature's disproportionate emphasis on system-level variables, deriving from the dominance of the realist approach to understanding international politics. However, recent theories regarding the mechanisms through which domestic political factors influence states' international behavior strongly suggest a need to correct this oversight, and this project represents just one step in that process. Rationalist theories of war hold that information failure is a primary cause of interstate conflict, while democratic peace theorists argue that the accountability of democratic leaders to their electorates allows them to peacefully resolve international disputes by, for instance, generating domestic audience costs.[27] Both perspectives emphasize the role of information transparency in mitigating international conflict. Yet, as we have argued, for information to be transparent, it must first be transmitted. The primary mechanisms for doing so are the mass media.

The evidence presented throughout this book thus clearly suggests a need to integrate more fully some aspects of political communication scholarship with research on international conflict and the domestic sources of foreign policy. Doing so will allow scholars to develop a more nuanced understanding of the effects of information transmission on states' international conflict behavior.

In an era of rapidly expanding and diversifying media, the potential is also increasing for media to influence foreign policy via their effects on citizen awareness of and attitudes regarding the activities of their leaders. Consequently, the accessibility and content of information transmitted via the media should be assessed alongside traditional realist variables in scholarly efforts to account for patterns of international conflict and cooperation.

Additional work might also consider alternative ways of conceptualizing and measuring opposition. We have argued and hopefully demonstrated that, particularly over spans of time and space, the number of opposition parties, particularly those holding seats in the legislature, represents the best and most reliable indicator of the extent of political opposition. That said, as we have discussed, this is clearly an imperfect measure. There are other places where

---

[27] Fearon (1994).

one could look to estimate the extensiveness of opposition, and though beyond the scope of this book, doing so would improve the robustness of the theory. One example would be the interaction between the proximity and the closeness (in terms of contestation) of elections. As some of our cases in chapter 6 demonstrate, elections, under the right circumstances, can interject an element of intense opposition into even low-party systems. Though our preliminary testing in chapter 5 of the effects on constraint of election proximity did not support this possibility, other research has found evidence that the timing of elections can influence democratic conflict behavior.[28] This potential mechanism thus warrants further exploration.[29] Alternatively, in systems where political power is split relatively closely we might see something similar emerge. That is, in two-party systems that are very closely contested there may be more constraint than in those in which one of the two parties is electorally dominant. By a similar logic, multiparty systems in which one party holds the vast preponderance of power might be less constrained than we would otherwise expect.

A potential example of this dynamic lies in the contrast between Tony Blair's experience seeking support for intervention in Iraq and his Conservative Party successor David Cameron's August 2013 debacle when attempting much the same thing for Syria. Where Blair was able to exercise his preference in the face of opposition, Cameron endured a humiliating rebuke from Parliament, which declined to endorse UK involvement in a proposed American-led intervention in Syria. The distinction, in part, likely emerges from the political power and position of the opposition. Where Blair faced an electorally weak opposition that lagged badly in the polls and actually supported his policy in Iraq, Cameron led a much more closely divided Parliament with an opposition on the rise and eyeing the next election. The point is that though the United Kingdom approximated a two-party system during both of these incidents, the extent and robustness of opposition still shifted due to variables outside our theory and analysis.[30] With the basic theoretical framework now established, future work would do well to incorporate such additional factors.

Those skeptical of the role of domestic institutions in international conflict have assailed literatures positing the distinctiveness of democracies as either empirical observations casting about for explanations (as in the democratic peace) or naïve theoretical constructs lacking meaningful empirical support (as in domestic audience costs). In the former case, such skeptics have argued that absent a clear mechanism accounting for what makes democracies differ-

---

[28] Gaubatz (1999).

[29] Part of the reason that we consider this a secondary story is that such a situation would not have the longer term implications for the composition of the media and its influence on public knowledge and engagement that we have argued are so important.

[30] It is worth noting that the vote and seat shares for the third largest UK party, the Liberal Democrats, increased slightly between 2003 and 2013, from 8 percent of the votes and fifty-two seats in the 2001 election to 9 percent of the vote and fifty-seven seats in the 2010 election.

ent, any number of other attributes of these states might actually drive the observed effect—be it shared Western political heritage, development, or some other factor that political scientists have not yet noticed. As Rosato argued in a prominent rebuttal to the causal logic of the democratic peace argument, "while there is certainly peace among democracies, it may not be caused by the democratic nature of those states."[31] Or, to put a finer point on it, as Friedman's "Golden Arches Theory" of the democratic peace posited, no two countries that both have McDonald's franchises have ever fought a war against one another.[32] Does this mean that McDonald's holds the key to perpetual peace? One suspects not.

Other critics have complained that while the audience cost story makes for an elegant theoretical model, there is little evidence that it actually ever plays a role in real-world international interactions.[33] Our findings are among the first to comprehensively address these concerns. By doing so in multiple conflict domains (initiation, reciprocation, and coalition formation) as well as across substantial geographical and temporal domains, our results suggest a robust mechanism capable of accounting for why *some* democracies behave differently in foreign policy. However, in doing so, we have also shown that the mechanism is complicated, and that there are differences among democracies in the extent to which the relevant institutional conditions hold. The implication is that the standard dichotomous treatment of autocracies and democracies only very poorly approximates the political realities that contribute to public constraint on leaders' foreign policy actions.

Our investigations make clear that democratic citizens *can* influence political decision making, even in the "high politics" arena of war and peace. To do so, however, they need help. This capacity does not automatically flow from free elections or the rule of law. Rather, an essential ingredient for generating democratic constraint is the presence of institutional arrangements—robust opposition and broad public access to media—that minimize a leader's capacity to manipulate the policy information available to citizens. Only when such arrangements are in place can we expect democratic foreign policy to be responsive to the will of the people.

---

[31] Rosato (2003: 585).

[32] Friedman (1999).

[33] E.g., Trachtenberg (2012); Snyder and Borghard (2011).

REFERENCES

Albarran, Alan B. 2009. *The Media in Spain*. New York: Routledge.

Aldrich, John H., Christopher Gelpi, Peter Feaver, Jason Reifler, and Kristin Thompson Sharp. 2006. "Foreign Policy and the Electoral Connection." *Annual Review of Political Science* 9:477–502.

Aldrich, John H., John L. Sullivan, and Eugene Borgida. 1989. "Foreign-Affairs and Issue Voting—Do Presidential-Candidates Waltz before a Blind Audience." *American Political Science Review* 83 (1): 123–41.

Almond, Gabriel A. 1950. *The American People and Foreign Policy*. New York: Harcourt Brace.

Altfeld, Michael F., and Bruce Bueno de Mesquita. 1979. "Choosing Sides in Wars." *International Studies Quarterly* 23 (1): 87–112.

Anderson, Christopher. 2000. "Economic Voting and Political Context: A Comparative Perspective." *Electoral Studies* 19 (2): 151–70.

Babst, Dean V. 1972. "A Force for Peace." *Industrial Research* 14:55–58.

Bagdikian, Ben H. 2000. *The Media Monopoly*. 6th ed. Boston: Beacon.

Balch-Lindsay, Dylan, and Andrew J. Enterline. 2000. "Killing Time: The World Politics of Civil War Duration, 1820–1992." *International Studies Quarterly* 44 (4): 615–42.

Baum, Jeeyang Rhee. 2011. *Responsive Democracy: Increasing State Accountability in East Asia*. Ann Arbor: Michigan University Press.

Baum, Matthew A. 2002. "The Constituent Foundations of the Rally-Round-the-Flag Phenomenon." *International Studies Quarterly* 46 (2): 263–98.

———. 2003. *Soft News Goes to War: Public Opinion and American Foreign Policy in the New Media Age*. Princeton, NJ: Princeton University Press.

———. 2004a. "Going Private: Presidential Rhetoric, Public Opinion, and the Domestic Politics of Audience Costs in U.S. Foreign Policy Crises." *Journal of Conflict Resolution* 48 (October): 603–31.

———. 2004b. "How Public Opinion Constrains the Use of Force: The Case of Operation Restore Hope." *Presidential Studies Quarterly* 34 (June): 187–226.

———. 2013. "The Iraq Coalition of the Willing and (Politically) Able: How Party Systems, the Press and Public Influence on Foreign Policy." *American Journal of Political Science* 57 (April): 442–58.

Baum, Matthew A., and Tim J. Groeling. 2009. *War Stories: The Causes and Consequences of Public Views of War*. Princeton, NJ: Princeton University Press.

———. 2010. *War Stories: The Causes and Consequences of Public Views of War*. Princeton, NJ: Princeton University Press.

Baum, Matthew A., and Samuel Kernell. 2001. "Economic Class and Popular Support for Franklin Roosevelt in War and Peace." *Public Opinion Quarterly* 65 (Summer): 198–229.

Baum, Matthew A., and David A. Lake. 2003. "The Political Economy of Growth: Democracy and Human Capital." *American Journal of Political Science* 47 (2): 333–47.

Baum, Matthew A., and Phillip B. K. Potter. 2008. "The Relationships between Mass Media, Public Opinion, and Foreign Policy: Toward a Theoretical Synthesis." *Annual Review of Political Science* 11:39–65.

Baum, Matthew A., and Yuri M. Zhukov. 2011. "What Determines the News about Foreign Policy? Newspaper Ownership, Crisis Dynamics and the 2011 Libyan Uprising." Paper presented at the International Studies Association annual meeting, San Diego.

———. 2013a. "Filtering Revolution: Reporting Bias in International Newspaper Coverage of the Libyan Civil War." Paper presented at the International Studies Association annual meeting, San Francisco.

———. 2013b. "Media Ownership and News Coverage of International Conflict." Paper presented at the annual meeting of the American Political Science Association, Chicago.

BBC News. 2002a. "Blair's Dossier Assessed.'" September 1, 2002. http://news.bbc .co.uk/2/hi/uk_news/politics/2228294.stm.

———. 2002b. "Iraq 'Growing Threat to Britain.'" September 1, 2002. http://news.bbc .co.uk/2/hi/uk_news/politics/2228294.stm.

———. 2002c. "Iraq Rebels Make Commons Protest." September 24, 2002. http://news .bbc.co.uk/2/hi/uk_news/politics/2279259.stm.

———. 2002d. "Protesters Stage Anti-war Rally." September 28. 2002. http://news.bbc .co.uk/2/hi/uk_news/politics/2285861.stm.

———. 2003a. "Blair Wins War Backing amid Revolt." March 19, 2003. http://news.bbc .co.uk/2/hi/uk_news/politics/2862325.stm.

———. 2003b. "Cook Wins Commons Ovation." March 17, 2003. http://news.bbc .co.uk/2/hi/uk_news/politics/2858957.stm.

Beck, Nathaniel, Jonathan N. Katz, and Richard Tucker. 1998. "Taking Time Seriously: Time-Series-Cross-Section Analysis with a Binary Dependent Variable." *American Journal of Political Science* 42 (4): 1260–88.

Belchior, Ana Maria. 2012. "Explaining Left-Right Party Congruence across European Party Systems: A Test of Micro-, Meso-, and Macro-Level Models." *Comparative Political Studies* 46 (3): 352–86.

Bennett, James R. 1997. "Perspectives: The Public Broadcasting Service: Censorship, Self-Censorship, and the Struggle for Independence." *Journal of Popular Film and Television* 24 (4): 177–81.

Bennett, W. Lance. 1990. "Toward a Theory of Press-State Relations in the United States." *Journal of Communication* 40 (2): 103–25.

———. 1995. "Seducing America—How Television Charms the Modern Voter—Roderick P. Hart." *American Political Science Review* 89 (1): 203–5.

Bennett, W. Lance, Regina G. Lawrence, and Steven Livingston. 2006. "None Dare Call It Torture: Indexing and the Limits of Press Independence in the Abu Ghraib Scandal." *Journal of Communication* 56 (3): 467–85.

Benson, Rodney. 2009. "What Makes News More Multiperspectival? A Field Analysis." *Poetics* 37:402–18.

Bentivoglio, Giulia. 2009. "Britain, the EEC and the Special Relationship during the Heath Government." In *The Two Europes*, edited by M. Affinito, G. Migani, and C. Wenkel, 281–93. New York: Peter Lang.

Berinsky, Adam J. 2009. *In Time of War: Understanding American Public Opinion from World War II to Iraq.* Chicago: University of Chicago Press.

Besley, Timothy, and Robin Burgess. 2001. "Political Agency, Government Responsiveness and the Role of the Media." *European Economic Review* 45 (4): 629–40.

Besley, Timothy, Robin Burgess, and Andrea Prat. 2002. *Mass Media and Political Accountability.* London: London School of Economics and Political Science.

Bloch, Yaeli, and Sam Lehman-Wilzig. 2002. "An Exploratory Model of Media-Government Relations." In *Media and Conflict*, edited by E. Gilboa, 153–73. New York: Transnational.

Bormann, Nils-Christian, and Matt Golder. 2013. "Democratic Electoral Systems around the World, 1946–2011." *Electoral Studies* 32:360–69.

Brecher, Michael, and Hemda Ben Yehuda. 1985. "System and Crisis in International Politics." *Review of International Studies* 11:17–36.

Bremer, Stuart A. 1992. "The Diffusion of War—A Study of Opportunity and Willingness." *American Political Science Review* 86 (3): 849–51.

Brody, Richard A. 1992. *Assessing the President: The Media, Elite Opinion and Public Support.* Stanford: Stanford University Press.

Bruegge, Chris, Kayoko Ido, Taylor Reynolds, Cristina Serra-Vallejo, Piotr Stryszowski, and Rudolf Van Der Berg. 2011. "The Relationship between Local Content, Internet Development, and Access Prices." Paris: OECD Information Economy Unit, Information, Communications and Consumer Policy Division, Directorate for Science, Technology and Industry.

Bueno de Mesquita, Bruce, and David Lalman. 1988. "Empirical Support for Systemic and Dyadic Explanations of International Conflict." *World Politics* 41 (1): 1–20.

Bueno de Mesquita, Bruce, James D. Morrow, Randolph M. Siverson, and Alastair Smith. 1999. "An Institutional Explanation of the Democratic Peace." *American Political Science Review* 93 (4): 791–807.

Bueno de Mesquita, Bruce, and Randolph M. Siverson. 1995. "War and the Survival of Political Leaders—A Comparative-Study of Regime Types and Political Accountability." *American Political Science Review* 89 (4): 841–55.

Bueno de Mesquita, Bruce, Alastair Smith, Randolph M. Siverson, and James D. Morrow. 2003. *The Logic of Political Survival.* Cambridge, MA: MIT Press.

Bush, George W. 2003. "Address at Whitehall, London, November 19, 2003." http://www.foxnews.com/story/2003/11/19/raw-data-bush-speech-at-whitehall-palace / (accessed September 3, 2014).

Campbell, Angus, Philip E. Converse, Warren E. Miller, and Donald E. Stokes. 1960. *The American Voter.* New York: John Wiley.

Carr, David. 2003. "War News from MTV and People Magazine." *New York Times*, March 27, B14.

Carter, David B., and Curtis S. Signorino. 2010. "Back to the Future: Modeling Time Dependence in Binary Data." *Political Analysis* 18 (3): 271–92.

Castle, Stephen. 2010. "British Voting Marks End of Labour's Hegemony." *New York Times*, May 7. http://www.nytimes.com/2010/05/07/world/europe/07iht-labour.html?pagewanted=all&_r=0.

Choi, Seung-Whan, and Patrick James. 2006. "Media Openness, Democracy and Militarized Interstate Disputes." *British Journal of Political Science* 37:23–46.

Cioffi-Revilla, Claudio, and Harvey Starr. 1995. "Opportunity, Willingness and Political Uncertainty Theoretical Foundations of Politics." *Journal of Theoretical Politics* 7 (4): 447–76.

Clawson, Rosalee A., and Zoe M. Oxley. 2008. *Public Opinion: Democratic Ideals, Democratic Practice*. Washington, DC: CQ Press.

Clinton, Bill. 1995. "A National Security Strategy of Engagement and Enlargement." http://www.dtic.mil/doctrine/doctrine/research/nss.pdf.

Cohen, Bernard C. 1963. *The Press and Foreign Policy*. Princeton, NJ: Princeton University Press.

Corbetta, Renato. 2010. "Determinants of Third Parties' Intervention and Alignment Choices in Ongoing Conflicts, 1946–2001." *Foreign Policy Analysis* 6 (1): 61–85.

Coughlin, Con. 2006. *American Ally: Tony Blair and the War on Terror*. New York: HarperCollins.

Cox, Gary W. 1990. "Centripetal and Centrifugal Incentives in Electoral Systems." *American Journal of Political Science* 34 (4): 903–35.

Dahl, Robert A. 1961. *Who Governs?* New Haven, CT: Yale University Press.

Daily Beast. 2010. "The Blair Witch Project." *Newsweek*, February 10.

Davis, Richard, and Diana Owen. 1998. *New Media and American Politics*. New York: Oxford University Press.

Destler, I. M. 2001. "The Reasonable Public and the Polarized Policy Process." In *The Real and the Ideal: Essays on International Relations in Honor of Richard H. Ullman*, edited by Anthony Lake and David Ochmanek, 75–90. Lanham, MD: Rowman & Littlefield.

Diermeier, Daniel, Jean-Francois Godbout, Bei Yu, and Stefan Kaufmann. Forthcoming. "Language and Ideology in Congress." *British Journal of Political Science*.

DiMaggio, Anthony. 2008. *Mass Media, Mass Propaganda: Understanding the News in the "War on Terror."* Lexington, MA: Lexington Books, 2008.

Döring, Holger, and Philip Manow. 2012. "Parliament and Government Composition Database (ParlGov): An Infrastructure for Empirical Information on Parties, Elections and Governments in Modern Democracies." Version 12/10. http://www.parlgov.org.

Dow, Jay K. 2001. "A Comparative Spatial Analysis of Majoritarian and Proportional Elections." *Electoral Studies* 20:109–25.

Downes, Alexander B., and Todd S. Sechser. 2012. "The Illusion of Democratic Credibility." *International Organization* 66 (3): 457–89.

Downs, Anthony. 1957. *An Economic Theory of Democracy*. New York: Harper.

Downs, George W., and David M. Rocke. 1994. "Conflict, Agency, and Gambling for Resurrection—The Principal-Agent Problem Goes to War." *American Journal of Political Science* 38 (2): 362–80.

Doyle, Michael W. 1983. "Kant, Liberal Legacies, and Foreign Affairs, Part 2." *Philosophy & Public Affairs* 12 (4): 323–53.

———. 1986. "Liberalism and World-Politics." *American Political Science Review* 80 (4): 1151–69.

Druckman, James N. 2004. "Political Preference Formation: Competition, Deliberation, and the (Ir)relevance of Framing Effects." *American Political Science Review* 98 (4): 671–86.

Ekman, Joakim. 2009. "Political Participation and Regime Stability: A Framework for Analyzing Hybrid Regimes." *International Political Science Review* 30 (1): 7–31.

Encarnacion, Omar G. 2006. "Bush and the Theory of the Democratic Peace." *Global Dialogue* 8 (3–4). http://www.worlddialogue.org/content.php?id=384.

Entman, Robert M. 2003. *Projections of Power: Framing News, Public Opinion, and U.S. Foreign Policy*. Chicago: University of Chicago Press.

———. 2004. *Projections of Power*. Chicago: University of Chicago Press.

Erbring, Lutz. 1989. "Nachrichten zwischen Professionalität und Manipulation." In *Massenkommunikation*, 301–13. Amsterdam: VS Verlag für Sozialwissenschaften.

European Commission. 2008. "Europeans' Knowledge of Economic Indicators." Special Eurobarometer/Wave 67.2. Fieldwork, April–May 2007. http://ec.europa.eu/public _opinion/index_en.htm (accessed June 5, 2014).

Everets, Philip. 2012. "The Netherlands." In *Public Opinion and International Intervention*, edited by R. Sobel, P. Furia, and B. Barratt, 83–108. Washington, DC: Potomac.

Ezrow, Lawrence. 2008. "Parties' Policy Programmes and the Dog That Didn't Bark: No Evidence That Proportional Systems Promote Extreme Party Positioning." *British Journal of Political Science* 38 (3): 479–97.

Fairweather, Jack. 2011. *A War of Choice: The British in Iraq 2003–9*. New York: Random House.

Fearon, James D. 1994. "Domestic Political Audiences and the Escalation of International Disputes." *American Political Science Review* 88 (3): 577–92.

———. 1995. "Rationalist Explanations for War." *International Organization* 49 (3): 379–414.

Flitton, Daniel. 2011. "Sky TV Trumps ABC in China." WAtoday.com, August 17.

Fraile, Marta. 2011. "Widening or Reducing the Knowledge Gap? Testing the Media Effects on Political Knowledge in Spain (2004–2006)." *International Journal of Press/ Politics* 16 (2): 163–84.

Friedman, Thomas. 1999. *The Lexus and the Olive Tree: Understanding Globalization*. New York: Picador Publishers.

Galtung, Johan, and Mari Holmboe Ruge. 1965. "The Structure of Foreign News." *Journal of Peace Research* 2 (1): 64–91.

Gaubatz, Kurt Taylor. 1999. *Elections and War: The Electoral Incentive in the Democratic Politics of War and Peace*. Stanford: Stanford University Press

Geddes, Barbara. 2003. *Paradigms and Sand Castles: Theory Building and Research Design in Comparative Politics*. Ann Arbor: University of Michigan Press.

Gelpi, Christopher, Peter D. Feaver, and Jason Reifler. *Paying the Human Costs of War: American Public Opinion and Casualties in Military Conflicts*. Princeton, NJ: Princeton University Press, 2009.

George, Alexander L. and Andrew Bennett. 2005. *Case Studies and Theory Development in the Social Sciences*. Cambridge, MA: MIT Press.

Ghosn, Faten, Glenn Palmer, and Stuart A. Bremer. 2004. "The MID3 Data Set, 1993–2001: Procedures, Coding Rules, and Description." *Conflict Management and Peace Science* 21 (2): 133–54.

Gilens, Martin, and Craig Hertzman. 2000. "Corporate Ownership and News Bias: Newspaper Coverage of the 1996 Telecommunications Act." *Journal of Politics* 62 (2): 369–86.

Gleditsch, Kristian Skrede. 2002. *All International Politics Is Local: The Diffusion of Conflict, Integration, and Democratization*. Ann Arbor: University of Michigan Press.

Gleditsch, Nils Petter, and J. David Singer. 1975. "Distance and International War, 1816–1965." Paper presented at the International Peace Research Association, Fifth General Conference, Oslo.

Gochman, Charles S., and Zeev Maoz. 1984. "Military Interstate Disputes, 1816–1976: Procedures, Patterns, and Insights." *Journal of Conflict Resolution* 28 (4): 585–615.

Goertz, Gary, and Paul F. Diehl. 1992. *Territorial Changes and International Conflict.* London: Routledge.

Golder, Matt. 2005. "Democratic Electoral Systems around the World, 1946–2000." *Electoral Studies* 24 (1): 103–21.

Goldsmith, Benjamin E., and Yusaku Horiuchi. 2009. "Spinning the Globe? US Public Diplomacy and Foreign Public Opinion." *Journal of Politics* 71 (3): 863–75.

Gordon, Stacy B., and Gary M. Segura. 1997. "Cross-National Variation in the Political Sophistication of Individuals: Capability or Choice?" *Journal of Politics* 59:126–47.

Graber, Doris A. 2002. *Mass Media and American Politics.* 6th ed. Washington, DC: CQ Press.

Green-Pederson, Christoffer. 2006. "Long-term Changes in Danish Party Politics: The Rise and Importance of Issue Competition." *Scandinavian Political Studies* 29 (3): 219–35.

———. 2007. "The Growing Importance of Issue Competition: The Changing Nature of Party Competition in Western Europe." *Political Studies* 55: 607–28.

Groeling, Tim. 2010. *When Politicians Attack: Party Cohesion in the Media.* Cambridge: Cambridge University Press.

Groeling, Tim, and Matthew A. Baum. 2008. "Crossing the Water's Edge: Elite Rhetoric, Media Coverage and the Rally-Round-the-Flag Phenomenon." *Journal of Politics* 70 (October): 1065–85.

Guo, Guang, and Laurence M. Grummer-Strawn. 1993. "Child Mortality among Twins in Less Developed Countries." *Population Studies* 47 (3): 495–510.

Habermas, Jurgen. 1996. *Between Facts and Norms: Contributions to a Discourse Theory of Law and Democracy.* Cambridge, MA: MIT Press.

Hallin, Daniel C. 1986. *The "Uncensored War."* Berkeley: University of California Press.

Hamilton, James T. 2003. *All the News That's Fit to Sell: How the Market Transforms Information into News.* Princeton, NJ: Princeton University Press.

Haumann, Wilhelm, and Thomas Petersen. 2004. "German Public Opinion on the Iraq Conflict: A Passing Crisis with the USA or a Lasting Departure?" *International Journal of Public Opinion Research* 16 (3): 311–30.

Henderson, Errol A. 1997. "Culture or Contiguity: Ethnic Conflict, the Similarity of States, and the Onset of War, 1820–1989." *Journal of Conflict Resolution* 41 (5): 649–68.

Herman, Edward. 2002. "The Media and Markets in the United States." In *The Right to Tell: The Role of Mass Media in Economic Development*, 61–82. Washington, DC: World Bank.

Herman, Edward S., and Noam Chomsky. 2010. *Manufacturing Consent: The Political Economy of the Mass Media.* New York: Random House.

Heywood, Paul M. 2003. "Desperately Seeking Influence: Spain and the War in Iraq." *European Political Science* 3 (1): 35–40.

Holmstrom, Bengt. 1979. "Moral Hazard and Observability." *Bell Journal of Economics* 10:74–91.

Holsti, Ole R. 1992. "Public-Opinion and Foreign-Policy—Challenges to the Almond-Lippmann Consensus Mershon Series—Research Programs and Debates." *International Studies Quarterly* 36 (4): 439–66.

———. 2004. *Public Opinion and American Foreign Policy*. Ann Arbor: University of Michigan Press.

Holsti, Ole R., and James N. Rosenau. 1984. *American Leadership in World Affairs: Vietnam and the Breakdown of Consensus*. Boston: Allen & Unwin.

Hummel, Hartwig. 2007. "A Survey of Involvement of 15 European States in the Iraq War 2003." PAKS Working Paper Series. Düsseldorf: University of Düsseldorf.

ICM Research. 2002. "August 2002 Poll."

International Telecommunication Union. 2010. "World Telecommunication/ICT Development Report 2010: Monitoring the WSIS Targets: A Mid-term Review." Geneva: International Telecommunication Union.

———. 2013. "Measuring the Information Society, 2013." Geneva: International Telecommunication Union.

Iyengar, Shanto, and Donald R. Kinder. 1987. *News That Matters: Television and American Opinion*. Chicago: University of Chicago Press.

Iyengar, Shanto, and Richard Reeves. 1997. *Do the Media Govern: Politicians, Voters, and Reporters in America*. Thousand Oaks, CA: Sage.

Jakobsen, Peter Viggo. 1996. "National Interest, Humanitarianism or CNN: What Triggers UN Peace Enforcement after the Cold War?" *Journal of Peace Research* 33 (2): 205–15.

———. 2000. "Focus on the CNN Effect Misses the Point: The Real Impact on Conflict Management Is Invisible and Indirect." *Journal of Peace Research* 37 (2): 131–43.

Jenkins, H. 2004. "The Cultural Logic of Media Convergence." *International Journal of Cultural Studies* 7:33–43.

Jentleson, Bruce W. 1992. "The Pretty Prudent Public—Post Post-Vietnam American Opinion on the Use of Military Force." *International Studies Quarterly* 36 (1): 49–74.

Joachims, Thorsten. 2002. *Learning to Classify Text Using Support Vector Machines*. Dordrecht: Kluwer/Springer.

Johnson, Karin L. 2012. "Germany." In *Public Opinion and International Intervention: Lessons from the Iraq War*, edited by Richard Sobel, Peter Furia, and Bethany Barrett, 137–56. Washington, DC: Potomac.

Jones, Philip Edward. 2013. "The Effect of Political Competition on Democratic Accountability." *Political Behavior* 35 (3): 481–515.

Kant, Immanuel. [1795] 1983. *Perpetual Peace and Other Essays on Politics, History and Morals*. Indianapolis: Hackett.

Kellner, Douglas. 2005. *Media Spectacle and the Crisis of Democracy: Terrorism, War and Election Battles*. Boulder, CO: Paradigm.

Kim, Woosang. 1991. "Alliance Transitions and Great Power War." *American Journal of Political Science* 35 (4): 833–50.

King, Gary, Michael Tomz, and Jason Wittenberg. 2000. "Making the Most of Statistical Analyses: Improving Interpretation and Presentation." *American Journal of Political Science* 44 (2): 347–61.

Kolmer, Christian, and Holli Semetko. 2004. *Media Content Analysis Framing the Iraq War: A Cross-Country Comparison*. Berlin: Media Tenor.

Krosnick, Jon A., and Donald R. Kinder. 1990. "Altering the Foundations of Support for the President through Priming." *American Political Science Review* 84 (2): 497–512.

Kumlin, Staffan. 2001. "Ideology-Driven Opinion Formation in Europe: The Case of Attitudes towards the Third Sector in Sweden." *European Journal of Political Research* 39 (4): 487–518.

Kunicova, Jana, and Susan Rose-Ackerman. 2005. "Electoral Rules and Constitutional Structures as Constraints on Corruption." *British Journal of Political Science* 35 (4): 573–606.

Laakso, Markku, and Rein Taagepera. 1979. "The Effective Number of Parties: A Measure with Application to West Europe." *Comparative Political Studies* 12 (1): 3–27.

Lake, David A., and Matthew A. Baum. 2001. "The Invisible Hand of Democracy: Political Control and the Provision of Public Services." *Comparative Political Studies* 34 (August): 587–621.

Lake, David A., and Donald Rothchild. 1996. "Containing Fear: The Origins and Management of Ethnic Conflict." *International Security* 21 (2): 41–75.

Larson, Eric V. 2000. "Putting Theory to Work: Diagnosing Public Opinion on the US Intervention in Bosnia." In *Being Useful: Policy Relevance and International Relations Theory*, edited by Miroslav Nincic and Joseph Lepgold, 174–236. Ann Arbor: University of Michigan Press.

Layne, Christopher. 1994. "Kant or Cant: The Myth of the Democratic Peace." *International Security* 19 (2): 5–49.

Leblang, David, and Steve Chan. 2003. "Explaining Wars Fought by Established Democracies: Do Institutional Constraints Matter?" *Political Research Quarterly* 56 (4): 385–400.

Lehmann, Ingrid A. 2005. "The Transatlantic Media and Opinion Divide over Iraq." *Peace Review: A Journal of Social Justice* 17 (4): 357–63.

Levendusky, Matthew S., and Michael C. Horowitz. 2012. "When Backing Down Is the Right Decision: Partisanship, New Information, and Audience Costs." *Journal of Politics* 74 (2): 323–38.

Levy, Jack S. 1987. "Declining Power and the Preventive Motivation for War." *World Politics* 40 (1): 82–107.

———. 1989. "The Causes of War: A Review of Theories and Evidence." In *Behavior, Society, and Nuclear War*, edited by Philip E. Tetlock, Jo L. Husbands, Robert Jervis, Paul C. Stern, and Charles Tilly, 210–333. New York: Oxford University Press.

Lijphart, Arend. 1999. *Patterns of Democracy*. New Haven, CT: Yale University Press.

Lippmann, Walter, and Charles Merz. 1920. *A Test of the News*. New York: New Republic.

Lipset, Seymour M. 1966. "The President, the Polls, and Vietnam." *Transactions* 3:20–22.

Livingston, Steven, and Todd Eachus. 1995. "Humanitarian Crises and U.S. Foreign Policy: Somalia and the CNN Effect Reconsidered." *Political Communication* 12:413–29.

Lodge, Milton, Marco R. Steenbergen, and Shawn Brau. 1995. "The Responsive Voter—Campaign Information and the Dynamics of Candidate Evaluation." *American Political Science Review* 89 (2): 309–26.

Lowi, Theodore J. 1972. "Four Systems of Policy, Politics, and Choice." *Public Administration Review* 298–310.

Lupia, Arthur, and Mathew D. McCubbins. 1998. *The Democratic Dilemma: Can Citizens Learn What They Need to Know?* Cambridge: Cambridge University Press.

Madison, James. 1787. *The Federalist Papers*. http://online.hillsdale.edu/file/constitution -courses-library/constitution-101/week-3/Federalist-10.pdf (accessed September 6, 2014).

Mansfield, Edward D., and Jack L. Snyder. 2007. "The Sequencing Fallacy." *Journal of Democracy* 18 (3): 5–10.

Maoz, Zeev. 2005. "Dyadic Militarized Interstate Disputes Dataset (Version 2.0)." http://psfaculty.ucdavis.edu/zmaoz/dyadmid.html (accessed July 10, 2012).

Maoz, Zeev and Bruce Russett. 1993. "Normative and Structural Causes of Democratic Peace, 1946–1986." *American Political Science Review* 87 (3): 624–38.

Maren, Michael. 1994. "Feeding a Famine." *Forbes Media Critic* 2 (Fall): 30–38.

McChesney, Robert W. 2000. *Rich Media, Poor Democracy: Communication Politics in Dubious Times*. New York: New Press.

McCubbins, Matthew D., and Thomas Schwartz. 1984. "Congressional Oversight Overlooked—Police Patrols versus Fire Alarms." *American Journal of Political Science* 28 (1): 165–79.

Media Tenor. 2004. "The War in Iraq on Television: A Split Reality." Berlin: Media Tenor.

Mermin, Jonathan. 1999. *Debating War and Peace: Media Coverage of US Intervention in the Post-Vietnam Era*. Princeton, NJ: Princeton University Press.

Meyer, David, Kurt Hornik, and Ingo Feinerer. 2008. "Text Mining Infrastructure in R." *Journal of Statistical Software* 25 (5): 1–54.

Miller, Gary J. 2005. "The Political Evolution of Principal-Agent Models." *Annual Review of Political Science* 8:203–25.

Milner, Henry. 2002. *Civic Literacy*. Hanover, NH: Tufts University Press.

Montgomery, Mark R., Michele Gragnolati, Kathleen A. Burke, and Edmundo Paredes. 2000. "Measuring Living Standards with Proxy Variables." *Demography* 37 (2): 155–74.

Moosbrugger, L. n.d. "Institutions, Information, and Political Sophistication: A Causal Model." Santa Barbara: University of California, Santa Barbara.

Mueller, Jonathan E. 1973. *War Presidents and Public Opinion*. New York: John Wiley.

New York Times. 2004. "The Times and Iraq." May 26.

Ordeix i Rigo, Enric. 2005. "Aznar's Political Failure or Punishment for Supporting the Iraq War? Hypotheses about the Causes of the 2004 Spanish Election Results." *American Behavioral Scientist* 49 (4): 610–15.

Organski, A. F. K. 1958. *World Politics*. New York: Knopf.

Organski, A. F. K., and Jacek Kugler. 1977. "The Costs of Major Wars: The Phoenix Factor." *American Political Science Review* 71 (4): 1347–66.

Owen, John M. 1994. "How Liberalism Produces Democratic Peace." *International Security* 19 (2): 87–125.

Page, Benjamin I., and Marshall M. Bouton. 2006. *The Foreign Policy Disconnect: What Americans Want from Our Leaders but Don't Get*. Chicago: University of Chicago Press.

Page, Benjamin I., and Robert Y. Shapiro. 1992. *The Rational Public: Fifty Years of Trends in American Policy*. Chicago: University of Chicago Press.

Palmer, Glenn, Tamar London, and Patrick Regan. 2004. "What's Stopping You? The Sources of Political Constraints on International Conflict Behavior in Parliamentary Democracies." *International Interactions* 30 (1): 1–24.

Patterson, Thomas. 1994. *Out of Order*. New York: Vintage.

———. 1998. "Time and News: The Media's Limitations as an Instrument of Democracy." *International Political Science Review/Revue internationale de science politique* 19 (1): 55–67.

———. 2000. "The United States: News in a Free-Market Society." In *Democracy and the Media: A Comparative Perspective*, edited by Richard Gunther and Anthony Mughan, 241–65. Cambridge: Cambridge University Press.

PBS NewsHour. 1999. "The Blair Doctrine." April 22, 1999. http://www.pbs.org /newshour/bb/international-jan-june99-blair_doctrine4-23/.

Peceny, Mark, and Christopher K. Butler. 2004. "The Conflict Behavior of Authoritarian Regimes." *International Politics* 41 (4): 565–81.

Pennings, Paul. 1998. "The Triad of Party System Change: Votes, Office, and Policy." In *Comparing Party System Change*, edited by P. Pennings and J. C. Lane, 79–100. London: Routledge.

Peterson, Susan, Michael J. Tierney, and Daniel Maliniak. 2005. "Teaching and Research Practices, Views on the Discipline, and Policy Attitudes of International Relations Faculty at US Colleges and Universities." Williamsburg, VA: Program on the Theory and Practice of International Relations, Wendy and Emery Reves Center for International Studies, College of William & Mary.

Pew Research Center for the People and the Press. 2010. "State of the News Media." Washington, DC.

Pickering, Jeffrey. 1998. *Britain's Withdrawal from East of Suez: The Politics of Retrenchment.* New York: St. Martin's.

Pohr, Adrian. 2005. "Indexing im Einsatz: Eine Inhaltsanalyse der Kommentare überregionaler Tageszeitungen in Deutschland zum Afghanistankrieg 2001." *Medien & Kommunikationswissenschaft* 53:261–76.

Popkin, Samuel L. 1993. "Information Shortcuts and the Reasoning Voter." In *Information, Participation, and Choice: An Economic Theory of Democracy in Perspective*, edited by B. Grofman, 17–35. Ann Arbor: University of Michigan Press.

———. 1994. *The Reasoning Voter: Communication and Persuasion in Presidential Campaigns.* Chicago: University of Chicago Press.

Potter, Philip B., and Matthew Baum. 2010. "Democratic Peace, Domestic Audience Costs, and Political Communication." *Political Communication* 27 (4): 453–70.

Powell, G. Bingham. 1982. *Contemporary Democracies: Participation, Stability and Violence.* Cambridge, MA: Harvard University Press.

———. 2000. *Elections as Instruments of Democracy: Majoritarian and Proportional Visions.* New Haven, CT: Yale University Press.

Powell, G. Bingham, Jr., and Guy D. Whitten. 1993. "A Cross-National Analysis of Economic Voting: Taking Account of the Political Context." *American Journal of Political Science* 37 (2): 391–414.

Powell, Robert. 1993. "Guns, Butter, and Anarchy." *American Political Science Review* 87 (1): 115–32.

Prat, Andrea, and David Strömberg. 2006. "Commercial Television and Voter Information." London: Centre for Economic Policy Research Discussion Paper 4989.

Prins, Brandon C., and Christopher Sprecher. 1999. "Institutional Constraints, Political Opposition, and Interstate Dispute Escalation: Evidence from Parliamentary Systems, 1946–89." *Journal of Peace Research* 36 (3): 271–87.

Pujante, David, and Esperanza Morales-Lopez. 2008. "A Political Action Against Popular Opinion: Aznar's Final Speech before the Spanish Parliament Justifying the War in Iraq (December 2003)." *Journal of Language and Politics* 7 (1): 71–96.

Putnam, Robert D. 1988. "Diplomacy and Domestic Politics—The Logic of 2-Level Games." *International Organization* 42 (3): 427–60.

Radziszewski, Elizabeth, and Wojtek M. Wolfe. 2012. "Poland." In *Public Opinion and International Intervention: Lessons from the Iraq War*, edited by R. Sobel, P. Furia, and B. Barrett, 69–82. Washington, DC: Potomac.

Rahn, Wendy M. 1993. "The Role of Partisan Stereotypes in Information-Processing about Political Candidates." *American Journal of Political Science* 37 (2): 472–96.

Ramsay, Kristopher W. "Politics at the Water's Edge: Crisis Bargaining and Electoral Competition." *Journal of Conflict Resolution* 48, no. 4 (2004): 459–86.

Ray, James Lee. 2000. "On the Level(s): Does Democracy Correlate with Peace?" In *What Do We Know about War?*, edited by John A. Vasquez, 299–316. Lanham, MD: Rowman & Littlefield.

Reiter, Dan, and Allan C. Stam. 2002. *Democracies at War*. Princeton, NJ: Princeton University Press.

Reiter, Dan, and Erik R. Tillman. 2002. "Public, Legislative, and Executive Constraints on the Democratic Initiation of Conflict." *Journal of Politics* 64 (3): 810–26.

Robinson, Piers, Peter Goddard, Katy Parry, and Craig Murray. 2009. "Testing Models of Media Performance in Wartime: UK TV News and the 2003 Invasion of Iraq." *Journal of Communication* 59 (3): 534–63.

Rosato, Sebastian. 2003. "The Flawed Logic of Democratic Peace Theory." *American Political Science Review* 97 (4): 585–602.

Rosecrance, Richard. 1986. *The Rise of the Trading State: Commerce and Conquest in the Modern World*. New York: Free Press.

Rosenau, James N. 1961. *Public Opinion and Foreign Policy*. New York: Random House.

———. 1962. "Consensus-Building in the American National Community: Some Hypotheses and Some Supporting Data." *Journal of Politics* 24 (4): 639–61.

Royed, Terry J., Kevin M. Leyden, and Stephen A. Borrelli. 2000. "Is 'Clarity of Responsibility' Important for Economic Voting? Revisiting Powell and Whitten's Hypothesis." *British Journal of Political Science* 30 (4): 669–98.

Rummel, R. J. 1979. *Understanding Conflict and War, Vol. 4: War Power and Peace*. Beverly Hills, CA: Sage.

Rumsfeld, Donald. 2011. *Known and Unknown: A Memoir*. New York: Sentinel HC.

Russett, Bruce. 1963. *Community and Contention: Britain and America in the 20th Century*. Cambridge, MA: MIT Press.

Russett, Bruce, and John R. Oneal. 2001. *Triangulating Peace: Democracy, Interdependence, and International Organizations*. New York: Norton.

Schampel, James H. 1993. "Change in Material Capabilities and the Onset of War—A Dyadic Approach." *International Studies Quarterly* 37 (4): 395–408.

Schmitt-Beck, Rudiger. 2003. "Mass Communication, Personal Communication and Vote Choice: The Filter Hypothesis of Media Influence in Comparative Perspective." *British Journal of Political Science* 33 (2): 233–59.

Scholz, John T. 1991. "Cooperative Regulatory Enforcement and the Politics of Administrative Effectiveness." *American Political Science Review* 85 (1): 115–36.

Schuck, Andreas R. T., Rens Vliegenthart, Hajo G. Boomgaarden, Matthijs Elenbaas, Rachid Azrout, Joost van Spanje, and Claes H. de Vreese. 2013. "Explaining Campaign News Coverage: How Medium, Time, and Context Explain Variation in the Media Framing of the 2009 European Parliamentary Elections." *Journal of Political Marketing* 12 (1): 8–28.

Schuck, Andreas R. T., Georgios Xezonakis, Susan Banducci, and Claes H. de Vreese. 2010. "Media Study Data Advance Release Documentation." www.piredeu.eu.

Schuck, Andreas R. T., Georgios Xezonakis, Matthijs Elenbaas, Susan A. Banducci, and Claes H. de Vreese. 2011. "Party Contestation and Europe on the News Agenda: The 2009 European Parliamentary Elections." *Electoral Studies* 30 (1): 41–52.

Schultz, Kenneth A. 1998. "Domestic Opposition and Signaling in International Crises." *American Political Science Review* 92 (4): 829–44.

———. 2001a. *Democracy and Coercive Diplomacy*. Cambridge: Cambridge University Press.

———. 2001b. "Looking for Audience Costs." *Journal of Conflict Resolution* 45 (1): 32–60.

———. 2012. "Why We Needed Audience Costs and What We Need Now." *Security Studies* 21 (3): 369–75.

Senese, Paul D. 1996. "Geographical Proximity and Issue Salience: Their Effects on the Escalation of Militarized Interstate Conflict." *Conflict Management and Peace Science* 15 (2): 133–61.

———. 2005. "Territory, Contiguity, and International Conflict: Assessing a New Joint Explanation." *American Journal of Political Science* 49 (4): 769–79.

Sharkey, Jacqueline. 1993. "When Pictures Drive Foreign Policy." *American Journalism Review* 15 (10): 14–19.

Sheafer, Tamir, and Gadi Wolfsfeld. 2009. "Party Systems and Oppositional Voices in the News Media A Study of the Contest over Political Waves in the United States and Israel." *International Journal of Press/Politics* 14 (2): 146–65.

Shi, Min, and Jakob Svensson. 2006. "Political Budget Cycles: Do They Differ across Countries and Why?" *Journal of Public Economics* 90 (8): 1367–89.

Singer, J. David. 1966. "Formal Alliances, 1815–1939." *Journal of Peace Research* 1:1–32.

———. 1972. "Correlates of War Project—Interim Report and Rationale." *World Politics* 24 (2): 243–70.

———. 1987. "Reconstructing the Correlates of War Dataset on Material Capabilities of States, 1816–1985." *International Interactions* 14:115–32.

Singer, J. David, and Melvin. Small. 1972. *The Wages of War 1816–1965: A Statistical Handbook*. New York: John Wiley.

Slantchev, Branislav L. 2003. "The Power to Hurt: Costly Conflict with Completely Informed States." *American Political Science Review* 97 (1): 123–33.

———. 2006. "Politicians, the Media, and Domestic Audience Costs." *International Studies Quarterly* 50 (2): 445–77.

Smith, Alastair. 1996. "Diversionary Foreign Policy in Democratic Systems." *International Studies Quarterly* 40 (1): 133–53.

———. 1998. "International Crises and Domestic Politics." *American Political Science Review* 92 (3): 623–38.

Smith, Michael. 2005. "Blair Planned Iraq War from Start." *Sunday Times*, May 1.

Snider, James H., and Benjamin I. Page. 2003a. "Does Media Ownership Affect Media Stands? The Case of the Telecommunications Act of 1996." Working paper, Institute for Policy Research, Northwestern University.

———. 2003b. "The Political Power of TV Broadcasters: Covert Bias and Anticipated Reactions." Working paper, Institute for Policy Research, Northwestern University.

Sniderman, Paul. 1993. "A New Look in Public Opinion Research." In *Political Science: The State of the Discipline II*, edited by A. Finifter, 220–45. Washington, DC: American Political Science Association.

Sniderman, Paul. M., Richard A. Brody, and Philip E. Tetlock. 1991. *Reasoning and Choice*. Cambridge: Cambridge University Press.

Snyder, Jack and Erica D. Borghard. 2011. "The Cost of Empty Threats: A Penny, Not a Pound." *American Political Science Review* 105 (3): 437–56.

Springford, John. 2003. "'Old' and 'New' Europeans United: Public Attitudes towards the Iraq War and US Foreign Policy." Centre for European Reform Background Brief.

Stein, Elizabeth. 2007. "Mainstream Newspaper Coverage: A Barometer of Government Tolerance for Anti-Regime Expression in Authoritarian Brazil." Joan Shorenstein Center on the Press, Politics and Public Policy Research Paper Series.

———. 2013. "The Unraveling of Support for Authoritarianism: The Dynamic Relationship of Media, Elites and Public Opinion in Brazil, 1972–1982." *International Journal of Press/Politics* 18 (1): 85–107.

Stephens, Philip. 2004. *Tony Blair: The Price of Leadership*. London: Politico's.

Stockmann, Daniela. 2012. *Media Commercialization and Authoritarian Rule in China*. Cambridge: Cambridge University Press.

Strobel, Warren P. 1997. *Late Breaking Foreign Policy*. Washington, DC: USIP Press.

Stromback, Jesper, and Daniela V. Dimitrova. 2006. "Political and Media Systems Matter: A Comparison of Election News Coverage in Sweden and the United States." *Harvard International Journal of Press/Politics* 11 (4): 131–47.

Swanson, David L., and Paolo Mancini. 1996. *Politics, Media and Modern Democracy: An International Study of Innovations in Electoral Campaigning and Their Consequences*. Westport, CT: Greenwood.

Tammen, Ronald L., Jacek Kugler, Douglas Lemke, Allan C. Stam III, Carole Alsharabati, Mark Andrew Abdollahian, Brian Efird, and A.F.K. Organski. 2000. *Power Transitions: Strategies for the 21st Century*. New York: Seven Bridges Press.

Tavits, Margit. 2007. "Clarity of Responsibility and Corruption." *American Journal of Political Science* 51 (January): 218–29.

Timmermans, Arco and Catherine Moury. 2006. "Coalition Governance in Belgium and the Netherlands: Rising Government Stability Against All Odds." *Acta Politica* 41:389–407.

Ting, Michael M. 2008. "Whistleblowing." *American Political Science Review* 102 (2): 249–67.

Tir, Jaroslav, and Paul F. Diehl. 2002. "Geographic Dimensions of Enduring Rivalries." *Political Geography* 21 (2): 263–286

Tomz, Michael. 2007. "Domestic Audience Costs in International Relations: An Experimental Approach." *International Organization* 61 (Fall): 821–40.

Tomz, Michael, Gary King, and Langche Zeng. 1999. "RELOGIT: Rare Events Logistic Regression." Version 1.1. Cambridge, MA: Harvard University.

Trachtenberg, Marc. 2012. "Audience Costs: An Historical Analysis." *Security Studies* 21 (1): 3–42.

Travis, Alan. 2002. "Voters Say No to Iraq Attack: 51% Oppose British Backing for US Action." *Guardian*, March 19.

Travis, Alan, and Nicholas Watt. 2002. "Blair Faces Defeat on Iraq." *Guardian*, August 24.

Tsebelis, George. 2002. *Veto Players: How Political Institutions Work*. Princeton, NJ: Princeton University Press.

Van Belle, Douglas A. 1997. "Press Freedom and the Democratic Peace." *Journal of Peace Research* 34 (4): 405–14.

———. 2000. *Press Freedom and Global Politics*. Westport, CT: Greenwood.

Verba, Sidney, Richard A. Brody, Edwin B. Parker, Norman H. Nie, Nelson W. Polsby, Paul Ekman, and Gordon S. Black. 1967. "Public Opinion and War in Vietnam." *American Political Science Review* 61 (2): 317–33.

Waltz, Kenneth N. 1979. *Theory of International Politics*. New York: McGraw-Hill.

Weeks, Jessica L. 2008. "Autocratic Audience Costs: Regime Type and Signaling Resolve." *International Organization* 62:35–64.

———. 2012. "Strongmen and Straw Men: Authoritarian Regimes and the Initiation of International Conflict." *American Political Science Review* 106:326–47.

Werner, Suzanne, and Douglas Lemke. 1997. "Opposites Do Not Attract: The Impact of Domestic Institutions, Power, and Prior Commitments on Alignment Choices." *International Studies Quarterly* 41 (3): 529–46.

White, David M. 1950. "The Gatekeeper: A Case Study in the Selection of News." *Journalism Quarterly* 27 (4): 383–90.

White House. 1996. "A National Security Strategy of Engagement and Enlargement." Washington, DC.

Wildavsky, Aaron. 1966. "The Two Presidencies." *Trans-Action* 4 (2): 7–14.

Wilkerson, John, Stephen Purpura, and Dustin Hillard. 2008. "The US Policy Agendas Legislation Corpus—Volume 1: A Language Resource from 1947–1998." Paper presented at the International Conference on Language Resources and Evaluation, Marrakech, Morocco.

Wlezien, Christopher, and Stuart N. Soroka. 2012. "Political Institutions and the Opinion–Policy Link." *West European Politics* 35 (November): 1407–32.

Wolfsfeld, Gadi. 2004. *Media and the Path to Peace*. Cambridge: Cambridge University Press.

Yamamoto, Yoshinobu, and Stuart A. Bremer. 1980. "Wider Wars and Restless Nights: Major Power Intervention in Ongoing War." *Correlates of War* 2:199–229.

Youngs, Tim, and Mark Oakes. 1999. *Iraq: "Desert Fox" and Policy Developments*. London: House of Commons Library.

Yu, Bei, Stefan Kaufmann, and Daniel Diermeier. 2008. "Classifying Party Affiliation from Political Speech." *Journal of Information Technology & Politics* 5 (1): 33–48.

Zaller, John. 1992. *The Nature and Origins of Mass Opinion*. New York: Cambridge University Press.

———. 1994. "Positive Constructs of Public-Opinion." *Critical Studies in Mass Communication* 11 (3): 276–87.

———. 1999. "Governing with the News: The News Media as a Political Institution." *American Journal of Sociology* 104 (6): 1819–21.

Zaller, John and Dennis Chiu. 2000. "Government's Little Helper: U.S. Press Coverage of Foreign Policy Crises, 1946–1999." In *Decisionmaking in a Glass House*, edited by Brigitte L. Nacos, Robert Y. Shapiro, and Pierangelo Isernia, 61–84. New York: Rowman & Littlefield.

Zuckerman, Ethan. 2013. *Rewire: Digital Cosmopolitans in the Age of Connection*. New York: Norton.

INDEX

Note: Page numbers followed by "f" or "t" indicate figures or tables, respectively.